PLAYING
THE OSTRICH

TALKING HEADS TALKING ARMS

*Conversations About Canada's Armed Forces at the
Beginning of the 21st Century*

Volume 3

PLAYING
THE OSTRICH

EDITED BY
JOHN WOOD

BREAKOUT EDUCATIONAL NETWORK
IN ASSOCIATION WITH
DUNDURN PRESS
TORONTO · OXFORD

Publisher: Inta D. Erwin
Copy-editor: Amanda Stewart, First Folio Resource Group
Designer: Bruna Brunelli, Brunelli Designs
Printer:Webcom

National Library of Canada Cataloguing in Publication Data

Talking heads talking arms/edited by John Wood.

Three of the 16 vols. and 14 hours of video which make up the
    underground royal commission report.
Includes bibliographical references and index.
Complete contents: v. 1. No life jackets—v. 2. Whistling past the
    graveyard—v.3. Playing the ostrich.
ISBN 1-55002-427-2 (v. 1).—ISBN 1-55002-428-0 (v. 2).—
ISBN 1-55002-429-9 (v. 3)

    1. Canada—Armed Forces 2. Canada—Military policy. 3. Canada—
Foreign relations. I. Wood, John. II. Title: Whistling past the
graveyard. III. Title: underground royal commission report.
IV. Title: No life jackets. V. Title: Playing the ostrich.

FC603.T34 2003   355'.033071   C2003-902307-6
F1028.T34 2003

1   2   3   4   5   07   06   05   04   03

Printed and bound in Canada.
Printed on recycled paper. ✪
www.dundurn.com

Exclusive Canadian broadcast rights for the *underground royal commission* report

intelligent television

Check your cable or satellite listings for telecast times.

Visit the *urc* Web site link at:
www.ichanneltv.com

About the *underground royal commission* Report

Since September 11, 2001, there has been an uneasy dialogue among Canadians as we ponder our position in the world, especially vis à vis the United States. Critically and painfully, we are re-examining ourselves and our government. We are even questioning our nation's ability to retain its sovereignty.

The questions we are asking ourselves are not new. Over the last 30 years, and especially in the dreadful period of the early 1990s, leading up to the Quebec referendum of 1995, inquiries and royal commissions, one after another, studied the state of the country. What *is* new is that eight years ago, a group of citizens looked at this parade of inquiries and commissions and said, "These don't deal with the real issues." They wondered how it was possible for a nation that was so promising and prosperous in the early 1960s to end up so confused, divided and troubled. And they decided that what was needed was a different kind of investigation — driven from the grassroots "bottom," and not from the top. Almost as a provocation, this group of people, most of whom were affiliated with the award-winning documentary-maker Stornoway Productions, decided to do it themselves — and so was born the *underground royal commission*!

What began as a television documentary soon evolved into much more. Seven young, novice researchers, hired right out of university, along with a television crew and producer, conducted interviews with people in government, business, the military and in all walks of life, across the country. What they discovered went beyond anything they had expected. The more they learned, the larger the implications grew. The project continued to evolve and has expanded to include a total of 23 researchers over the last several years. The results are the 14 hours of video and 16 books that make up the first interim report of the *underground royal commission*.

So what *are* the issues? The report of the *underground royal commission* clearly shows us that regardless of region, level of government or political party, we are operating under a wasteful system ubiquitously lacking in accountability. An ever-weakening connection between the electors and the elected means that we are slowly and irrevocably losing our right to know our government. The researchers' experiences demonstrate that it is almost impossible for a member of the public, or in most cases even for a member of Parliament, to actually trace how our tax dollars are spent. Most disturbing is the fact that our young people have been stuck with a crippling IOU that has effectively hamstrung their future. No wonder, then, that Canada is not poised for reaching its potential in the 21st century.

The *underground royal commission* report, prepared in large part by and for the youth of Canada, provides the hard evidence of the problems you and I may long have suspected. Some of that evidence makes it clear that, as ordinary Canadians, we are every bit as culpable as our politicians — for our failure to demand accountability, for our easy acceptance of government subsidies and services established without proper funding in place, and for the disservice we have done to our young people through the debt we have so blithely passed on to them. But the real purpose of the *underground royal commission* is to ensure that we better understand how government processes work and what role we play in them. Public policy issues must be understandable and accessible to the public if they are ever to be truly addressed and resolved. The *underground royal commission* intends to continue pointing the way for bringing about constructive change in Canada.

— Stornoway Productions

Books in the *underground royal commission* Report

"Just Trust Us"

The Chatter Box
The Chance of War
Talking Heads Talking Arms: (3 volumes)
No Life Jackets
Whistling Past the Graveyard
Playing the Ostrich

Days of Reckoning
Taking or Making Wealth
Guardians on Trial
Goodbye Canada?
Down the Road Never Travelled
Secrets in High Places
On the Money Trail

Does Your Vote Count?
A Call to Account
Reflections on Canadian Character

Fourteen hours of videos are also available with the *underground royal commission* report.
Visit Stornoway Productions at www.stornoway.com for a list of titles.

TABLE OF CONTENTS

FOREWORD

Playing the Ostrich is the third volume of *Talking Heads Talking Arms*, a collection of conversations about the state of Canada's military and its place in Canadian society as we move further into the uncharted waters, jungles and deserts of the post–cold war era. The interviews were originally recorded for the Stornoway Productions documentary *A Question of Honour*.

Because Canadian soldiers have recently been front and centre alongside the Americans in Afghanistan, the media, and therefore the public, is hopefully more interested in and more aware of the activities of our Armed Forces than usual. What many of us don't realize is that we have soldiers stationed in many other parts of the world as well. These troops are working hard, living in difficult environments, and are often caught up in situations just as dangerous as those faced by our soldiers in Afghanistan. But we don't know much about them. Most of us don't even know where they are or why they are there. It is true that we have become more aware of the military since September 11, 2001, but we focus almost exclusively, led by the United States, on the war on terrorism. The situation that existed prior to the attacks in New York and Washington has not changed. Only our awareness of the problems has increased.

In general, we have not really heard much or asked many questions about Canadian soldiers over the past 10 years, unless, of course, they have been involved in some kind of scandal or other public relations disaster. Why is that? Why has the military disappeared from the radar screens of most Canadians? And why has a society that once valued, respected and prayed for its soldiers now become almost unconscious of their existence?

The eclectic group of people who discuss these and many other questions in *Playing the Ostrich* represents a wide cross-section of Canadian experiences from within government, the military and the academic world. There are also several outside perspectives from the United States. Although all contributors came to the table with different points of view and sometimes revealed different versions of the same situation, they shared a deep understanding of the problems facing our military at this crucial time in our history. As we now contemplate another U.S.-led war on Iraq, we should listen as carefully to those who spoke prior to 9/11 as we do to those who were interviewed after the attacks.

I believe, perhaps because I grew up during the Second World War, that pride in our military is part of the emotional glue that has held the country together. If we throw away traditions and forget the importance of our soldiers in the growth of Canada, we will be without history. If we allow government officials to play fast and loose with our soldiers' lives for the sake of personal ambition or campaign promises, we will become accomplices to these politicians. And if we use words like pride and honour only when we win medals at the Olympics, we will be without either.

John Wood
Stratford, Ontario
December 2002

PART ONE

American Views

MAX CLELAND
2001 (Pre-9/11)

Max Cleland is Georgia's senior senator, first elected in 1996. Senator Cleland currently serves on four Senate committees, including the Committee on Armed Services where he is chairman of the Subcommittee on Personnel. In this position he has sought to improve the quality of life of active and retired military personnel. Trained in the Airborne, he volunteered for duty in Vietnam in 1967. He was then promoted to the rank of captain, but was severely injured by a grenade at Khe Sanh in 1968. In 1970 he was elected to the Georgia Senate. In 1977 when President Carter appointed him to head the U.S. Veterans Administration, Cleland was the youngest VA administrator and the first Vietnam veteran to head the agency.

There's an old saying that came from one of Wellington's troops after the battle of Waterloo:

> In time of war, and not before,
> God and the soldier men adore.

> But in time of peace, with all things righted,
> God is forgotten, and the soldier slighted.

What we have here, worldwide, is an era of relative peace. We don't have the Russian Bear bearing down on Western Europe, which is what created NATO and Canadian involvement in NATO in the first place. We don't have the Chinese out there, proffering wars of national liberation as they did 35 years ago when I was a young soldier, a young lieutenant on the ground in Vietnam, trying to forestall that war of national liberation. You had Milosevic in the Balkans, but he's in jail in The Hague, after a 78-day war. The war in the desert — 30 days of bombing and 100 hours on the ground.

So in some sense the world is more at peace now, without any major threat to a major part of the world, than at any time in recent history, certainly any time since, say, the beginning of the 20th century. So for the first time in more than 100 years the world is relatively at peace. Now, what that does is drop strong defence as an issue to the bottom of the pile — in America, in Canada, in Europe.

In America, if you ask, "What are the top 10 serious issues facing America?" defence comes last, which has led to a problem here, where despite the fact that we led and won the desert war in the early 1990s, and led and won the Balkan war just a year or so ago, the fascinating thing is that America has an under-300-ship navy for the first time since before Pearl Harbor. Seventy-five percent of the United States Army's equipment is beyond half-life or better. And the average age of our planes, naval and air force planes, is between 18 and 22 years of age. We are still flying B-52s that were created in the 1950s. We've been flying B-52s for more than 50 years. And we're still thinking about extending the life of B-52s. That's just an example. So we haven't modernized our forces. We haven't done what we needed to do, say, in the last five to 10 years since the cold war has been over.

NATO
But I guess we have the responsibility for leading NATO, the command responsibility, but we are overextended. We haven't lessened our commitments, but we have cut our forces since the end of the cold war by a third, and yet expanded our commitments by 300 percent. Now Canada, I think, finds itself in a similar position. It doesn't have a

strong impetus politically to put defence high up on the list for expenditures. Other expenses come into play. Health care. Education. Basic infrastructure of government. So defence for Canada is always, I think, going to be a relatively low priority, unless there's a shooting war going on somewhere.

Secondly, Canada is one of those wonderful nations in NATO that grabs an oar, you know, and pulls the ship forward, but it's one oar among 19 nations. And they are not in the command position; the United States is, with the four-star commander à la General Clark. It doesn't have the resources, and it has not invested in modernization to the level that the United States has.

You find the same situation among the NATO allies in Europe. Germany, particularly. France. These countries, when we went to war in the Balkans, were found desperately underfunded, undertrained and unready, really, for major combat. And so the first big sorties in the air war were American sorties. And still, after we laid on 1,000 sorties a day we were still the majority package, with the big strategic aircraft, the B-52s, the B-1s and precision weapons. The countries in NATO didn't have that equipment. Canada didn't have that kind of equipment, and they don't plan to invest in it.

So, you know, peace has broken out around the world. Defence is very low in priority for all of the legislatures involved, including the United States Congress. And yet all of us have to maintain a certain vigilance so we can respond to crises when they occur.

They had been able to escape for the last 30 years, basically saying, "Never going to happen." All of a sudden they started being deployed by the government into various places. It's really the question of the government not paying attention to what exactly they had let the military slip to and then deploying them anyway. And the military, being good, "Can do, sir" kind of guys, saying, "Yes, we will go take that mission," and then they go take that mission.

Senator Pat Robertson of Kansas and I took the floor last year in five or six different rounds of debates, trying to call the Senate's attention to the fact that we were overcommitted and underfunded. And that we had to begin sorting out what was in the vital interests of the United States and what was not, what needed to be done and what was nice to do. We could not do everything. We could not be Gulliver and get trapped up in every little Lilliputian commitment around the world. That was exactly what was happening.

But that wasn't necessarily welcomed. We spoke to virtually an empty chamber. No attention to it in the press. It was a big yawn, a big ho-hum. We couldn't energize anybody about looking at the increasing divergence between our commitments and our resources to meet them. Now this new administration has actually gone further. For a number of years Americans postulated our defence on the two-major-theatre war scenario. Basically you've got to be ready to go to South Korea and fight on the Korean peninsula and reinforce the 37,000 American troops that are already there. And those 100,000 troops in the Pacific reinforce that. Then you have to be able to fight another war, say, reinforce Kuwait, maybe Saddam Hussein tries to break out of his box again, or Iran, or whatever. The two-major-theatre scenario.

Well, I think there has been at least an admission now that we can fight, as Americans — anywhere, anytime — in the world and win one theatre. It is unrealistic, based on our resources now, to expect us to fight two at the same time. I think we're beginning to acknowledge that. So we're beginning to realize, "Look. We may be great, one place, one time, right now. But we can't be great two places, two times, right now." We have in effect allowed ourselves to slip to that point. We don't have the resources to even re-fight the desert war of 1991! And the administration's looking to further cuts in order to gin up some improbable (that's using a nice term) Star Wars missile defence against, I think, a pretty much nonexistent enemy.

Terrorist Attacks and Tax Cuts
Certainly the attacks on the United States would more likely come from terrorist attack, rather than some Third World nation, Fourth World nation launching a third-stage rocket attack, an intercontinental ballistic missile with a nuclear warhead. So we are out of position here. It's not just Canada and NATO nations, but we are out of position because we haven't modernized. We have let the commitments run far ahead of our resources. And now we're overcommitted and underfunded, and facing further underfunding of our conventional forces for an aberration in perception of what's really the threat, which is this National Missile Defense ginning up. Which I don't support.

The $1.3-trillion tax cut over the next 10 years has virtually wiped out the surplus. That and the downturn in the economy. By next year the United States won't have a surplus in its budget and yet we still have $30 billion of unfunded requirements. So we're in a world of hurt ourselves. And one of the reasons is that after the cold war when the Soviet Union imploded, it created a power vacuum in so many parts of the world. In Eastern Europe. In the Balkans. In the Middle East.

Now, invariably America, because it was the only major superpower other than the Russians, began to fill that void. NATO began to fill that void. It wasn't exactly all that calculated and planned; it was just there. I voted for NATO expansion, or enlargement, to include Poland, the Czech Republic and Hungary. But I'm very cautious about any further expansion of NATO because that would expand our commitments when our own countries can't fund the commitments that we've already made. And the chiefs, the service chiefs in the United States tell us that.

You can't have a 57 percent increase in some National Missile Defense technology and underfund the service chiefs by $30 billion. That's absolutely the wrong direction. I would much rather have less money in National Missile Defense. I'd rather, first of all, focus on theatre missile defence. It's more practical, more mobile and is not locked down in concrete. And it doesn't abrogate the treaty, doesn't upset the Russians and the Chinese. Boost up the conventional forces, I think that's what we need. But getting the president and the secretary of the Defense Department in this administration to go that way is like pulling teeth. So we hold our hearings, those of us who believe this. We hold our hearings, we try to point these things out, but we're running up against a stone wall here.

What you have here from the administration is the cart before the horse. You have it backward. They come out with a budget that is driven by budget cuts, not by strategic thinking. And it's ready, fire, aim. There is no strategy. It's just budget cut here, buildup there. Build up your National Missile Defense and undercut conventional weapons and conventional forces. What's the strategy in that? That's all done before the strategic review is done. So I don't see any strategy in place, except undercut conventional forces, which have already been undercut and overcommitted. And we are headed for a crisis. We're going to have to end some of our commitments abroad. We can't do everything, everywhere now.

The Senate

Our constitution, particularly in terms of the United States Senate, says, "advise and consent." The president can't appoint a general, the president can't appoint an ambassador, without the advice and consent of the United States Senate. The president can't go to war without the consent of the Senate. The president can't fund the army, navy, air force and the Marine Corps, can't spend one dollar without the consent of the United States Senate. The Senate was designed under our framework to be the counsellor to the president, particularly in terms of foreign policy. You can't have a treaty, you can't have expansion of NATO, unless you get a two-thirds vote of the United States Senate.

So the Senate plays a very strong role in foreign policy and defence of that foreign policy. You can't, willy-nilly, just run over the Senate, run over the chiefs and say, "We're going to go out here and build our National Missile Defense thing, come hell or high water." You can't run off to NATO and tell all of our European allies that and demonstrate that you're going to do whatever you're going to do, regardless of the advice and consent of anybody. I think that's one of the political problems the president has. He's got to get his own team here at home to support him before he starts broadcasting — to Putin and the Chinese and the Europeans and to NATO — what he's going to do. That team is not together in the Pentagon. It is split. It is not together here on Capitol Hill.

American Commitments

I will say on Kosovo that I felt very much peeved because we only spent two days debating it and then we took a vote. The truth of the matter is, it was a vote on air and missile strikes. It was not an authorization for ground attack or our land-based effort. I voted for air and missile strikes against Milosevic to stop the killing. But what that has resulted in is some long-term, open-ended commitment. We're going to be there now for years, again with our NATO allies, and the United States Senate didn't vote for that.

Again, overextension of commitment. I think personally that it's time for the United States to remove its combat forces from the Balkans, Bosnia, Kosovo and Macedonia, and turn that over to the Europeans and their European security-defence initiative. We've still got the defence in the Pacific. Europeans — and Canada — don't have that role, but that is a role the United States has assigned itself.

The United States constitution is fuzzy, and maybe deliberately so. The point is, it's probably OK to be fuzzy because the truth of the matter is, the Congress declares war and funds the army and the navy and the military. But the president is commander-in-chief. In other words, once troops are committed it really is out of the hands of the national assembly. And that is a fuzzy area. Once the horse is out of the barn it's hard to rein that horse back in. You can have oversight hearings; you can tighten up on the budget; you can threaten fund cutoff and all that kind of stuff. But the president still is the commander-in-chief here and can deploy forces once you say that first "aye."

In 1964 there was a classic example. Lyndon Johnson got the Congress hooked; then he could do whatever he wanted to in Vietnam. President Clinton came to the Senate and got the Senate hooked on air-missile strikes against Milosevic, and then that war took off. And you know, as Napoleon said, "Wars are a lot easier to start than they are to end." And so the National Assembly, or the Parliament, once they authorize the chief executive to do something it's pretty much out of their control.

Canada and the United States are the same. We're both democracies. When you go to war you have to carry your people with you. Clausewitz, the German theoretician on war in the early 1800s, said this, in effect. You've got to carry your people with you. You've got to explain why you're going to war. In a democracy you've got to have the Parliament or the National Assembly with you. You can't just say, "This is what I'm going to do. Everybody fall in behind me and let's march." You've got to explain why you're doing something, what it means to the country, that it is in the vital interest of Canada or the United States or our allies, or our cause, and explain that this is the direction we're going to march in. Then you've got to get a validation vote.

DAVID JONES
2001 (Post-9/11)

During his 30-year career David Jones held numerous postings dealing with politico-military affairs and congressional relations. He was the minister counsellor for political affairs in the American embassy in Ottawa from 1992 to 1996. From 1989 to 1992 he served as foreign affairs advisor to the chief of staff of the army in Washington. Jones contributes articles on the Canadian political system and U.S.–Canada relations to the National Post, The Hill Times *and* Ehgloo.

I went through ROTC at university. My military experience started with two years on active duty and I continued on as a reserve officer for another 26 years.

It was an objective of mine at university to be involved with international relations, and one of the things that I became aware of was the opportunity to enter the foreign service. At the same time I also had a military commitment. So before I went into the foreign service I did my two years of active duty with the military, and when I went on foreign service duty I continued to have the reserve obligation. It usually meant two weeks of active duty a year, which I performed, normally, in Washington. If I had been called up, I would have done military analyses for the Defense Intelligence Agency as an army attaché, in one post or another around the world, on a country with which I had some background, such as Greece, Turkey and Cyprus. Or since I had had some experience in France, I might have been assigned to replace the army attaché in Paris. So an individual with that kind of background would have been released for more active and dramatic duty.

During the time that I was the foreign affairs advisor to the chief of staff of the army, we had the reversal of the dictatorship in Panama and the entire Gulf War experience, along with the collapse of the Soviet Union following the collapse of the Berlin Wall. That was a particularly interesting period in which to be a fly on the wall watching how our military really worked from the inside.

A Political Counsellor in Ottawa

The Canada assignment was an interesting one. It came immediately after I was at the Pentagon with the chief of staff of the army. I had not had previous experience with Canada but it fell in with work that I had done with NATO and arms control issues because there were issues of that nature in play bilaterally between the United States and Canada.

A political counsellor works essentially in two directions.

The political section first presents a wide variety of bilateral issues of American concern to the Canadian government. This could be everything from seeking assistance on a particular vote in the UN or seeking, perhaps, support on Haiti or things of this nature. Or just to tell the Canadian government what the United States is doing in a wide variety of places and the issues. It might be global warming. It might be African assignments or issues. It could be developments in central Europe. What we want under those circumstances is for the Canadian government to understand what the United States is doing, support it if you're able to, or at least appreciate the concerns that we have. That's the one side of the political section's effort.

The other side is internal domestic analysis. We look at Canada and we try to determine what is happening at each and every level across the country, assisted by a number of consulates that provide their input and analysis as to local conditions in the provinces. We do what you would consider, let's say, a good journalist would do. If you're going to have an election, we outline how this election will evolve, make a judgment of who's likely to win or lose, what the results of one party's victory or defeat would mean.

Also, of course, we studied very carefully the Quebec issue as it evolved and was evolving during the four years that I was in Canada. Without going into that, it was certainly an extremely interesting period of time to be in Canada. Indeed, I guess I would say that anyone who thought that Canadian politics were dull would be satisfied only with blood in the streets. During the time I was there, there was a national referendum, a national election, a reversal of a national party at the federal level, a major election in Quebec in which there was a reversal of the party status in Quebec, and then a referendum in Quebec. That was about the most interesting and exciting time that a political analyst could find anywhere.

To try to assess the character of the people is probably something that's deeper than we would be doing on a day-to-day basis. Our points are almost invariably tactical. The Department of State takes the given situation as we have it and we attempt to work within it. What are the limits of the possible? — which is what diplomacy is all about. You do not change great societies, great countries, by spinning them on a dime. Short of revolutions, you don't reverse courses or make alterations of more than a few degrees, any more than you spin supertankers on a dime.

The character of the Canadian nation, like that of the United States, has evolved and continues to evolve. In both countries we're far more multiracial, multiethnic societies than we were 50 years ago. Although the United States likes to talk about itself as a melting pot and Canada talks about itself as a mosaic, we are both much richer and more complicated societies than we were 50 years ago. I consider the United States and Canada alternative North Americas. The issues and problems that turn up in one society are very likely also to return and rebound in the other society, whether these are issues such as gun control or health or, say, the degree to which drugs are managed or handled. Each of these are issues that are North American, and Canada and the United States have slightly different skews and approaches on them.

The Canadian System

When I first came to Canada I found the parliamentary system very interesting. I thought that there were certain aspects to it, particularly the ability of the governing party to govern, that were very interesting, shall we say. I'm more of a child of the executive who would like to get things done, and a parliamentary system definitely can get things done.

On the other hand, if you talk about accountability, particularly accountability to the people, the more I looked at the Canadian system of government, the better I liked the American system. The American representative system means that each representative is more directly influenced by the people, and the interests and the desires and the demands of the people. This makes for a very messy situation in which you constantly are dealing with pressure groups and individual groups that have special interests.

But these special interests are very reflective of democracy, and if you don't have the people making their points clearly and vigorously known to their congressmen, who are responsible to them every two years in the electorate, you lose a vital element of democracy itself. The executive in the United States is a major, even a primary, actor. But it is by no matter of means the only actor. Nor is it the dominant actor. Just about every-thing that the executive does or tries to do is subject to check, vigorous check and defeat by Congress, without any specific defeat on any partic-ular topic being life threatening, so far as its ability to govern is concerned.

All right, you've made a miscalculation. You took a nasty licking by trying to put this particular individual forward for the Supreme Court or for your cabinet. OK, you take two steps back, you wipe off your wound and you go at it again. What it does is keep a constant level of humility, regard-less of whatever lack of humility you may see in American executives. There is a humbling nature in trying to govern in the American scene.

When you try to develop a consensus for anything across the society, the society in a democracy by and large will get what it wants. If it wants enor-mous attention delivered to the health of its citizens, a very high percent-age of the public revenues will be devoted to public health care. If the consensus is that the first welfare of a welfare state is the security of the society, you're going to pay greater attention to defence. The Canadian population has not shown any special interest in defence and consequently there is absolutely no requirement by Parliament, other than a nominal one, to pay specific attention to defence or defence concerns.

Defence in Canada has become a niche issue rather than a societal issue. The absence of military issues cross-cutting in Canadian society means that Canadian society has no special interest in it. You don't look at your prime minister and say, well, he served at such and such a time.

You don't look at any of your prime ministers and say, well, he was a famous general during World War X or in the Civil War or whenever. You look at American society, and one of the paths to political promi-nence in the United States has always been military expertise, and one of the societal values which voters have seen as important in their rep-resentatives politically has been to have performed military service.

If you are going to be a politician and think of the ultimate good of your society, have you also been willing, as a soldier, to put yourself in the front ranks of the defence of the society? Now, you can get too far into this, but one illustration that you are willing to sacrifice for society has been military service.

An American View of Canada's Defence
I think Canadians have looked at the situation concerning defence in a very realistic and perhaps even self-serving way. What they have seen is the basic argument that anything large enough and nasty enough to threaten Canada is also going to be viewed by the United States as a threat to us and that we are going to have to do something about it and consequently defend Canada in responding to this threat. At the same time Canadians have realized that there is no way that Canada could defend itself against a hostile, aggressive United States. So Canadians have come to the judgment that they could either be inadequately defended expensively or inadequately defended cheaply. And they've come to a rational judgment that spending less money is the way to go.

Now, whether that has a long-term societal effect on Canadians' psyche or self-worth or anything of that nature, I don't know, I'm not a Canadian. I haven't been placed in this position. I haven't implicitly sur-rendered my defence to somebody else. There is no Roman Empire to defend the United States of America, no galactic freedom league to defend Earth. So the United States, throughout my lifetime, has been the implicit defender of the kinds of rights, freedoms and liberties that the West puts in the forefront of our desires and being. And throughout my professional lifetime as a diplomat, and even as a reserve officer, I recognized that if we failed in this effort, if our abilities were wanting, there was a serious chance that there would be an apocalypse that would be totally destructive.

As a minor military historian I've reviewed Canadian military history and seen it with great respect. Indeed, during World War I Canadian losses were greater than American losses. In World War II Canadian participation was at least proportional to that of the United States, and the fact that almost all of your Forces were volunteers up until the very end, and certainly virtually all of your Forces overseas were volunteers, I consider that participation even greater than that of the United States.

So Canadian ability to handle military issues and concerns has never been in question. Indeed, if Canada had continued on anywhere near proportional levels (the military commitments that they had made during World War II) and backed up these commitments throughout the cold war, it would have been very helpful. It would have been money and resources that the United States would not have had to spend.

What you do in situations like this, though, in the end, is that you see what has been done, what is available. We have gone at this constantly over decades to try to encourage Canadian expenditures for defence purposes to increase, but all of our urging and all of our efforts haven't worked. Canadian defence expenditures have remained on the low end of the NATO scale and that is simply something that we accept in political-diplomatic terms. You work with what is available. Diplomacy is the art of the possible, working with what Canada has. And what Canada's willing to contribute is what we will work with as a team, as an alliance, as a coalition, as whatever the grouping happens to be.

My regret continues to be that Canadian personnel abilities and the basic, historical expertise that the Canadian Forces have demonstrated is something that is being lost as a resource for the West.

What we have been doing for years and decades is encouraging — urging — the Canadian Forces to spend more, to build up their resources, to note the fact that there are problems and shortcomings. Ten years ago when I was with the chief of staff of the army and we visited Canadian counterparts on the army side, we said, in effect, "Our warehouse is open to you. Come, let us help you, let us work together on training or co-ordination." We really have to be able to do these things together if we are ever going to do them in combat.

The problem that we began to note — and have been noting for years and years — is that the Canadian Forces are not working and not co-ordinating and not equipping themselves at a level that makes this productive effort likely. I mean, when you have a situation, as General MacKenzie has pointed out, in which you have not trained as a brigade in nine years, you simply have no brigade capability. Technically you may have a brigade on paper, but you don't have a brigade. If you are going to be an effective military unit, you have to train at every level, all the time. You cannot sit down and say, "Well, we have a battalion," but not train your battalion. Your companies in your battalion can't be drawn from four different areas. They don't know each other, they don't know how to co-ordinate, they can't co-operate effectively and they simply will get themselves killed if they go into combat.

The same is true for a brigade and we recognize this. Our military attachés have gone out and seen the degree of training that is taking place and we know what Canadian capabilities are in this regard. And we've noted over the years the degree to which Canada has set aside capabilities and reduced their force levels.

After the end of World War II, to go back once again into what is really almost ancient history, you had aircraft carriers and a heavy bomber force and were able to manufacture your own jet fighters and could have become a nuclear power if you had wished. These are all capabilities that are so far in the past that Canadians don't even realize they existed. If Canadians wished to develop, say, an aircraft carrier battle group, it would take between 10 to 15 years at the absolute minimum. You would have to start all the way over from the beginning. Capabilities just do not leap like Athena from the brow of Zeus. You simply don't have them unless you work from the bottom up: squad, platoon, company, battalion, brigade, division.

And it's true in the United States. During the Desert Shield buildup we had a brigade that was supposed to be a round-out brigade for the 2nd

Mechanized Division. This was a Southern-based unit, so you can see there was a heritage aspect to it. They were people that had gone out to train with the 2nd Infantry Division. When the 2nd Infantry Division was called up and was one of the first units to go overseas, the round-out brigade wasn't ready. So they stuck an independent brigade under the 2nd Division and they kept training the round-out brigade. They trained and they trained and they replaced the entire senior echelon of reserve officers and they kept on training. More than six months later they were still in the training process and they were not ready to go. This is a long, extended explanation of just how difficult it is to sustain a capability, even when in theory you have a substantial societal focus on it.

NATO

The Canadian commitment to NATO was a clear and effective commitment throughout the cold war. In the late 1970s during a Reforger exercise, I had the opportunity to visit the Canadian brigade during the exercises in Germany. At that time it was led by Brigadier-General Fox. It was an outstanding unit. It was very effective; it was very highly regarded.

The situation with the end of the cold war has seen Canadians, as was the case with many Americans, decide that there simply is no equivalent threat. There is no need to be prepared to stand shoulder to shoulder with German and American armies. As a result of the accurate recognition that this level of threat no longer existed, Canadian ability to put a brigade together simply evaporated. And the Canadian air units that were forward deployed were withdrawn.

I think any military analyst will tell you that Canada could not in any near-term prospect put a brigade into Europe. What has happened over a period of time within NATO is that, since it remains primarily a military alliance, those countries without forces of any significant weight have less of a hearing. It's not that Canada equals Luxembourg by any manner of means, but the Canadian ability in NATO to drive its political points is certainly weakened because of the absence of the essential coin of the NATO realm, which is military forces.

There was a study that has just come out which rated Canada not even as high as Belgium, so far as military equipment was concerned. That may or may not be important to Canadians. What it does do is give you an illustration of the weight that Canada would have in military terms if you were to put a value on military forces.

Peacekeeping

Throughout the cold war Canada had a special relevance in peacekeeping. There was a particularly adroit divide that Canada could manage between Warsaw Pact forces and real American or British forces. They were seen as competently and effectively pro-Western, but balanced, in an acceptable in-between fashion.

The real point, though, was that during the cold war period Canadian peacekeepers were effective because they were first effective soldiers. And it is a baseline that peacekeepers in the abstract don't want to recognize, but to be an effective peacekeeper, first you have to be an effective soldier. And Canadians had this long, historical reputation for military excellence and professionalism on which they could draw for their peacekeeping forces, and these peacekeepers were indeed very good, in Cyprus and elsewhere in the Middle East and literally in almost every place around the world. Canada took great pride, and deserved pride, in having participated in virtually every peacekeeping mission, UN or otherwise, around the world.

The problem for Canada has been that the paradigm has shifted, that you no longer have this strong reservoir of very effective military personnel, while at the same time you have continued to put your Forces forward into increasingly complex and even more hostile peacekeeping exercises. Peacekeeping has become more than a little bloody-minded. It's not the equivalent of putting a policeman in a uniform and directing traffic. And in situations where units are questionably trained or questionably equipped, you could find yourself in a catastrophic situation.

While I was in Ottawa, I won't say that I had my heart in my mouth, but I definitely had my fingers crossed on some of the positions in which Canadian units were being placed in Bosnia. You could have run into a situation very easily in which a large number of people died, with the result being intense investigation as to whether training, leadership or equipment was really the cause.

A circumstance like that happened to the United States in Somalia. Our problem was not that our people were incapably equipped, trained or led, but that we got ourselves into an impossibly stupid tactical situation. The point is that we won tactically. We killed hundreds of Somalis in this fight, uncounted losses as far as the Somalis were concerned, but the result was a strategic disaster for us. If something comparable had happened to Canadians, where not only you had taken these losses, but you had to question yourself on every echelon of leadership, training and equipment, would you have been able to shrug this off and do anything further? I don't know.

Questions on Policy

Every society gets the political system that it really desires. If there had been an intense desire to investigate Somalia or Bosnia or Kosovo through the parliamentary system, the mechanisms are certainly there for the government to have as full, open, detailed and effective inquiry as it wished. I mean, your Question Period could have been devoted to it every single day if there had been a desire on the part of the opposition to ask question after question after question on Somalia, until either everybody died of complete boredom and exhaustion or the government was forced to respond in a manner that was ultimately viewed as effective.

So Question Period is a device for accountability and an interesting one. The fact that Question Period in my view has become the equivalent of melodramatic farce is something else. But that's not the way it could have been or even should be.

There is no question that Congress would have called for an investigation. And whether it was the minority that was holding hearings or the majority that was holding hearings, or a joint session of congressional committees, you would have had congressional hearings in intense detail on specific issues of concern.

One of the analogies that I've worked through is the degree to which we would review a treaty. At the end of 1987 the Intermediate-Range Nuclear Forces (INF) Treaty agreement was reached between the United States and the Soviet Union to eliminate a couple of classes of nuclear-armed missiles in Europe. The Senate, and for that matter the House, were somewhat skeptical of this. There were significant numbers, even of the president's party, Republicans who were dubious about any agreement with the Russians. They started hearings on this treaty. They presented more than 1,000 questions to the administration.

Each one of these questions had to be specifically answered and returned to the individual senators or committees that had asked them. They called the negotiators up to testify. They called other elements of the administration involved with intelligence acquisition to testify. They called in our military leadership to ask whether the executive branch was twisting their arms. They held full sets of hearings in both the committees on Foreign Relations and Armed Services, and from there they moved to days of debate within the Senate on whether this was a good treaty or not. At one point they thought that they had found a flaw in the negotiations and they sent the negotiators back to Geneva to renegotiate a point with the Russians.

To show that we were not hiding anything within the executive branch, the Senate insisted that the entire negotiating record and all of the classified material that went back close to 10 years be available for them to review. Now, this was done under appropriate classification and security terms, but there was as comprehensive and total a review from both Democrats and Republicans of this particular agreement as could be conceived. I don't think there had ever been anything comparable done, but it wasn't considered to be extraordinary or something that was without possible precedent in the future.

Anybody looking at our systems learns quickly that it is not necessary to gather together in Canada a sort of coalition of members of Parliament to try to deliver pressure and to convince a wide range of political membership in Parliament that you are right. It's useful and helpful, of course, and you always want to do that. But if you want to get something done, you go to a minister or you go to the Prime Minister's Office. You try to reach the prime minister. Obversely, any Canadian diplomat very quickly knows that even though he has the president onboard, it is the beginning of his effort and not the end of it. He really has to work harder. He has to go throughout our government and work very hard to build these full sets of coalitions and find the individual points of persuasion. It's easier sometimes to work with a parliamentary government if you're a diplomat and the government agrees with you.

One of the things that puzzled me was the unwillingness of those who are most critical of the United States to spend so little on Canadian defence. If the United States is indeed your explicit — not even your implicit — defender against all threats foreign, then what happens to

Canadian self-reliance? I would have thought that those who were the most skeptical of the United States and its interests would have been those who were the most devoted to as strong a Canadian defence establishment as possible. Their logic in this escapes me except to conclude that viscerally they know that the United States is not a threat. Therefore dissing us is irrelevant. Nothing is going to happen. So not spending money on defence frees up money that can be spent on social causes. It's a very logical, very rational type of judgment, whether it has a long-term societal effect on Canadian self-esteem is something that Canadians themselves have to answer.

I think your paradigm has changed. Until relatively recently you were able to continue to run on momentum, the residual expertise that you had for decades — that you could indeed send people off to do peace-keeping, that your Forces were strong enough to do this, that the prime minister, who grew up without any military background, or frankly, in my view, without any interest in the military, took this as much as a given as pure water in Ontario.

You had this resource and you could call on it. Well, the reservoir's gone dry and the prime minister has only haltingly, I would say, become aware of this. Because most militaries will, when their bosses say, "Can you do this?" most militaries say, "Yes, sir."

And until there is a horrible shock the prime minister or the leadership in any society doesn't know what they don't know. They don't know that they can't do it anymore until suddenly the system fails, and then they realize that the paradigm has shifted. Now, gee whiz, we can't do robust peace-keeping. We can only do light-housekeeping peacekeeping. OK. Well, that means that you have to recut your suit to fit the cloth that you have available. Are you going to reopen a textile factory? Well, that's a Canadian societal question. Is it going to become a societal value again in Canada to be able to do heavy-duty peacekeeping, or are you going to continue to be satisfied with a steadily lower level of military-style peacekeeping?

This is your society's choice. It's highly unlikely that Canada is going to be faced with a World War II–type challenge in which you are going to have to take that horrible deep breath and start all over again and learn very painfully that, gee, this guy who was a great first lieutenant can't command a battalion because he just lost two companies in action trying to do a river-crossing operation for which he had never been trained. The United States has had catastrophes of that nature.

Canada and the U.S.

Yes, the Canadian military are embarrassed, and they're embarrassed for good reason. But that doesn't mean that they're not respected in the United States. It's more that the United States military feels sorry that these people, who clearly would like to do more and are intellectually and professionally and historically capable of doing more, can't. Running a volunteer military is expensive. In the United States personnel costs, both present and past, run better than 50 percent of our budget. I mean, this is a gigantic amount of money. And at the same time you can't go back to a draft military because society and the militaries are so complex that you can't get people up to speed with a two-year draft.

America could not exist by itself. America cannot exist without the support of democratic countries around the world, whether they are militarily powerful, such as France or England, or militarily weak like Costa Rica or Paraguay. You bring to the table the assets that you have. If you will not develop assets to a level that we would like you to, this is regrettable. If the challenge were at the level of World War II and you did not bring to the table or the battlefield commensurate resources, that could be fatal to you in a societal sense. But that is not the case today. So all we can do is continue to urge you to bring up specific military resources to the degree that your society will permit you to. And to aid us with the assets in a particular conflict to the extent you are able to. Your finances, your intelligence, your economic assets, your political resources and your ability to persuade people because you're not Americans are valuable, and there is no reason to say that these are unworthy contributions because they aren't military contributions. They are contributions that we need, that we desire and that we hope will be committed.

Political Comparisons

It's been interesting for me, looking at the difference between Canadian politics and American politics. No Canadian prime minister has ever been a general. When I was first looking at the Canadian parliamentary bios I saw that there were only a tiny handful, of the governing party in particular, that had any military experience at all. The path to political leadership simply does not lie through military service in Canada.

The level of congressional military expertise is a reflection of interest. You are going to be interested because it is a major thread in the warp and woof of your political and social life.

The people in Congress know that society is interested in things military. A number of them have had military experience themselves. It is a valued element of American society. We are not a society in which the prevailing ethic is that you don't make good men into soldiers. We are still happy when good men become soldiers. And our Congress recognizes this.

They also recognize that there's an enormous defence industrial complex that reaches down into every constituency, every riding. As a result, they are interested not only in the economic aspects of it, they're also interested in making sure that the systems work and will continue to work.

So, that said, there are people who know more about the military than they know about farming, or hydroelectric facilities, or pick your subject of expertise. The people who are most interested in a subject will clump together to reinforce their own interest and to demonstrate it. That's the best way to explain why you're going to find some people who are quite knowledgeable about it. I've heard that General MacKenzie was impressed by the knowledge of those he met from the Congress. Maybe he met people that really wanted to show off that day.

General MacKenzie is an impressive individual. I've heard him speak. I have a lot of respect for him. I thought that years ago when he was just out of the Canadian military. He was a straight shooter. He hasn't changed the trajectory of what he has been firing since 1993, when I think he said there were more Toronto policemen than there were Canadian infantry. And that was before the Canadian Forces dropped even further than they have today.

JOHN HAMRE
2001 (Post-9/11)

Dr. John Hamre is a specialist in the congressional budget authorization and appropriation process, and has been president and CEO of the prestigious Center for Strategic and International Studies in Washington, D.C., since 2000. Prior to that he served as U.S. deputy secretary of defense and as undersecretary of defense. In that position Dr. Hamre was the principal assistant to the secretary of defense for the preparation, presentation and execution of the defense budget. Before serving the administration Dr. Hamre worked for 10 years as a professional staff member of the Senate Committee on Armed Services, responsible for oversight and evaluation of defense research and development programs.

Politics is how you take the ideas in one person's head and turn them into a national commitment, something that you're going to do as a nation. It's pretty easy to figure out how politics works in a monarchy. The king wakes up, decides we're going to do this, you go off and do it.

But whether it's an American democracy or a Canadian democracy, it's a lot more complicated, and I personally believe that despite the gun-smithing differences between how government works in Canada and how government works in the United States, they absolutely serve an identical purpose.

It's the way in which you take an individual idea of a minister or a pres-ident or a senator, and you turn it into a national commitment. You've got to have a mechanism that does that, one that turns it into something that the entire country's going to go off and do. In our system that's done by the president working with the Congress. In your system it's done with a prime minister taking a program forward through his party and passing legislation.

The Senate Committee on Armed Services
When you think of America, the nation, you think of the president. When you think of the phrase "we the people," you think of the Congress. That's how it works in our system. The president embodies the larger sense of nationhood but it's our Congress that embodies the sense of individual Americans and their commitment to our goals. I worked for 16 years for the Congress, six years in a support organization to the Congress and 10 years working as the deputy secretary for one of the committees of the Congress and the Senate.

And my job in working for the Senate Committee on Armed Services was to oversee the elements of the defence budget where we bought hard-ware. We bought weapon systems and we spent money for the develop-ment of new things. That was my primary responsibility. My job was to build a better Defense Department. Every day that was my job. Now, part of that was to criticize what came forward if it wasn't good. And a lot of it was to defend the things that were good and to improve it.

Oversight is not just standing back in critical isolation. You become an advocate for what's important and good and you use the credibility you get by being an advocate for reform and changing what you think is weak. And that's the nature of oversight in our system.

We had a staff of about 25 professionals on the Senate committee. We had behind us resources that you could draw on from the General Accounting Office, and there were 700 or 800 people, I suppose, over there. Over at the Congressional Budget Office there were probably 30 to 40 people that you could draw on. Congressional Research Service you could draw on, and then there was a huge army in people in town here who are always trying to change your thinking about things. Some of them are lobbyists, some of them are think-tank types, always trying to change how people think about things.

Of course you've got the contractors who are always trying to give you their point of view on things. In all candour I got my most useful information from inside the department itself, where I found the greatest power was a kind of venue for the true counterbalancing of truth. Because there's never a case where everybody's right on one side and everybody's wrong on the other side. Invariably there are cases where you've got good arguments and weak arguments on both sides of an issue. So you pit them against each other. And our role was to pit divergent views against each other in a constructive environment. That meant a lot of my best sources of information came from the Defense Department. Even though they knew I was going after them, they knew I was going to be fair.

I was very lucky. I worked for probably the most bipartisan committee in the Congress. During the second half of the 1980s and the first part of the 1990s the Senate Committee on Armed Services was one of the most bipartisan committees. I hardly ever had a partisan battle. I can't even remember a partisan battle where it was Republicans versus Democrats or vice versa.

We had battles and there may have been more Republicans on one side and more Democrats on the other, but it was never a partisan issue. Ours is a system where there's so much contentiousness, a counterpoising of facts is ultimately the only thing that you can really resort to. What's the most compelling case? Can you support your argument with compelling facts? That really is what the nature of oversight is in our system. But the American congressional environment has deteriorated over the last eight to 10 years. It's not nearly as collegial and bipartisan as it was when I worked there.

Deputy Secretary and the Defense Department
I think I was effective as deputy secretary in large measure because I came from the Hill community. I was in the brotherhood. There was a willingness

to let me talk to them in ways that somebody who comes from the outside just will never enjoy. So I was at an unbelievable advantage. I knew them all. I knew the Republicans as well as I knew the Democrats and I could call them up and say, "Look, I've got to just talk turkey on this one; here's where we really are." And I'd always tell them what was going on too. I'd never play games with them. And that gave me a huge advantage.

In our system you can't only choose to involve yourself in the productive oversight. It just doesn't work that way. People that don't know the Congress and the Defense Department resented being hauled up to the Hill. I always said, "Look, we have a very asymmetrical relationship with the Congress. They have the money and we want it. If you want the money, you're going to have to go up and deal with the people that have the money, period."

Money has too much dominated the way in which the Congress has tried to manage the Defense Department over the last 10 or 15 years, frankly to Congress's loss. Congress has far more influence if it really focuses on big issues rather than getting lost on 1,000 little issues. But, believe me, its power is astounding because it controls the budget.

I was the comptroller for the Defense Department, the chief financial officer for four years. I had to go get the money every year from the Congress, and I know a lot about how it works. Our constitution specifies that only the Congress can make appropriations. The president cannot generate his own money. He can't raise his own revenue and he can't spend it. Congress spends it; the president has to approve it.

In our system the source of integrated policy is the executive branch. The resident's the integrator of public policy and Congress is the disintegrator. It breaks it up into all these committees and they figure out what they want to do.

Inside the Defense Department program the president would say, "You guys get to spend X billion dollars." When I was the comptroller I'd build the budget for the department, for the secretary. It was the secretary's budget. We would spend the year getting the Congress to approve, not just the total but also all the pieces, and that meant an enormous amount of interaction on a day-to-day basis with our oversight committees. Because ultimately they decided.

You'd have to sometimes do things you didn't think were the highest priority but Congress did. If they have the money and we want it, you've got to put up with the way they give it to you. But you've got to take their role very honestly and very seriously, and if they think you're an honest broker, they'll work with you. Every year we were able to come back with 98 percent of exactly what we wanted.

The most important purpose is not just to get Congress to give you the money, but to get their commitment on behalf of the American public to what you're trying to do. You can't sustain a defence program unless the public is behind you.

We have annual appropriations every year, when you've got to go up and get money for things and explain what you're trying to do. Yet your average program takes 12 years to develop, then 20 years to buy. You keep that long-term commitment by getting the Congress to argue with you, understand and ultimately come to an agreement. You all say, "That's what we're going to do as a country." You take one person's idea and turn it into a national commitment. We do it through our Congress and through the way in which we interact with our Congress. You have a little different system.

Oversight
Primary oversight in our system is through two armed services committees, two defence appropriation subcommittees, two intelligence committees and a host of other committees that would claim some jurisdiction. I probably spent one-third of my time, when I was the deputy secretary working the congressional accounts, keeping relations positive, moving ahead, working through problems. Oversight is intense and time consuming. But what you are doing is building a national basis of support for your program.

I think that it's preferable to have our system, for such a big and diverse country as ours, if you're going to try to get a program that you can hold together over long periods of time. You can make big mistakes in our system if you move too quickly. I always say the biggest mistake that we make is not debating something in America. Spend a lot of time debating it if you want to understand as much as possible beforehand. In that sense I think our form of checks and balances is preferable. In a parliamentary system you can go charging off and make some pretty big mistakes that accumulate over time and are hard to get out of.

There are enormous oversight powers. When I was up on Capitol Hill I underestimated how much time and attention people were paying to what I thought. When I was over in the Pentagon I spent all my time trying to figure out, where are these Congress guys? What are they trying to do? How do I get them to see it in a different way? Congress has much, much more power than they realize. Subpoena power is a powerful tool. They have the power to withhold funds. They have the power over nominations.

That doesn't mean you just figure out what it takes to buy them off. I've fought a lot of battles. I've gone right to some Congress members and said, "We're going to fight you every step of the way on this. You're wrong and we're going to have to fight it." But you have to be up front about it and honest in how you deal with it. It's not because you don't like them, it's because there's something wrong with their idea and you've got to explain why.

When I was comptroller I said to Congress, "You don't ever have to ask for anything, just tell me what you want. I'm never going to make you have to use power to get something from me. I'll give it to you. I also expect you to hold the line against people who want to use power to do the wrong thing. But you'll never be in that position; I'll give you whatever you want." And I never once was asked to do a bad thing, not once in seven years.

I'm a big believer in the seniority system. People trash the U.S. seniority system, where you get more power because you've been there longer. I'm a big fan of that because in our system everybody's running for office all the time. You get elected and the first thing you do is hold a fundraiser for your next election.

The longer you're here, the more secure you are in your seat. Seniority tends to translate into confidence and you don't have to spend so much time trying to get back to town. You hold the levers of power, and when that happens people tend to become more national and less parochial. Every member of Congress has a sense they're a national leader and a local leader. "I'm here to get the chestnuts and bring 'em back and bury 'em in the forest in my little district." But they also have a sense that they're here for a national purpose. Conversely, it's hard to not be parochial when you are very junior. The more senior you are, the more national you become. I'm a big fan of seniority.

Gaining Power

In the American system you commit early on in your career in the Congress to where you're going to build your mighty fortress or how you're going to have power in Washington. It's all about power. Our Congress is organized around standing committees and you jockey and manoeuvre until you get on committees that you think match your personal interest, your constituents' interest and where you think you can get maximum leverage in Washington. That's our system. That's good. This is not a problem.

In our system people spend time developing substantive knowledge to become powerful, politically powerful. That's a pretty good thing and that reinforces the public good and personal good. People want to do the public good because it's helping them personally. There's nothing better than being able to totally overlap public good and personal initiative. That's fabulous.

That's how it works in our system. Our problem now is that people tend to get into those powerful jobs before they have good judgment, so we have a lot of very inexperienced young chairmen that tend to use muscle ahead of judgment, to be candid. That causes problems. I'm a big fan of the traditional, historical system, the way that Congress worked in the past.

This is one of the fault lines in the American constitution. We say we want an effective executive and so we put the ability to go to war in the hands of the president. But we try to hold him accountable by saying he can't pay for anything unless the Congress gives him money. Occasionally this gets to be a real problem. It did when I was comptroller.

I had a number of instances where a Democratic president felt it was important for national security to get the military involved in operations, and in this case a Republican Congress didn't like the idea much. They tried to stop it by choking us off, trying to hold the money down on our side. Very awkward. I had a number of battles like that.

Kosovo was one and before Kosovo it was Bosnia-Herzegovina. That was a far bigger problem. Kosovo was a little later and by then there was not as much of a fight over it. While I was the comptroller I think we had $15-billion to $16-billion worth of operations internationally for which the Congress didn't give us any money. They didn't agree with it. We went ahead. We did things. Then we had to find ways to pay for it out of our own accounts. Again very awkward, but this is one of the fault lines in the American constitution.

I was involved in deciding to go ahead without congressional approval, but I still tried to be objective. I think we made a mistake in the administration by not going through the very hard process of building a consensus. That made it a lot harder. But my experience in the Defense Department was that we were able to work with Republicans who didn't like the Clinton administration. I found it was possible to work with them. I thought that's what we should have done. You're a lot better off if you do that. But that was one of the real friction spots. And of course during the impeachment thing it got to be very hard.

Canada
Canada's always had a problem. How are you going to remain an independent sovereign nation next to this giant, the United States? For the first 60 years of the last century the solution to that was by being a bridge between Britain and the United States. That really worked up through World War II and after, up to the creation of NATO. But the U.K. started to diminish as a global player and all of a sudden Canada's role started to slip. That traditional defined role started to erode.

Lester Pearson created a new concept, saying, "We're going to be the bridge to the UN," and you defined your larger role as world peacekeepers. That gave you status, a standing in the international community. Over time that diluted. Now it's kind of a vague, "Well, we're going to lead in the world of ideas."

That's about where the Vatican is, OK? Now, it's not unimportant. I don't say that with any disparagement. But that's just about where the Vatican is. You lead with moral suasion. But take it for what it is.

You know, Al Capone said, "A smile will get you a long way in life, but a smile and a gun will get you further." I don't play down the importance of the military. What the world needs right now more than anything is not armies but policemen. You know, most of the real problems of the last 10 years were caused by the breakdown of law and order in society. And unfortunately, because the U.S. doesn't have mobilizable or deployable policemen, we've tended to send armies instead.

There is a very valid role for peacekeeping. I'm not of the view that peacekeeping is somehow less manly than fighting in real combat. I don't believe that at all. I think the world needs that. Having said that, I think it's a serious mistake if you want to be a serious player, if you want to be a G8 kind of country, not to have the ability to put an army in the field. If you can't put boots on the ground, you aren't going to be a real player. Now, that doesn't mean that peacekeeping's unimportant. It's very important and we need that, we very much need that. And Canada can play a very important role in doing that.

In my personal view — and I shouldn't be lecturing Canada, that's not my business, but I'll say it as a friend — I want Canada to be stronger so that it really can sit at the table.

The Future

The security epoch ended when the Berlin Wall came down. We drifted for 10 years until the new one developed on the 11th of September. We in the U.S. call it "homeland defence," but it really is a very different sort of security challenge. Security challenge for all countries. You know, they could have just as easily been aiming for the CN Tower as aiming for the World Trade towers.

What do you do when you have people who are prepared to kill themselves for the sake of making a political statement? Unfortunately they can put their hands on what's left over, the residue of the cold war. The terrible things they did on the 11th of September could have been worse if they'd gotten their hands on a nuclear device left over from the cold war, or on a biological weapon left over from the cold war. It's different from the classical security eras, at least over the last 200 years, because it's not as clearly a case of nation states posing the security threat. We now have the prospect of transnational actors. You can't intimidate them and deter them the way we did in the past. This is going to be a challenge.

America has a pretty strong bipartisan consensus on defence in general. It tends to become less focused when you get into real activities. But by and large Americans want a strong, capable military. They want to have the ability to act globally. They want to be able to conduct a fairly full spectrum of defence capabilities, deter nuclear war, intercede in a civil war to save Americans or Canadians or Western hostages, rescue people if there's an earthquake or a hurricane, fight another Desert Storm. Where you'll get some problems are the individual projects that tend to be contentious. National Missile Defense. That will be one that'll be hotly debated.

The questions are, "Is this the highest priority? Is it worth the money?" Not, "Do you want to basically be able to block the bad guys that want to attack you with missiles?" I think this has now shifted the focus a good deal. How capable are we at integrating intelligence and law enforcement and things here in the home front, and are we able to share information across these lines? I think there is a bipartisan consensus for that.

There's a bell curve. Some very, very capable people in our Congress know a lot, and then you get some guys that really don't know very much. So frankly, you'd find a fair number of people that are pretty uninformed in our Congress. But they're not taken seriously until they take it seriously. People tend to write you off if you don't seriously engage in the issue.

In our system you tend to be taken seriously if you take the job seriously. Because defence is still seen as an important national goal, you find members that feel that they've got to do that. I think this is a matter of party leaders. This comes with leadership. Bill Clinton fundamentally changed the Democratic Party. He changed welfare reform, for example. He created a new way of thinking about the problem and he led Democrats to a position you would think they never would have gone before.

It's very possible, but you must lead. The party leadership has to be the one that says, "For Canada to sit honourably at the big table and be taken seriously, we must do something about defence. We can't just have a uniformed Salvation Army." You've got to be able to put boots on the ground. You've got to be able to make a difference where you have to make a difference. If the party leaders say that, and you have a bunch of guys say, "Why should we do that? The public doesn't want it," then you lead. You know, the public didn't ask Margaret Thatcher to privatize British industry, but she did it. And she totally transformed the way U.K. society is today. And that's what leadership's about. Forgive me, that's very pretentious for me to say, but it's about political leadership!

You have such a proud tradition. God, just think, nobody fought more courageously on Normandy than the Canadians. Nobody bled more than the Canadians. I don't think there were Canadians who were worried about being Canadians back on D-Day. Everybody knew what the hell they were doing.

The reason that you have standing in NATO is not because of your strength, it's because you're willing to fight. You've had troops on the ground. But when Canada decided to pull out of Europe, you pulled away from a big commitment. If you aren't a real player on the world stage, it's pretty hard to keep a sense of sovereign control, a sense that you *are* a real player on the world stage.

Canadians spend time asking, "What does it mean? How do we stay next to this big giant to the south?" Well, you know, be a proud partner with us. The best way to do that is to have a strong military. You can fight right beside us.

PART TWO

Views on the Balkans

KIM RICHARD NOSSAL
2001 (Pre-9/11)

From 1976 to 2001 Kim Nossal taught international relations at McMaster University, where he was chair of the Department of Political Science from 1992 to 1996. In September 2001 he became head of the Department of Political Studies at Queen's University. Professor Nossal lectures and writes widely on international relations. He is the author of The Politics of Canadian Foreign Policy, *a definitive textbook on the subject which is now in its third edition. He recently co-edited* Diplomatic Departures: The Conservative Era in Canadian Foreign Policy, 1984–93.

Foreign Policy/Defence Policy
You have to keep in mind that the Canadian government works in an international system. It has to deal with as many as 195 different sovereign governments, a large number of international actors of all sorts from international organizations, multinational corporations and different kinds of groups that operate on the world stage. So the idea is that the policy gets made within the confines and constraints and imperatives of that external environment.

At the same time foreign policy is always very much a matter of domestic politics with governments, members of Parliament and Cabinet ministers responding to pressures that emanate from within the Canadian polity.

And finally there is a governmental side to this, how all of the folks in Ottawa who are responsible for thinking about what kinds of policy responses the Canadian government should take on a particular issue deal with one another. One has to look at the way in which different bureaucrats in different departments deal with one another, fight their fights and put forward different perspectives of what they consider to be the national interest.

You can't find the root or the source of policy in just one of those settings. All three of them have an inevitable impact on what eventually the government does, and that is what policy analysis is all about.

In the post–Second World War period, one of the things that we've seen is the growing importance of the international system and in particular the struggles between the great powers. In the last 25 years or so, one of the things that we've seen grow in importance is the question of human rights and the way in which governments treat their citizens and the way in which citizens treat each other in other countries. That's very much an outgrowth of our own rights consciousness in Canada. That rights consciousness, it can be argued, is rooted in the growth of rights consciousness in the United States. So when you look at the longer term, one can see that the external environment continues to be an important element in those longer-term fashions in Canadian foreign policy.

Any country's foreign policy is always and inevitably going to be a reflection of the particular men and women who hold particular positions at any time. So when you look at fads and fashions in policy, you can't help but look at the individuals who are holding positions, whether it be the prime minister or the foreign affairs minister or even the senior bureaucracy. These folks bring to their positions particular ideas, particular notions of what is right and wrong, what is in the national interest, what is not in the national interest. That's where your fads and fashions come from. There's a limit, of course, to how far those fads and fashions can be shaped by any one individual. There are broader imperatives that the Canadian government and all Canadians have to face that no single individual can possibly do anything about. But always it's important to look at particular individuals.

Canadian policy is marked, always, by continuity. The fact is that we're a deeply conservative, a deeply bureaucratic community, and because of our stability, you're not going to see large changes, even with changes of government and changes of personality. So the essence of our existence as a political community does not shift and change when we get changes of party, changes of leader, changes of personality.

One of the persistent problems that Canadians have in dealing with the outside world is knowing exactly how much to spend on their military establishment, and there's no good answer to that question. It seems to me that politicians over the course of many generations, not just at present, have understood their constituents and the desires of those constituents. There isn't a great deal of support within the Canadian political community for spending on defence.

The reality is that the political culture of this community is one that does not value our Forces. It does not value our spending tax dollars on the Forces and politicians come to understand that. So those governments who come to power thinking that they are going to be the ones to change the fortunes of the Canadian Forces discover extremely fast that there's no percentage in it. If you look at the Mulroney government's record over the course of the 1980s, in modern Canadian history there has been no party, no government, no prime minister who has come to office better disposed to the Canadian Forces and its needs than Brian Mulroney and the Progressive Conservative Party. And yet over the course of the 1980s Mulroney and his ministers and the party came to understand that the demands of the Forces simply were too out of whack with the desires of constituents not to spend money.

As Desmond Morton of McGill University has said, and it seems to me so apt, "Canadians come by their cheapness, with regard to defence, quite honestly," and over the course of long historical experience as a political community, we are incredibly fortunate that we've never seriously been threatened by anyone. As a consequence Canadians understand that, really and truly, we don't need to spend on defence and that we can get away with spending as little on defence as our allies will allow us. And it seems to me that's a long-term continuity in Canadian policy.

PLAYING THE OSTRICH

We are always prepared to be criticized simply because criticism from allies at a NATO summit, or at a prime ministerial–presidential summit in the case of the United States, is limited pain.

One can put up with a lot of criticism. That short-term pain of having to suffer the slings and arrows of your annoyed allies, when you come back home you realize that it's all worth it because you don't have to face the considerable difficulties of spending a great deal of money on defence and then having to justify that to always quizzical taxpayers.

One of the interesting things about Canadian defence policy, and Canadian foreign policy more broadly, is that Canadian politicians and indeed Canadians have always liked the fact that we have a seat at the table and that we are members of a large number of groups in international politics. We're a member of the G7, the G8, we're a member of NATO, we're a member of the United Nations. And once in a decade we get to sit on the Security Council.

Canadians and their politicians love that for all sorts of fairly obvious reasons. Canadian politicians like it because it affords them an opportunity to operate on the world stage. Canadian parties like it because it provides an opportunity to present themselves to the electorate as active on the world stage. And keep in mind that the electorate for many comes from different parts of the world. For Canadians themselves there is a nice, warm and fuzzy feeling of being well regarded in international affairs and international politics.

But here of course is the paradox. The fact is, it actually costs virtually nothing to remain as part of all of these groups simply because everyone is far too polite to throw any recalcitrant or cheap member out of a particular club or coalition. Canadian politicians have grown to understand, by sheer dint of experience, that in fact you don't have to spend large to be able to enjoy the seat at the table.

The government understands that one of the prices for the seat at the table for international activism is that you occasionally have to put your money where your mouth is, you actually have to use your national resources to try and achieve what you claim you want to achieve. Here is where the Canadian government got into difficulty after the end of the cold war. The first government to experience it was the Mulroney government, and the Chrétien government followed immediately.

The problem was that Canadians and the Canadian government love to make commitments, but we were quickly confronted with the reality that the Canadian Forces simply didn't have the kind of force structure, the kind of equipment necessary to undertake all of the commitments that the political masters were committing Canada to. So very quickly the Canadian Forces discovered that they were everywhere, trying to do a great deal, operating in conditions that were fundamentally unlike the conditions of the cold war peacekeeping operations. And very quickly it ran the government into serious difficulty.

The question of what kind of a power Canada is, whether it's a large power or a principal power, or a medium power, middle power, small power, or indeed a stooge of the United States, is a question that very much depends on who's doing the asking. Canadians themselves like to comfort themselves with the idea that we're a middle power. We're not big enough to be large and imperial like other countries. We're not so small that we're inconsequential. Therefore sitting in the middle is a nice place to be. It very much depends, though, on the kind of issue that you're talking about. A number of Canadians will recognize that their government always needs to respond to the pressures of the United States.

We often feel constrained to respond in a positive way simply because there is a fundamental recognition that our interests are linked to good relations to the United States.

Our membership in the G7 imposes a special kind of obligation on us. The obligation that all Canadian governments have to toe the G7 line on important political issues. That, after all, is the price of membership. It's the way in which the G7 operates. It doesn't mean that everyone has to be marching in lock step, but it does mean that if you want to go to the G7, if you want to have an impact on the other leaders there, one can't be on the periphery and on the margins shouting for your own position. If you're going to have an impact on the other leaders, it has to be done through very quiet diplomacy, so that at the end of the day when the leaders are all lined up for their ritualistic photographs, there is in fact a commonality of ideological purpose, even if there are severe policy differences in the backrooms.

The Cold War and the "Gap"

The huge changes that began in 1989, and continued through 1990 and 1991, caught Canadians off guard. There was in fact a considerable amount of enthusiasm in Ottawa. The government of Brian Mulroney embraced the change quite enthusiastically. Mulroney himself was enthusiastic about the prospect of new world order being promulgated by George Bush.

After the Iraqi invasion of Kuwait Mr. Mulroney embraced the new generation of peacekeeping very enthusiastically, in the early 1990s until he left office in 1993. That enthusiasm was picked up by the Chrétien Liberals, in particular after Lloyd Axworthy became the foreign minister. If you look at the way in which Canadian policy responded to those massive changes in the international system, what you see is a certain degree of enthusiasm by governments of both stripes, by both the Conservatives and the Liberals, for Canada's new moral authority.

One of the persistent issues in Canadian defence policy is what during the cold war period came to be known as a commitment-capability gap. The reality is that well before that phrase was coined in the cold war era, Canadians had had a commitment-capability gap.

Canadians, given the geography that we occupy, have never been able to defend our country. So from the beginnings of Confederation in the 1860s we've always had a commitment-capability gap. In the cold war period what we saw was an intensification of that gap, as the Canadian government continued to embrace a set of military commitments while at the same time driving down expenditures on the military. During the cold war period that was always a source of considerable criticism by our allies.

In the post–cold war period, interestingly enough, the commitment-capability gap continues, but it takes a slightly different form. Today our commitment-capability gap revolves around the fact that the Canadian government, first the Mulroney Conservatives and then the Chrétien Liberals, embraced a set of commitments to the post–cold war order that the Canadian Forces simply did not have the capacity to fulfill. They don't have the personnel capacity. All you have to do is to talk to serving members of the Canadian Forces who are on such tight rotations now because of the large number of operations that the Canadian government has committed them to.

Our Forces used to be up around the 80,000 to 90,000 mark, and they're drifting ever downward. There are some people in Ottawa who are thinking about a force of 40,000 or 50,000 people. Trying to be in as many places as we are creates difficulties of all sorts. Some people argue that this commitment-capability gap in the post–cold war era is a fundamentally bad thing because it corrodes the capacity of the Forces and it creates the kind of difficulties that attract criticism.

I have the slightly different view that being able to spread the Forces as thinly as the Canadian government has done has actually been a great success. Think of it from a slightly different perspective. Instead of thinking about what the Canadian Forces are actually doing in the field, think about where the government can say we are in the world. As long as we are able to participate in a particular operation in this country or that country, does it really matter whether or not we have troops there that are hopelessly stretched? Does it really matter that the people on the ground are stressed out because of the rapidity of their rotation? Are they really concerned about the inadequacy of some of the equipment that they're sent out into the field with?

Well, from a politician's point of view — and I don't want to sound overly cynical here, but I think it's important to look at it from a politician's point of view — we are getting a tremendous bang for our buck, to use the American expression. With a very small base of Canadian Forces the Canadian flag flies in a lot of places. Is it always effective? No. On the other hand, does that really matter from a politician's perspective? And that's where we get another important gap. The politicians are too removed from the realities in the field which are confronted by members of the Canadian Forces on an ongoing and real-time basis.

There's a general calculation that it's good to be places. It's good to try and affect international politics and to commit ourselves to different operations. However, there is a tendency to place greater importance on the act of being there rather than on what is necessarily done there.

Canadian governments have been lucky. In the case of Somalia, of course, they were not at all lucky. They put folks into the field without actually thinking through what the unified task force was actually doing in Somalia. They deployed a contingent that was actually quite appropriate for the nasty operation that Somalia represented. Where the government got unlucky was that some members of this contingent behaved in a way that previous peacekeeping operations simply never had the inclination to do.

The Gulf

The Gulf War didn't start off as a war. It started off as the "Gulf conflict" in August of 1990, and the nations that joined the United States in opposing Saddam Hussein and the Iraqi occupation of Kuwait never dreamed that they would be entering a war situation. There was a great degree of enthusiasm. We tend to forget just how enthusiastic countries were, governments were, leaders were, in August of 1990, about what was happening.

We tend to forget how unusual it was to see the U.S. secretary of state and the Soviet foreign minister standing side by side, giving a joint press conference, and how unusual it was to see large numbers of countries from different ideological, religious, cultural and economic perspectives coming together to form this grand coalition of something like 34 different countries, to impose sanctions on Iraq in an effort to get the government of Iraq to withdraw from Kuwait. Those were heady days. All of the countries who got involved, including Canada, never really dreamed that they would be climbing on a roller coaster whose trajectory they actually could not control in any reasonable way. Because the United States government decided that it was impossible to continue simply to have forces in the Gulf region to protect Saudi Arabia against a potential Iraqi attack. They either had to withdraw those forces, which would have been a disaster in political and diplomatic terms, or use them.

So in November of 1990 the government of George Bush decided to shift the nature of the coalition from being a defensive coalition to being an offensive coalition. That decision, a unilateral decision taken by the administration in Washington, presented every single one of the governments who were onboard the coalition with an unenviable choice. Do you get off and withdraw from the coalition, or do you hang on tight and see where the ride takes you? No one withdrew from the coalition.

Some governments were less than enthusiastic. The government of Australia, for example, was not at all enthusiastic about being involved in what was quite clearly going to be a war. Some governments, particularly where there were large Islamic populations, chose to retain as low a profile as they possibly could.

The Canadian government actually was not unenthusiastic. It was concerned, but the Mulroney government understood what the constraints and imperatives were at this particular point. There was a considerable amount of enthusiasm, in particular at the prime ministerial level, but versus a considerable amount of concern at other levels about the possibility of committing our Forces.

Relative to other countries, the contribution that Canada made was a normal to above-normal contribution, compared to other middle powers. Needless to say, when you compare our contribution to that of the United States, of France, of Britain, of Syria, of Egypt, no, it was nothing like that. The "two and a half ships" that that we allocated to the Gulf region were one frigate and one destroyer and the supply ship. When you look at the ships that we allocated to the Gulf, when you look at the CF-18s in Qatar and when you look at the field hospital, this was a fairly positive and solid contribution.

Looking at the reactions to the various contributions, there wasn't much harping against the contributions of smaller countries like Canada, mainly because there was so much harping about what the Japanese and the Germans were not doing. So some of the American annoyance at their allies was diverted. One has to recognize that Canada wasn't alone in fighting a war in which there were no casualties, in which there was no loss of equipment, in which there were no actual nasty combat offensive operations conducted by Canadians. A large number of countries were in exactly that kind of situation.

A large number of countries joined the coalition, put together over a two-week period by the Americans and by NATO, for a variety of reasons. The first and, I think, the most important reason was that what the government of Iraq had done to Kuwait was truly unique in modern diplomatic history.

Lots of countries invade other countries. Lots of countries use force against other countries. But with the lone exception of the disappearance of Tibet in 1950, no other country had eliminated the sovereignty of one of its neighbours. So fundamental a threat to the existing legal order in international politics was the disappearance of Kuwait that there was an inexorable logic to climbing onboard a sanctioning coalition. That's why it's important always to keep in mind that this thing started off not as a war coalition against Iraq, but as a coalition to sanction Iraq into abandoning its occupation of Kuwait.

Probably there was a considerable push within some parts of the military to take advantage of the opportunity offered by the transformation of the coalition from a defensive to an offensive coalition, to say, "This is what we exist for. Please use us." On the other hand — and this is where we come back to the importance of domestic politics — the Mulroney government understood and understood completely, and Joe Clark gave voice to this concern in a speech that he made, that it would be extremely difficult for a Canadian prime minister or a Canadian defence minister or a Canadian foreign minister to have to explain to the parents and relatives of dead Canadians precisely why their son or daughter had died in the Gulf.

There was in the Mulroney government's perspective the same kind of casualty avoidance that we now come to associate with the way in which we fight wars. That is, if you're going to commit your citizens to be put in harm's way to be potentially killed, then you'd better have a really good reason for doing so.

Responsibility and Luck
The responsibility in Canadian legal and political practice is that the executive, in other words the prime minister and Cabinet, have the sole responsibility of committing and using the Canadian Forces and committing the Canadian Forces to combat. Very simply this is a legal precept that goes back to Westminster practice, that the Crown has the responsibility for fighting wars. To the extent that the executive is sustained in power in the House of Commons, it may do with the Forces more or less what it wishes.

Now, there is a requirement under Canadian legislation to call Parliament if the Canadian Forces are being committed to combat, but the Canadian Parliament doesn't need an explicit vote of approval to make that commitment. Normally, however, Canadian governments do not commit their citizens to war without seeking the approval of the Canadian Parliament. Canadian governments, generally speaking, have not sought explicit parliamentary approval for committing our Forces to peacekeeping. Somalia, I would argue, is not the same as either the Gulf in 1990 or Kosovo in 1999.

Canada has been bluffing up to a certain point, and those who control the shape and nature of the Canadian Forces understand full well, in my view, what they're doing. They understand that as long as we are there in some form or other, it will simply be enough. Moreover, their capacity to withstand embarrassment seems to be limitless. Think about the Timor intervention, for example.

Now, quite clearly the Canadian government was interested in participating in the Timor mission that was put together by the Australians, but they had significant difficulties in doing so. There weren't enough forces. The transport kept breaking down. The inability to deploy Canadian forces very quickly, and remember that international forces were needed on the ground very quickly, was a significant problem. But think of the outcome. The reality is that the Canadian government did not face a barrage of either domestic or international criticism for not being able to be there in time.

So often the Canadian government has gotten extremely lucky in this kind of situation. The Somalia case, I think, demonstrates the lone exception to that. Even in the case of the former Yugoslavia. The Canadian government had been extremely lucky that so few members of the Forces were harmed in that mission.

I think that the fundamental tension in Canadian foreign and defence policy is that the aspirations of the politicians and the aspirations of the foreign policy makers will always be out of whack with the capabilities of the defence folks who have to actually deliver the policies, who actually have to implement them. Very simply, in order for the Defence Department to do the full range of what our foreign policy calls for, it would require such a massive increase in the defence budget that it simply isn't conceivable. One of the difficulties of being a defence planner or a defence policy maker in Canada is the fundamental reality that Canadians, generally speaking, and their representatives in Parliament do not consider defence to be important enough to devote large amounts of national treasure to it. And that's a reality that every defence planner intrinsically knows. They may moan about it, but they understand.

PLAYING THE OSTRICH

The Bookends — Suez and Zaire

Some have argued that the Suez crisis in 1956 and the Zaire crisis in 1996 represent bookends in Canadian peacekeeping operations, that from the high of Suez that netted Lester Pearson the Nobel Peace Prize, we've seen this tragic descent in Canadian peacekeeping operations, to the experience in Zaire where we wanted to be there but couldn't be.

I have a very different perspective. Suez represented a triumph of Canadian diplomacy, not Canadian military policy. It actually didn't matter whether we had folks there on the ground or not. As it turned out, the folks that we did send to the Suez mission, to the United Nations Emergency Force, weren't the ones that you might have originally thought. What was important in Suez was not the military capability, it was the idea. It was the idea of putting a force in place.

In Zaire it was likewise not a great disaster because of the lack of capability, but because the idea wasn't as good as it had been in 1956. The idea of inserting a force into what was still a potential civil-war situation was an idea whose time very definitely had not come. The Americans recognized this immediately, and it was American opposition to the Canadian idea that scuttled that mission, not the lack of Canadian capability. If Canada had had its own global airlift capacity and a large contingent of combat-capable forces able to be inserted into a civil-war situation, the Canadian government very simply would have faced a true disaster. The only way to make the Zaire idea work was to get Americans and others onboard, and the Canadian government failed to do that.

The Zaire conflict represents an important lesson in having folks on the ground who are able to provide a separate and independent assessment so that you are not so deeply linked to the great powers that they are able to run your foreign policy.

Decisions about committing the Canadian Forces often tend to be made at the political level, where the prime minister or the foreign affairs minister or someone else decides that this would be a good thing to do. If you think about the commitment-capability gap, there tends not to be any long-term thinking about what the consequences and implications of saying yes to a commitment actually are, largely because for the most part the Canadian contribution is always symbolic. We are always an add-on to someone else's taking the lead.

The Zaire case is a nice example of what happens when we try to take the lead, expecting that others are actually going to be there on the ground. Our often token, or sometimes symbolic, contribution gets easily scooped into a larger operation.

What does it mean to lead an operation like the Australians led in Timor? They had to think through all of the operational and logistical requirements of mounting that kind of operation. One of the interesting consequences of Canada's long-term dependence on NATO and the United States is essentially that we've not had to do this in any serious way. That's why the Zaire mission in 1996 was not such a hot idea. Because we lacked the capability to follow through on our idea.

Foreign Policy and the Prime Minister

We got into trouble in the mid-1990s because we had explicitly embraced an idea about foreign policy that was so expansive that it would almost guarantee running into trouble: Lloyd Axworthy's idea of human security. If you take human security seriously, and Mr. Axworthy took the notion of human security seriously, this implies a vast commitment of resources. Because if you take human security seriously, you must be concerned about all of those refugees in Goma. Every single one of them.

What it implies is that you actually have to commit Canadian resources and put Canadians in harm's way to protect the security of those individuals. That of course is an utterly impossible policy objective. There are, among the six billion human beings in the world, simply far too many hundreds of millions of them who lack elemental security. Thirty-three million Canadians can't possibly begin to address the vast canvas that the human-security agenda implies.

Historically Canada's role has never exceeded being an add-on. Our involvement in peacekeeping is far more symbolic than the vast majority of Canadians realize, and that is precisely the way the politicians like it. Canadians are comforted as long as we believe that we are this great peacekeeping, peacemaking nation. Those people in the Canadian Forces who know the reality on the ground have a rather different perspective.

There's no doubt that over the course of the last 30 or 40 years the Department of Foreign Affairs and its minister have experienced a decline in prestige, in political importance. Most of the time we remember Foreign Affairs for its signal success in the post–Second World War period, placing Canada as a global actor. We remember the success of Lester Pearson's diplomacy at Suez. We remember the Nobel Prize. We remember Pearson going from being foreign minister to being the prime minister of the country.

Since that time there have been a number of changes. One of the changes has been the declining importance of high diplomacy in world politics in the 1980s and 1990s. In the post-1945 period in the decade after the war, international diplomacy was important simply because it was directed at trying to avoid the re-emergence of conflict between two great powers that now had awesome tools of destruction. By the 1960s and 1970s those weapons of mass destruction had grown so massive that, ironically, high diplomacy was less and less necessary as it became very clear that so awesome was the destructive capability of nuclear weapons, war between the U.S. and the USSR was fairly unlikely. There was always grave danger, but there was a certain lack of reality about thinking of a nuclear exchange between the great powers.

By the 1980s and 1990s international economics was much more important for global politics, so you see a transformation in Canadian bureaucratic structure. The Department of External Affairs becomes the Department of Foreign Affairs and International Trade, as it became in 1993. We've also seen a change in the foreign minister's importance in Cabinet. Sometimes the foreign minister is appointed as a way of getting a political rival out of one's hair, if one is the prime minister. If you look at the pattern of appointments to External Affairs, going really back to Paul Martin, Sr., in the 1960s, one can see the willingness of prime ministers to basically give a prestigious portfolio to political rivals. The classic case, of course, is Brian Mulroney giving External Affairs to Joe Clark.

The Prime Minister's Office, the Privy Council Office and the Department of Finance have really inserted themselves much more into foreign policy. You're no longer dealing in high diplomacy. The kind of diplomacy that Pearson engaged in, in 1956, didn't require very much, other than some excellent interpersonal skills, a good budget to support receptions and diplomacy at the United Nations. In essence there wasn't the need for a large expenditure of funds for that. As a consequence the involvement of central agencies, which are all about the allocation of resources, wasn't so important.

The received wisdom is that Canada was the third-largest country as far as armed forces were concerned in the 1940s, and therefore we were a player in 1956 because of it. No.

Very quickly our Forces were demobilized. Very quickly we began to run down the military budget, as one might expect after spending so much on wartime military. Canada was a player insofar as Canadian diplomats were active at the United Nations in alliance circles. The fact that Canada didn't have big military capacity really wasn't that important. We were a marginal player in the Korean War. I don't want to minimize what the Canadian contribution was or minimize the contribution of those 300 Canadians who lost their lives in that conflict. But we weren't the lead player and we've never been the lead player, ever, in any international conflict. I don't think Canadian government, from the St. Laurent government of the 1950s to the Chrétien government of the 1990s, has ever really conceived of Canada being the kind of lead player that the United States or Britain or France, the big powers, tends to be.

Some people have argued that Cabinet has become less important in foreign policy making over the years, and that the prime minister has become more important. I'm sorry to say that this is quite a historical view. If you look at the broad sweep of Canadian history, you will find Canadian prime ministers are always more important than their Cabinet colleagues in crucial decisions involving the Canadian state. Whether it be Mackenzie King's long tenure in office or Louis St. Laurent's involvement as prime minister or Lester Pearson's. Pierre Trudeau, Brian Mulroney and Jean Chrétien all have been inclined to want to make important decisions by themselves without consulting, or without formally calling Cabinet together.

Think about how we got involved in the Gulf coalition. It was essentially Brian Mulroney flying down to Washington to have dinner with George Bush. Out of that came our commitment. His defence minister, his foreign minister weren't around. Prime ministerial prerogatives in foreign policy making remain as pronounced as they always have been, and that is largely because it's the prime minister who is the focus of so much policy. It's the prime minister who gets to go to international summit meetings and it's the prime minister who ultimately is responsible for the broad directions of the government that he or she leads.

Some people argue that one of the reasons why the prime minister is as powerful as he is in the Canadian system is because Parliament is not as involved as it might be. But the prime minister and the members of the Cabinet are all members of Parliament. So what exactly do they mean when they say "Parliament"?

Parliament is always involved in policy making, and indeed Parliament is always involved in the centralized nature of the prime minister. It's involved on an ongoing basis every time the prime minister walks into the House of Commons and his ministers line up with all of those backbenchers. That is a daily act of involvement in the centralized process. Anytime Parliament wanted to, it could insert itself into the policy process by simply denying the prime minister confidence in his capacity to govern.

I'm sorry to be so constitutional about this, but it's really important, when you think about the role of Parliament in the policy process, to think about the origins of our political system so we understand that there are particular reasons why those masses of Liberal backbenchers sit on their hands, day after day, allowing the prime minister to have the kind of powerful and central point in the policy process that he enjoys.

Different Systems
There's no doubt that the way in which our system is structured creates severe problems for people's conceptions of democracy and the ability to influence the decisions and acts of government that have an impact on their lives.

On the other hand, it doesn't necessarily follow that there is a lack of democracy just because you have a system of government where after an election a large number of backbenchers sit on their hands and allow the prime minister and Cabinet to have the kind of inordinate power that they enjoy in our system — and in all Westminster systems like ours. What does follow is that people get turned off by such a system simply because they recognize the futility, and in the Canadian case there's an additional problem in that all Canadians have a sense of how things run so very differently down south.

They see members of Congress and senators impede the power of the president. They see that their local representative goes to Washington and has the kind of impact on the policy process that the average back-bencher on the government side, or on the opposition side, never has in Ottawa. So there tends to be built up a sense that the Americans do it better, and that they're more democratic. My view is that they just do it differently. It would be a fundamental error to give Canadian parliamentarians the kind of powers enjoyed by the Congress of the United States for one very simple reason. Unless there is a constitutional separation between the members of Parliament, as legislators, and the executive in whose hands the fates of individual legislators rest, then — and I hate to say it — it's a mug's game. The case of John Nunziata really says it all. The fact is that if you're serious about opposing the executive, then you must have the freedom to oppose and to survive punishments inflicted on you by the executive.

A member of the United States Congress can oppose the executive, and there isn't a thing the executive branch can do about it in any serious way. By contrast, in the Canadian case if, as a member of Parliament, as a backbencher, I oppose my front bench, eventually my front bench is going to throw me out.

Generally speaking, electors in this country will not elect independent members of Parliament. They like to elect folks who are able to hang around their necks a party sign. Unless you're able to restructure the essence of our system to give members of Parliament a political existence that is utterly independent of the prime minister and the Cabinet, then anything you do is simply going to be a kind of elaborate Potemkin village.

Say you do create committees of Parliament that will be given real oversight responsibilities, really and truly. The oversight responsibilities will last about as long as it takes a committee of Parliament to become independent minded. To openly oppose the prime minister, to make the prime minister look bad, what parliamentary committee is going to do that? What parliamentary committee filled with people who run the serious risk of being excommunicated from the party that is after all responsible for bringing them to Ottawa is going to change this? All of the structures are all wrong. You can't create a Congress out of a Westminster Parliament. It is impossible.

Committees play a very important role in giving governments an opportunity to explain themselves in detail, an opportunity that they're not going to find in the House of Commons with its tight agenda. It gives parliamentarians an opportunity to contribute to the policy-making process. It provides ordinary people with an opportunity to present their views to the governing structures of our community. I don't want to suggest that parliamentary committees in and of themselves are useless. What I do want to suggest is that parliamentary committees in a Westminster system cannot be given the kind of powers that congressional committees enjoy in Washington.

Parliamentary committees have different uses than the ones in Washington. The congressional committees in Washington are all about constraining the power of the executive. Because after all that's what the genius of the United States constitution was designed to do — to stop the kind of tyranny that is implicit in a British parliamentary system.

The North Atlantic Treaty
Originally the North Atlantic Treaty was set up to ensure that the United States would use its massive power to defend Western European countries against what was seen to be a threat of attack by the Soviet Union. That's what the concern of all the little countries of Western Europe was after the Second World War. The effort to involve the Americans in the defence of Western Europe was really what the North Atlantic Treaty was all about. The North Atlantic Treaty of 1949 was transmogrified into the North Atlantic Treaty Organization in the early 1950s, after the Korean War broke out, largely to try and institutionalize and organize the collective efforts of the North American partners, Canada and the United States, and all of the Western European partners.

That essential purpose never changed over the entire 45 years of the cold war. There was a fundamental continuity of purpose, of keeping the Americans in and the Russians out. It was also to involve West Germany in an alliance and bind them in so that never again could the Germans threaten the peace of Europe as they had done in the 1930s. And those purposes remained unchanged.

With the disappearance of the Soviet Union in December of 1991, the essential purpose of the organization changed fairly dramatically. If you've organized an alliance against a particular enemy and that enemy disintegrates, you would think that there was no longer any need for the alliance. Instead of going out of business, as some might have thought it should have or could have done, NATO reinvented itself as an international organization committed to the same kinds of goals, even without an enemy in the form of the Soviet Union. It committed itself to maintaining the peace of Europe and also committed to keeping the Americans in.

Very much, NATO is designed to keep the Americans engaged and involved in the peace of Europe, even though it may not have the same kind of military commitment on the ground that it used to have during the cold war. Although the Soviet Union has disappeared, European peace is not quite yet so totally apparent.

Back in the 1940s the Canadian interest in the North Atlantic alliance was identical with those of the Western Europeans. Canadian diplomats made the calculation that the only way that there was going to be a European peace was if the Americans were involved, and Canadians worked just as hard as Western Europeans did in trying to secure the willingness of the United States to commit its forces to the defence of Western Europe.

Now, it is true that once the treaty was signed and the organization was in place Canadians recognized that there were lots of benefits to being involved in NATO. It was a seat at yet another table. It was an opportunity to be institutionally involved in Europe. It was an opportunity not to be left alone with purely the Americans in North America. And that has always been an abiding concern of Canadian governments, that we are already dependent enough on our dealings with the United States in terms of trade and continental defence. This provides a little opportunity to be involved elsewhere.

Kosovo broke new ground for NATO, in large part because it was the first time that NATO forces had ever been used in an out-of-area operation. It broke new ground in the sense that this was not in any sense an attack on NATO or on NATO countries by a foreign power. This was not an alliance organizing itself in mutual defence. This was an international organization that took upon itself the responsibility, if you want to think of it in those terms, of bringing order to a particular region to its immediate southeast for the purpose of maintaining the broader European peace.

It was clear that the United Nations was not going to become involved in the conflict in Kosovo in the way that it had allowed in the conflict in the other provinces of the former Yugoslavia. It was quite clear that the Russian Federation and the Chinese would block any move to use NATO-led forces to intervene in the province of Kosovo. And it can be argued that the United Nations doesn't exist to involve itself in civil wars in other countries.

In fact, Article 2 (7) explicitly prohibits it from involving itself within the jurisdiction of one of its member states. To the extent that the province of Kosovo is a part of the Federal Republic of Yugoslavia, then what NATO forces did is something that the United Nations, unless it is a Chapter VII operation, would normally never have done.

Keep in mind that, although we've had long involvement in Yugoslavia since it collapsed into civil war in 1991, that involvement hasn't been uniformly enthusiastic. There's no doubt that the Progressive Conservative government of Brian Mulroney was an enthusiastic participant in the early 1990s. In fact he is the only Canadian prime minister who is on record as advocating the use of force by United Nations troops for the purposes of human rights.

One of the interesting consequences of the Conservative defeat in 1993 was that it brought to power a prime minister and a party considerably concerned about the implications of being involved in the former Yugoslavia. And if you look at Canadian policy in the mid-1990s, in the first couple of years of the Chrétien government's tenure, you will see a distinct lack of enthusiasm. The Chrétien government did not want to participate in the use of NATO air strikes to coerce the government in Belgrade, on a number of occasions.

That policy only changed once two things happened. One was the slaughter in Srebrenica, when thousands upon thousands of Muslim men and boys were slaughtered by Serbian forces and everyone knew it and stood by. The second thing, and it's not unrelated, was the very different attitude that Lloyd Axworthy brought to the Department of Foreign Affairs in 1996. It's clear that Mr. Axworthy was very much affected by the standing to one side in Srebrenica, and to a lesser extent in Rwanda.

Mr. Axworthy in his previous public statements had always appeared fairly ambivalent about the use of force under certain circumstances. During the Gulf War in 1991 he was clearly on the record as opposing the use of force against Iraq, wanting to give sanctions more time. However, in 1999 there's no doubt that Mr. Axworthy understood full well the implications of what was happening in Kosovo, and he did not hesitate to embrace the logical implications of his own human-security agenda and to embrace the use of force by NATO, and indeed justify it and resist the criticisms of NATO policy as illegal, as illegitimate. He was a staunch defender of that particular use of force. The thing is that Mr. Axworthy, when the chips were down, and they certainly were down in Kosovo in March of 1999, stood right there and stressed what had to be done, very simply because the Kosovo operation was led entirely by the United States.

What the Canadians did or said about it actually would have made very little difference to the dynamic of how that conflict was unfolding. Let's face it, that conflict had already unfolded by the time that the Americans insisted on the terms of the Rambouillet agreement. That agreement was designed, in my view and the view of some others, to provoke a war. So whether or not Mr. Axworthy was on side was relatively immaterial.

My sense is that Mr. Axworthy, judging by his comments, was indeed affected by the slaughter at Racak, Kosovo, in January 1999, and that he feared that the massacres that had gone on in Kosovo would lead to another Bosnia. So when the United States pursued its policy around Rambouillet, my sense was that Mr. Axworthy was very much onboard.

Canada and the World
Canadians are inevitably affected by what goes on overseas, given the luxury of the security that we enjoy in North America. We have been moved on numerous occasions to involve ourselves and to welcome it when our governments involve us in international conflicts. There are some Canadians who argue that we actually don't need any of this. We derive virtually all of our wealth from our incredibly huge trade with the United States. We live in a part of the world that is, generally speaking, unaffected by the quarrels of others, and therefore we shouldn't really be engaged. The difficulty with that perspective is that it goes against something that is now deeply ingrained in Canadian political culture, and that is that it is wrong to behave as we did in the 1920s and

1930s. In the 1920s and the 1930s Canadians took the view that the quarrels of Europe are "over there" and that 60,000 Canadians who died from 1914 to 1918 fighting European quarrels need not have died.

The difficulty is that the Second World War always looms large in arguments about why Canadians need to remain engaged, and this is one of the primary ways that we have found to keep ourselves engaged in world politics. That is the reason why you'll never find a Canadian government, at least not in the recent past and I would venture to say not in the foreseeable future, that will say, "We actually don't want to do peacekeeping anymore. Leave that to others."

What we will find are Canadian governments who will say, "Let us leave the actual implementation of peacekeeping operations to those folks from poor countries who derive considerable foreign exchange from selling their operations to peacekeeping. Let us put a symbolic number of Canadians in the field to contribute to the operations."

"Let us," as the current defence minister has said, "be first in but first out."

We'll be the first in there because that's when the cameras are on us. But once we're in there we'll leave it to someone else to actually engage in the exceedingly messy, often very expensive — and here's the important bit — rather dangerous business of involving one's self in other people's quarrels. Because after all that's really what peacekeeping is all about. It's inserting oneself into someone else's business.

And Canadians haven't really thought very much about that part of it. Occasionally Yugoslavs and Somalis like to remind Canadians about what exactly they're doing there. But nonetheless, it's so deeply part of Canada's political culture and it is used to such good political effect by our political parties of all different stripes that there's no party, not even the Bloc Québécois (which of course is devoted to the dismantling of this country) that will say a bad thing about Canadian peacekeeping.

It would be wrong to think about the dynamic of getting involved in other people's quarrels as overt hypocrisy. I think a better way to think about this is that we have not been thinking things through. We involve ourselves in what looks on the surface to be a good thing, but without thinking about what we're actually doing. When we insert ourselves as we did in Somalia, or in Haiti, or in the former Yugoslavia, or in Timor — and there will be numerous other places where we will insert ourselves — we haven't really thought clearly and bluntly about what we're doing. We're basically inserting ourselves into someone else's politics. That means that there are going to be winners and there are going to be losers and the losers are not going to be terribly well disposed toward us at all.

The winners may well be. But the losers will be occasionally so annoyed that they may decide to take a couple of potshots at Canadians, and this is something that is of course a marked difference from cold war peacekeeping. When we went in we were in effect going in as an adjunct to a political settlement that had already been reached. We were going in there with the consent of both warring parties. We weren't on one side or another. In the post–cold war period we've been involved on one side rather than on the other. And the other side has not been happy about that.

Because, after all, what is warfare except the infliction of cruelty and pain and suffering and hurt on a people to get them to bend to your will? If it means that that you've then got a force coming in to prevent you from inflicting such pain, then your objectives have just been stymied by well-meaning Canadians.

It may well be that when all is said and done we actually want to behave in such a fashion. But we've got to then be prepared to be called imperialists for doing it, and we've got to be prepared for admitting to ourselves that we're doing to other people what we would never stand to have done to us. Ever. It entirely depends on whose portrait at the end of the day is remembered, to the extent that you can paint a particular portrait of a particular operation in a certain way. To have no one confront it, oppose it or decry it, then you've won.

This of course is one of the reasons why the Chrétien government has been lucky. The Liberal Party was able for many years to characterize the Conservative foreign policy of Brian Mulroney in whatever way it wished. But it has faced no serious foreign policy opposition from the benches across the way since 1993, largely because there were only two Tories left to challenge that version of events and neither of those, neither Jean Charest nor Elsie Wayne, had any interest in foreign policy at all. And for their part the Bloc Québécois and the Reform Party, and later the Canadian Alliance, had very little capacity in foreign and defence policy matters. So as a consequence the spin that the government put on its peacekeeping operations, on its use of force internationally, was not able to be counterspun by others.

An effective opposition that had been, let's say, left over from the Mulroney period would at least have known enough to be able to put a different spin on it. When it comes to the involvement of Parliament in a commitment to the use of force, one of the persistent claims of the Chrétien Liberals in the mid-1990s was that the Mulroney government never went to Parliament to secure approval for the use of force abroad.

In the case of Somalia that is indeed the case, but in all other cases the Mulroney Conservatives in fact held numerous parliamentary debates on peacekeeping and peacemaking operations. The classic debate in Canadian Parliament is the huge three-day debate in January of 1991 on the issue of the Gulf War. So it matters whether your spin-doctors actually win in the end. Winners always write the history.

The prime minister in a Westminster system, whether in Canada or New Zealand, Australia or Britain, has awesome potential political power very simply because everything rests in the prime minister's hands that sustains that power, notably, the ability to throw people out of the party, out of caucus. Without the approval of the party in our electoral system, you are nowhere.

If we had a different electoral system, one that was a little more sensitive to voter preferences, unlike the antiquated and hopeless system that we have now, you wouldn't need the party that much. But in our system you need the party endorsement. And without that you're finished.

When this awesome amount of power is used carefully and accurately it manages to sustain prime ministers in power for an awfully long time. Think about Mackenzie King, who became prime minister in 1921 and, with one very brief absence, remained prime minister into his dotage, until 1948. He had awesome power and he used it very carefully and very wisely.

On the other hand, as all party leaders know, leadership and confidence in one's leadership is an exceedingly fragile thing, and confidence in leadership can be easily withdrawn. Talk to John Diefenbaker about how easily a prime minister, regardless of the awesomeness of his power, can find that people are walking out the door.

That is how one should think about power in a Westminster system.

SEAN MALONEY
2001 (Post-9/11)

*D*r. *Sean Maloney is a military historian specializing in Canada in the cold war and post–cold war period. He has had extensive experience in the Balkans and Middle East and teaches in the War Studies Programme at the Royal Military College in Kingston. He is the author of* War Without Battles, Canada's NATO Brigade in Germany, *the official history of 4 Brigade. Two of his forthcoming books,* Canada and UN Peacekeeping: Cold War by Other Means 1945–1970 *and* Chances for Peace: The Canadians in UNPROFOR 1992–1995, *provide a new perspective on Canadian peace support and stability operations. Maloney is also in the process of writing* Operation KINETIC: The Canadians in Kosovo, 1999–2000.

Sheer apathy characterizes the way Canadians approach the military.

The people who are handling the formulation of Canadian national security policy are not thinking in terms of a long-term vision for Canada. Everything seems to be geared toward media spin, immediacy and instant gratification, not long-term economic benefits, long-term social benefits, long-term moral benefits and things of that nature. There are a lot of vague pronouncements on these things, but there's no stated Canadian policy and thus there's no real vision.

It's clear that if Canada does not develop and articulate a vision, somebody else will definitely impose theirs on us. It's very clear who that might be, given the sheer weight of cultural product crossing the border.

The Balkans
Kosovo and Canada's involvement in it has to be placed within the context of an almost decade-long commitment to that region, and that cannot be divorced from Canada's involvement in Europe and in NATO. In many respects Canadian involvement in Kosovo and the earlier operations is linked to our precipitous withdrawal from stationed forces in Europe in 1992. Our influence has been reduced. We need to be seen to be doing things. Not only do we need to be doing things, we need to be actually doing them effectively with salient forces that can contribute to these efforts. Canadian interests are in fact wider than many people believe, particularly in the Balkans.

Our objective initially in the Balkans was to contain the violence and the instability that existed in the early 1990s. That was very difficult to do but we pulled it off, once NATO eventually replaced the UN forces. The efforts of the alliance to protect the hard-won peace under the 1995 Dayton accords was obviously threatened by the events in Macedonia and in Kosovo.

The larger issues of the 1990s, the other elements of the stabilization campaign that helped propel us into this conflict, include the failure in Somalia, the failure in Rwanda, the failure in Zaire in 1996, and a whole litany of problems of Western intervention, globally. We in the West could not be seen to be messing this up again. There was a lot of media pressure to ensure that the right thing was done. This forced the alliance and Canada into a position where we had to do what we did. And the results were the air campaign and the introduction of KFOR into Kosovo.

We don't know enough about the air campaign yet; the work has not been done on it. There is an image of the air campaign that does not necessarily jive with the results on the ground. The KFOR forces, when they moved in, did their own assessment of what the air campaign had done to the deployed forces on the ground. The political objective, that is, getting the Serbian forces, the VJ and the MUP, the special police forces, to withdraw from the region, was accomplished. The VJ is the Serbian army, as opposed to the JNA, the Yugoslav National Army, which was the pan-Yugoslav army of the earlier period. Now that fragmentation has taken place, the JNA is now called the VJ.

However, there was no long-term plan for that particular region. We are seeing the effects of that now. We went in and stabilized the region after forcing out the one particularly belligerent force that was behaving very aggressively. Yet the basic problems of Kosovo and its relationship to Belgrade, and its relationship to Maccdonia and Albania, are still under debate and have not been solved.

In terms of alliance strategy in the region it's very clear from the work that I've conducted that one of the problems is that of spillover. That instability in one particular area will spread to other areas and this will set up a series of precipitating or cascading events that will have an effect on NATO and thus on Western and Canadian interests as well.

The situation in the Balkans has an earlier analogy in Cyprus. Cyprus is not as complicated and it is fairly contained geographically. But what was the purpose of the introduction of UN peacekeeping forces into Cyprus in 1964? The context was the cold war. UN peacekeeping was used to stabilize the region and work toward a political solution, but the primary aspect of any intervention was to stabilize it because the concern was that any situation like that could escalate in the larger scheme of the cold war. We got used to inserting stabilization forces into these hot spots and just leaving them there because we weren't sure how long the cold war was going to last or what the larger effects on the region would be.

When we got into the stabilization campaign of the 1990s we didn't have a sophisticated understanding of our previous stabilization operations. We got used to doing the same thing: insert people into a region, stabilize it and then hope for the best. So that's probably the best way of looking at what we were doing in the 1990s. We were following the same path that we had previously taken, just outside of a cold war context.

We need to actually delineate or differentiate between the types of deployments that did occur in the 1990s. The pure humanitarian aid missions that do have an armed component are one thing. Actual stabilization operations with the full range of military activity are another. So, for example, Somalia is one form of it. And an SFOR deployment or IFOR deployment to Bosnia is another. They appear to be the same, but they are in fact very different and they have different agendas.

If maintaining stability in the Balkans is a long-term Canadian objective, then we are going to be into this for the long term. But that's very different from firing 50 guys into the Central African Republic just to tell the UN we're doing something.

Then we have the problem of jihad-oriented mujahideen who are deeply involved with the UCK and the other groups in the region. Those people are linked to our current problems in the Gulf and elsewhere. You can't divorce the Balkans from the Gulf, and particularly the Middle East. There are links, there are connections, and policy in one area has an effect on policy in the other.

In the early period in the Balkans when the UN forces were deployed, they did not have a credible level of force with the belligerents. They were outgunned. In the case of Kosovo we weren't going to allow that to happen again — no way. We were going to go in with the maximum level of force possible, given proportionality in that region. We wanted the ability to meet them at the level of force they were going to use. KFOR was structured in part to deter Serb or VJ mechanized incursions into Kosovo and to a large extent it did.

If, hypothetically, we'd introduce an UNPROFOR-like organization, the credibility of it vis-à-vis what the VJ is capable of doing would have been minimal.

During that whole decade of the 1990s Canada incrementally involved itself in many aspects of operations in the Balkans. We were part of the European Community Monitoring Mission right off the bat, in 1991. We provided UN military observers. We provided forces to UNPROFOR I and II. UNPROFOR I was in Croatia; UNPROFOR II was in Bosnia. We then contributed forces to UNPREDEP, which was the UN force in Macedonia.

We also provided air intercept operations. We had F-18s in Italy as part of the NATO contingent supporting the UN. We had Canadian ships as part of the NATO Maritime Interception Force in the Adriatic during the UN period. In addition Canadians were involved with surveillance and intelligence, and as we progressed throughout the 1990s we were increasingly involved in one way or another. Nobody questioned the deployments as each piece was added. Then we got to the IFOR-SFOR period after 1995, and these pieces tended to consolidate.

When we got to the 1990s it looked as if Canada was going to become isolationist in the so-called new world order of the day. We were going to pull out of Europe, which we did, and we weren't going to participate effectively on the ground in the Gulf War. We sort of sat back and said we'd conduct some low-risk activity over here, and we'd have a debate about how offensive we should be on the ground there.

Once the Yugoslav drama kicks in we already have forces deployed on the ground in Germany, though they are withdrawing. Suddenly somebody came up with an idea that we can become involved in the Balkans. We already have forces in Europe. We can contend that those forces deployed to the Balkans, under the UN banner, are really NATO forces when we go to the table in Brussels. Well, we tried that and we were basically laughed out of the room. However, we did regain, incrementally, some influence within the alliance and with our European allies by these other steps and forces that we sent in. The naval interception force and the air interception force are a couple of examples.

When Canada was not asked to be part of the larger contact group, the diplomatic organization designed to help solve or ameliorate the problems in the Balkans, the people that did the incremental deployments decided that maybe we should take our toys and go home. So we wound up backsliding again, not thinking in terms of the larger aspects of things.

People think we're caught in a cold war mindset. We're not: we're caught in a Second World War mindset about how the world functions because we don't have an adequate historical understanding of what Canada was all about during the cold war. And that involves peacekeeping and NATO deployments and how the game worked within NATO. Until we have an understanding of that, how can we base any policy on anything? It has to be reactive and in some cases the people don't want to know what we were doing because it might conflict with their current personal or policy agendas. I don't have the answer about why there is no larger debate about this in the public forum. I would suggest historical ignorance is definitely part of it.

Operation Kinetic was Canada's deployment as part of KFOR. Almost every one of the troops had been involved with Cyprus, everybody had had an UNPROFOR tour, everybody had an IFOR-SFOR tour under their belt and their attitude was, "Here we go again. Why are we doing this? These people want to kill each other. What is the reason for us being here?" Nobody had any adequate answer. "We're doing this because we're Canadian soldiers and we're good at it."

Canada's involvement in the Kosovo crisis began with something called the Kosovo Verification Mission, or KVM. This was the non-UN or OSCE observation force that was put on the ground to monitor the Rambouillet accord. When that failed the KVM was withdrawn and the air campaign was initiated. Operation Echo was the deployment of CF-18s as part of the NATO aerial armada to conduct those operations. The Canadian component to KFOR that was to go in on the ground was called Operation Kinetic in Canada. NATO had a pretty clear idea about what was going on, on the ground, who they were dealing with, and they had to walk a fine line because they knew the UCK were no angels.

Now, I think we have to clearly understand who the players are on the ground. On one hand we have the Serb forces, the VJ, the former JNA or Yugoslav National Army, now in Serbian colours. We have the MUP, which are special police forces. The term "special police forces" in the Balkans has special meanings, like the Einsatz group in Germany during World War II. These are pretty nasty people. On the other side we have a collection of factions, loosely called the Kosovo Liberation Army, and there is some debate about how centrally controlled it was. Like the bin Laden organization we're dealing with now, or the Calle cartel down in Colombia, when you are dealing with the KLA you're dealing with a widespread network that does a wide variety of illegal and criminally oriented activities to achieve its aim. It's very clan based; it's very decentralized. It's not the Resistance of the French during World War II. This is a unique type of organism with people in it that have multiple agendas. It can boil down to a blood feud that may determine policy or activity in a particular region. So when you're dealing with the KLA, in a propaganda sense it would be nice to paint them as the resistance of Kosovo, but in fact it's not the case.

NATO and Canada knew that going in. We were very hesitant to prop up the UCK or KLA against the Serbs. I mean, all things being equal, if the KLA had been a legitimate resistance movement, say like the mujahideen in Afghanistan in the 1980s, we would have provided mass military support and training. We would have backed them against the other side. In the environment of the Balkans you can't do that. We couldn't do peacekeeping in our traditional sense because that would mean getting between the two sides.

So you had this problem, this legacy of the 1990 stabilization campaign where we'd go in, we're too impartial, all sorts of problems erupt and the peacekeeping force winds up getting targeted by everybody. The compromise in this case was Operation Allied Force. We had to walk this fine line. We had to be able to take out the Serbian threat to coerce Belgrade into backing off. On the other hand we couldn't let the KLA completely go to town on the VJ and the MUP; we had to hold them back. The result was the introduction of KFOR into Kosovo, which functioned like IFOR in Bosnia, to keep everybody suppressed. Arguably it's probably a better peacekeeping force than we had deployed before, in terms of maintaining or reducing the level of violence to nearly minimum.

It gets far more complicated in terms of the specific makeup of the belligerent forces. It's neat to sort of lump these people together as Albanians, but it's far more complicated than that. You have mujahideen from overseas involved. You have a whole variety of other people with varying agendas involved. To say, as some do, that we switched sides, one would argue that we were never really on the KLA side in the first place, totally. Maybe we supported them, but you can't go, "Well, they're on our side. It's our tree fort versus their tree fort." It's not like that. It's far more complicated than that.

Understanding Canadian Policy
This level of complication is something that Ottawa does not understand. There are individuals within the structure that tend to understand it, but there's no place to fuse that into the policy process.

The Canadian policy during the Axworthy regime has been referred to as "soft power." The soft power mantra steers away from the use of coercive military force because the proponents of soft power believe it to be a wrong. The reality is that in the soft power mechanisms that Canada employed in various parts of the globe in the 1990s — we can point to Zaire in 1996, we could look at UNTAC in Cambodia — our participation in these coalitions of the willing were less than effective. When we attempted to use those types of mechanisms in the Balkans they were useless because we were dealing with some very crafty people who were very aware of how perception functions within the Western media and Western cultural standpoint. And they failed. Finally Axworthy had to use coercive force to achieve humanitarian aid, and that basically demonstrated the policy of soft power was bankrupt.

There is a Canadian cultural belief that we're this sort of ship that's buffeted, first by the British ocean and then by the American ocean. That belief took root sometime in the 1960s, and definitely during the Trudeau area of the 1970s. Where the Trudeau government tried to chart a third course, it was called the third option. The reality of the situation is, if you go back and look at Canada's development and deployments throughout the 20th century, our learning curve has been pretty good. Initially we're going to participate because we're part of the Empire. You could jump ahead and say if the UN is the new empire, we're doing the same thing we were doing in the Boer War or the First World War.

However, if you look at the development of Canadian national security policy, particularly in the early cold war period where it's the most critical, we do have a very strong policy. We have the means to implement that policy. That gives us influence within the alliances and coalitions that we're part of. It also allows us to protect our troops from being misused because we have a vertical integrated structure that's based on salient Canadian Forces.

If you have troops that are capable of contributing effectively in unique ways, that have unique capabilities, then this allows you access to certain planning levels, which in turn allows you access to certain political levels. If you do not have effective deployed forces as a basis for your policy, then you're not going to have much of a policy because you have nothing to stand on. Everybody in NATO recognizes this.

It even seeps into UN operations. For example, to ensure that the Canadian Forces were not misused in the Congo or in Cyprus, significant forces, credible and salient forces, were deployed on those operations to allow us the command slots in those operations. So suddenly Canadian troops couldn't be ordered to do things that were against Canadian national policy. We almost lost that, particularly during the Trudeau period. Those principles, which were developed over decades, were thrown away by allowing the Canadian Forces to, as we refer to it, rust out and not modernize, and then not deploy anything that's salient. The Canadian Forces, particularly in the 1970s, became almost symbolic.

But we're back to this cultural bent that started in the 1960s where some people thought that the use of force is somehow wrong. There is that old anti-American stream in Canadian culture, that the use of force, or lack of use of force, differentiates us from the Americans. We're not going to be nasty Americans, so we're not going to do the nasty things that they do, like use intelligence, covert operations and coercive military force. That's the sort of mindset that developed, particularly in the Trudeau period. There's this naive concept that Canada is going to be the shining beacon on the hill. "Be like us; we're going to behave in nice ways." But the rest of the world's staring at us, asking, "What planet are you people on?"

But violence is part of that language we understand, particularly in the regions that we've been involved in: the Balkans, the Middle East, Europe, particularly dealing with the Soviet threat. The only language they understood was our ability to give them a nuclear bloody nose when we developed that ability. And Canada had that capability, and we didn't seek it reluctantly. We had that coercive ability. And did they attack us? No.

In Kosovo we selected capabilities, particularly the Coyote reconnaissance squadron, the helicopter squadron, specifically so that we could have influence within the British and thus the KFOR command structures. Again, saliency was a principle that was in play here. If, hypothetically, the UN had done it, the UN just would have asked Canada for, say, a light infantry battalion, and then it would have not been integrated effectively within the command structure. In this case, in NATO, there was a dialogue between NATO and Canada. What can you send? What do you want? Well, we want these capabilities. We have these capabilities, but we want to add those capabilities so that we have a salient structure in place. That dialogue did take place. It had not taken place in the same way throughout the 1990s, particularly.

The forces that we deployed there were salient. We had access to the levers of command if we needed them. There were always mechanisms to ensure that our troops were not misused and those had developed throughout the 1990s as well and they hearkened back to the problems we had in Dieppe and in Hong Kong when we didn't have control over our troops.

Throughout the cold war we developed this concept of operational influence. When we look at the deployment of the Canadian brigade group in NATO, you know, it had unique capabilities. It was involved in unique planning. It allowed us positions in the higher command structures that oversaw it.

Yet there were always escape valves. There were always escape mechanisms to ensure that it was not misused. That mechanism and its relationship to the larger game of political influence within NATO was disrupted throughout the 1970s. It was barely existent. The reconstruction of it started in the 1980s, but for a variety of reasons, not least of these the budget in 1989, the government put an end to it. Yet some of the principles still remain in the system. It's just a question of continuously educating the commanders and the political people making the decisions that these are the principles that we operate by.

We're about to find out if we are capable of matching our strategic with our tactical means now, after the events of September 11. We now are being asked to be part of a coalition and we are being asked to commit something that is going to be effective, something that is going to be useful and something that is not symbolic. Now that North America has been attacked directly, this is no longer a problem that's just "over there."

Canada's Strategic Tradition

The principles of forward security, which is a Canadian strategic tradition going back to the early part of the 1900s, are now and always have been in play. Arguably we could take this all the way back to the Boer War. There are Canadian interests overseas. Canada is not an island. We are part of a globalized culture; we're part of an economic globalized system. We have to participate in what's going on. We are not just the recipient, the passive recipient, of goods or services or culture or violence. We are part of a larger system, however you want to define that system, and because of Canadian geography, part of that system is overseas.

Now, when threats appear to that system, no matter what they are — Communism, fascism, extremism, instability in the 1990s — it has always been incumbent on Canada to be involved in alliances and coalitions in these overseas areas to ensure that the instability and violence in those areas does not affect Canadian interests either at home or abroad. You can track that for every overseas deployment we were involved with, from the Boer War, the First World War, the Second World War, particularly the cold war and almost every cold war peacekeeping operation. Arguably elements of the stabilization campaign of the 1990s fit within forward security, particularly the Balkans. Some of them don't. Some of them are very dubious and don't fit into this, but forward security is a Canadian strategic tradition that goes back a long time. This is something we've always done. We're about to find out how far we're going to go with this after the events of September 11.

Canada's withdrawal from the KFOR commitment in 2000 was related to a process we refer to as "Balkans rationalization." Balkans rationalization was predicated on an economic problem where we have two separate commitments in the Balkans, both requiring an extensive logistic structure. It would have been cheaper for all concerned if we'd retained a base area in Germany. But in any event, consolidating the Canadian Forces in the Balkans in one area, allowing the British to consolidate in Kosovo, was seen to be an economic reality of the time. The actual policy spinoffs from this, we don't know yet. There has been very little discussion of that.

So did we retire in shame? Probably not. Should we have pulled out of KFOR? Probably not the entire contingent. When I spoke with the British they really missed the Coyote reconnaissance capabilities; there was nothing else like it. This is an example of a salient Canadian contribution. In the past weeks we've reintroduced a Coyote squadron into Macedonia to help with the Macedonian situation. So we're back to this problem of logistic support for several deployed contingents in a geographical region.

The actual physical withdrawal from KFOR, I should say redeployment of Canadian troops from Kosovo, was a bit of a mess. The need to economize within DND throughout the 1990s led to an increased reliance on alternate service delivery, or ASD. We have to rent strategic lift to move our people around. Most of the strategic lift that we rented is former Soviet or Russian Antonov aircraft. This causes all sorts of havoc if the company that owns these things goes belly-up, or if Canada wants to deploy to a region that the Russians don't think we should deploy to and they just deny us access to the aircraft. This is a serious impingement on national sovereignty. It means that we can't pick up and deploy whenever we want, wherever we want.

We can wind up in an embarrassing spectacle like the GTS *Katie* affair, where the ship, on the way back from Greece with Canadian Forces armoured vehicles onboard, was trolling around the Atlantic for weeks waiting for its American owners to allow it to proceed to Montreal to unload because it was in a financial dispute with a Montreal-based company that had the DND contract.

If we go back to the 1950s when we had a merchant marine, we had a lot of strategic airlift (the RCAF had substantial numbers of transports, tactical and strategic) and we had the ability to conduct strategic deployments throughout that entire period on our own. We didn't need anybody else to do it. Now we're reliant on another power.

Canada's part of the G8 and we can't build our own operation support vessels. Why can't we build three amphibious ships, lift ships, to drop our guys off somewhere? Three ships. Canada can't build three ships? It's utterly ridiculous. There's just no will to do it. Canada could build or buy C-17s or any other strategic lift aircraft if we so desired. But we entered into a sharing arrangement with the Americans so that, hypothetically, if we want to deploy somewhere and it's not within American interests, they just turn off the planes.

This belief that Canada's some kind of impoverished Third World country that has no industrial base, and therefore we can't build our own amphibious lift, is insane. If we build the amphibious lift ships in Canada, we're going to employ people. That means more money's going into the economy through those people who are being employed. Everybody wins. We get the ships we need. The politicians get the votes they want, depending on where they want to build the ships, probably in Quebec.

In Operation Assurance, in Zaire in 1996, there was this belief that we could lead this coalition of the willing but not provide anything other than command and control for it. You have to have something on the ground to command before you can actually say, "We're in command." We can't just provide a bunch of command-and-control troops and say, "Hey, everybody, pony up your troops. We'll lead you." We attempted to do that and it was a disaster. We looked idiotic. We didn't have the strategic airlift even to move our own command-and-control personnel to that region and sustain them. We were dependent on everybody else in the coalition. It was almost the old free rider concept in microcosm, where we're going to provide these people and then everybody, "Just give us your resources, we'll command them for you in this very dangerous part of the world. But since we don't have our own strategic airlift, we're not going to be able to extract when things go really wrong."

As I understand it from talking with participants, the ASD aircraft scheduled to repatriate the troops from Kosovo was another disaster. Disaster is probably the wrong word, but we wound up having troops left on the ground, troops shuttled to countries like Greece and left there for several days. They had people arriving in the wrong order and being forced to fend for themselves until someone could collect them and sort them out.

Historically this has happened before. We've often had problems with our strategic lift system, going back to the Boer War!

LENARD COHEN
2001 (Post-9/11)

*D*r. *Lenard Cohen is a professor with the Department of Political Science at Simon Fraser University. He is a graduate of the University of Illinois and received his doctorate from Columbia University. He also studied political science in Belgrade and conducted field research in Yugoslavia and the former Soviet Union. He is the author of* Broken Bonds: Yugoslavia's Disintegration and Balkan Politics in Transition *and* Serpent in the Bosom: The Rise and Fall of Slobodan Milosevic, *soon to be republished in an expanded and updated edition. Professor Cohen's recent works include "'Living an Illusion': Political Transition in Kosovo," an article published in the* Canadian Military Journal, *and a new, co-edited book,* Alliance Politics from the End of the Cold War to the Age of Terrorism.

Facing the 1990s

The whole international community after 1990 was sort of making it up as they went along. The United States was ill at ease with the whole situation after the kind of dyad of two major powers facing off, or preventing their facing off, through mutual assured deterrence during the long cold war. But after 1990 there were, as they call it, asymmetric kinds of conflicts, low-level conflicts, which were hardly low level. They were ethnic conflicts, regional conflicts, very new, really, to both the old Soviet Union and to the United States.

We got involved in the Balkans primarily because Canada had a very good record of peacekeeping around the world. Here's a Balkan situation and the spectre that "Europe's on fire." Canada felt very strongly for humanitarian reasons, and felt because of experience, that it should be in the forefront. There were other factors too. I suppose the prime minister and the government were also very sensitive to the area because of connections with the Slavic community. These things impelled Canada to be among the first to offer to go into Croatia.

Canada, a traditional peacekeeper that had always gone in when there had been a cease-fire and when peacekeeping troops had been invited in, found itself in the Balkans when there was barely a cease-fire. Perhaps it wasn't fully appreciated that the situation on the ground in the Balkans was different, but that can't be construed as a criticism because all countries were reacting to a new situation. We had never been in this situation before. You're trying to use the tools and the skills that you've honed, and certainly Canada had honed those skills in previous decades. But it was a new situation on the ground and you had to adapt.

Canada had been trying to retrench in terms of military commitments in Europe and had been doing so for some time in the late 1980s. To some extent Canada was compensating for its retrenchment from Europe by getting involved in this particular action, which the Canadian government and many other governments thought would be a short-term commitment and would not be the quagmire it turned out to be. It still goes on today. We saw it cascade from Slovenia into Croatia, from Croatia into Bosnia, Bosnia into Kosovo, and most recently Macedonia. We've been living with this for more than a decade. This wasn't foreseen and it couldn't have been reasonably foreseeable at that particular point.

The Balkans
In hindsight I think the UNPROFOR mission did have some severe problems in terms of what was necessary on the ground. Here's a lightly armed military force that goes in to maintain, impartially, a sit-

uation in which there's an expectation there'll be peace on the ground. And there isn't peace on the ground. One side certainly had a more aggressive posture, maybe two sides out of the three in Bosnia, and more clout. More heavy lifting was necessary, which would ultimately lead, of course, to American involvement.

It's quite right to suggest that the Americans were loath at the beginning of the Clinton administration to get involved in the Balkans at all. The premise in Washington, as I remember Bill Clinton's initial phrase, was, "It's the economy, stupid." Clinton didn't want to get involved in international ventures. This was on European soil — in southeastern Europe. Initially Clinton thought he could leave it to the Europeans for various reasons: lack of experience, lack of will, lack of treasure, lack of consensus. But the Europeans weren't able to put out this fire in Bosnia, which began to be quite a large fire after 1992.

Learning lessons for government organizations and government officials is always difficult because so much of political involvement in these kinds of situations is reactive. You have to react very quickly and there is no cookie-cutter approach that can be used everywhere, for example, in Rwanda and Somalia and Yugoslavia — or for that matter in different places right inside of Yugoslavia. It's hard to really learn lessons and apply them.

I think it's rather dramatic to say, as some people have, that peacekeeping died after this experience in Bosnia. Soon we'd have to find another kind of cookie-cutter for Kosovo or for Macedonia, and we will — down the road — have situations that will resemble our Cyprus involvement or involvements in other areas. What you have to have is a repertoire of different kinds of approaches for different kinds of tension areas and crisis zones, and you have to apply the appropriate one, which is really the art of leadership and good sense.

It's difficult for politicians and officials to ever call a spade a spade when they're accountable in an office and facing new elections as they go along. I find it difficult in 20/20 hindsight to criticize politicians who are dealing with the realities of their public. Unfortunately it's the rare politician that is immediately transparent with the facts and takes the blame and responsibility.

Medak and Srebrenica

The Medak Pocket incident of September 1993 was really the largest battle fought by Canadian troops in the post–World War II period. What happened, as it unfolded, was that Canadian troops were being deployed in this area south of Gospic known as Medak. Croatian troops were being deployed in the same area and were very anxious to drive some of the Serbs in that area out of that pocket. Canada was trying to serve as a buffer between the Serbian side, which was in rebellion against Croatia, and the Croatian authorities and their troops. So it was a confrontation, a 15- to 20-hour battle that ensued between Canadian troops and Croatian forces, in which a number of Canadian troops were injured and some Croatian troops were killed. The Canadian troops on the ground got firsthand experience in the kind of antagonisms, animosities and savageries of this kind of interethnic struggle between Croats and Serbs, right in Croatia.

By the time the Medak Pocket incident occurred in September 1993, the situation in Bosnia had deteriorated to a very great extent and all of the governments involved in UNPROFOR were searching about, rather embarrassed that they hadn't foreseen all of the difficulties, and were starting to think about how to extricate themselves.

In our wisdom the international community decided to create certain safe haven areas in Bosnia to try to protect the local population. The idea was that we and the Dutch troops could provide a buffer, in the case of Srebrenica, between the Serbian military and the paramilitaries of the Muslim forces, and between the local populations which then of course were quite antagonistic and not getting along together. This was obviously — and it's an understatement to say it — a great failure.

It was a great failure that the Dutch have had to deal with because they were on the ground when the massacre of Muslim men occurred, and they've gone through a tremendous catharsis in the Netherlands asking themselves, "Could we have done more?" Should they have done more? How should they have done more? What's wrong with their peacekeeping activities? We've asked ourselves the same questions as part of the community and the forces that were there with UNPROFOR. There's no way to apologize for it. It was a great mistake at Srebrenica that more troops were not put in there and that they didn't act more aggressively to protect the local population. The Srebrenica massacre was a tragic mistake.

After UNPROFOR

UNPROFOR was the United Nations, and Canada was very much for the UNPROFOR formula: the dual key that no action should be taken against hostile forces on the ground unless both the United Nations and NATO agreed with both their keys to the operation. This of course makes the whole process of reacting more lengthy and more difficult and more bureaucratic.

UNPROFOR effectively ended after the Dayton agreement. The Dayton agreement was essentially orchestrated by Richard Holbrooke in the United States, in an American air force base, where he knocked some heads together and brought some of the local culprits and some of their sponsors together. It was a formidable achievement that ended the savage war in Bosnia, and after that a new force went in. The Implementation Force under the Dayton agreement replaced UNPRO-FOR, which was extracted from the area. Canada took part in the new operation, IFOR, which eventually became SFOR and is still in Bosnia helping to maintain the Dayton peace agreement.

I think Richard Holbrooke had an agenda and that was to end the war in Bosnia for President Clinton, who wanted to get this war off the front pages so it wouldn't affect his re-election campaign for the presidency of the United States. In doing so Holbrooke had to act and work with only the big powers, so to speak, and he left out the small fry and the middle fry in order to get his peace conference going at Dayton. In retrospect he's been proven correct. Holbrooke was insistent that he had to work through the great powers, especially in respect to the role of the United States. He wanted to sideline the UN to a certain extent. That meant sidelining Canada and anyone that would ask for a major UN role in this.

That's most disagreeable, when a country that's played a disproportionate role, as Canada had in helping to deal with the Balkan situation, doesn't have a voice at the table when the actual decisions are being made to end the war. But in reality what Canada did is paint over their blue helmets and then adopt green helmets and take part in the next activity to help maintain the Dayton peace agreement. We played our role in the next phase as well, and were much needed and have done a good job at that. We're still there.

It is a tragic irony that there were more casualties in the Balkans with UNPROFOR than there were in the whole Gulf War. I think these casualties and the difficulties faced by UNPROFOR gradually led to a certain public frustration in Canada and in other countries with the whole venture — a fatigue and a desire to get out of the Balkans.

By the time the U.S. administration decided to take the driver's seat in the peace negotiations, sidelining Canada's influence, most of the public was just terribly anxious to get out of the Balkans. It wasn't considered to be such a slight to Canada in the opinion of the public, although in retrospect it is something that we have to guard against — being used and not being at the table.

Those who have studied the area closely and observed it suggested that once we went into Bosnia we were going to have to stay a long time. This is a very difficult zone. It's easier to go in than to extract yourself from it. And once you commit yourself, as the international community did at Dayton, to managing and economically developing and reconciling all of these nation-building aspects, it becomes an even more protracted kind of venture.

It means that essentially we create a quasi- or semi-protectorate, even if you don't call it a protectorate. Subsequently we have created protectorates, as in Kosovo, and we have kind of semi-protectorates because of our association with the Macedonian government and perhaps even with the Albanian government. Those are sovereign governments, but there's a semi-protectorate relationship to the extent that we assist them in dealing with their ethnic problems.

So we have this long-term, perhaps multigenerational, commitment to southeastern Europe. In the United States one sees a constant desire to extract the United States, especially after the events of September 11. With this terrorist action the United States is compelled to deal on a wider landscape with other matters than just Balkan reconstruction. But the United States and Canada and other countries now have to support the venture that they began in the Balkans, and it's very difficult to see how we can get out quickly.

Kosovo
My question about Kosovo at the beginning of 1999 was, "What is our goal?" If we want stabilization and democratization in the area, will that

be achieved by bombing Yugoslavia and Serbia? My answer to that was no. These negotiations shouldn't have been set up in such a way that you really couldn't get agreement between the Serbs and Albanians. I opposed the war and I felt that we should go on at Rambouillet.

If it was necessary to deal with the devil in order to achieve our overall goal of stabilization and democratization, it might have been necessary to prolong our negotiations with Slobodan Milosevic at Rambouillet, or even go directly to see him and make some kind of compromise, which at the time I think he was ready to do. But Mrs. Albright and the American administration were reluctant to do this because they had already come to the conclusion he was part of the problem, not part of the solution.

Now, it's easy in retrospect to say it might have worked. But we saw what happened to the Albanian population, not only at the hands of Serb paramilitaries, but also during the bombing. Many people had to leave so tragically. During the Rambouillet negotiations there was already suffering on the part of the Albanian population. Many thousands had already been displaced, and when the bombing started hundreds of thousands of Albanians were forced to leave their homes and even to cross borders into other countries. Ultimately they came back and there was a revenge syndrome against the local Serbian population.

We saw what's happened once the Kosovo Liberation Army came to the idea that they could use our air force, and the American air force and NATO air forces, as their air force in order to solve their Albanian problem in the Balkans. We then had the destabilization in 2001 in Macedonia, which we may be able to now look at as something that's behind us, but I think we're going to see aspects of it and episodic violence down the road. This will be controversial for some time to come. But that's my read on it — that we probably could have done more to prevent that NATO bombing of Yugoslavia that occurred for 78 days in 1999.

Anyone who assessed the Kosovo situation in 1999 knowing Serbian history, knowing the history of that region and Serbian-Albanian relations, would know that it couldn't possibly have been the kind of war that would end in a few days. This was self-delusion and a mistake when President Clinton and Mrs. Albright suggested it would be a quick war that would be over in three days. They knew something about the area but they didn't know enough and they didn't talk to enough people and think it through, or else they decided to roll the dice in order to get rid of Milosevic.

After 78 days Milosevic had not capitulated, NATO was fraying at the edges in terms of its consensus and there were real difficulties inside the alliance. Mind you, I wouldn't be so dramatic to say that if the war had gone on for another 30 days or 100 days, NATO would have disintegrated. NATO was 50 years of age during the war and NATO was determined that its credibility and legitimacy were on the line. Some countries, but perhaps not the whole NATO alliance, would have seen this through and ultimately a 19-country alliance can prevail over one country like Serbia. NATO was bound and determined to win. It would have won.

I think the decision makers who took the action to carry out a NATO attack against Yugoslavia in 1999 saw Kosovo through the lens of Bosnia. President Clinton said a number of times that he viewed the entire situation in Kosovo through the lens of Srebrenica and Bosnia. I feel very much that each case has to be considered on its own merits and demerits. If you react quickly one time, the next time doesn't necessarily suggest that you shouldn't prolong negotiations in order to achieve a better end.

There are many countries that have different kinds of political subcultures and each case has to be dealt with differently. Each province of a country, section of a country has a different demographic makeup. It's the same thing for the solution you are trying to obtain. The level of antagonism in Kosovo between Serbs and Albanians was far deeper than, say, the level of antagonism that existed before the war in Bosnia, where there had been a lot of intermarriage. So the solution — trying to rebuild Bosnia — is perhaps easier than trying to get Serb-Albanian cohabitation and to create a multicultural state in Kosovo.

The international community not only went in for reasons that were very similar to Bosnia — even though the cases were different — but started to talk the idea that you could create a multiethnic state in Kosovo. That hasn't been worked out yet. This is a complicated zone. Most multiethnic countries, large or small, are complicated and you have to look at this in a sophisticated way before you take action.

The problem of being a member of a 19-member alliance that has to act quickly because of difficulties in different crisis zones is that you are often forced to react before you've thought through the particular case fully. You regret it later on, as some officials have in retrospect. This is the problem of reacting in a dangerous world and being the members of an alliance in which you have to cut bait when you are required to. You are asked by the other countries in the alliance to take action. You place your bets and take your chances. Unfortunately people die when you do so.

The thing about expertise as an input into government decision making is that there are always experts on both sides. You can find experts to support almost every fallacy. Politicians have their own agenda in terms of getting re-elected, and even though they may be experienced, they have to react within the context of an alliance. So things move ahead, and the experts who are most appropriate to the decision that's already been reached for political imperatives are often the experts that are brought into play. Time is of the essence very often; you don't have much time to respond. I would hope there would be more contact between the academic experts of various kinds and governmental decision makers. This discussion about philosophers and kings has been around since Platonic times and I don't think we've ever been satisfied by the linkage.

The Canadian contribution in Kosovo was designed mainly so the alliance could say that this was an alliance-wide attack on Yugoslavia by 19 countries that were appalled by the humanitarian situation on the ground. Any one country that held back in NATO and didn't provide planes wouldn't have affected the overall bombing campaign launched from various NATO bases.

NATO was 50 years of age. Political leaders and delegations of NATO had made a decision. The more consensus that you have, the more the image of what you're doing has the kind of rightness and appropriateness that you need to convince public opinion to support you during a campaign like that. Mind you, I think the Canadian population was polarized on the question of war and there were certain reservations earlier about the Gulf war.

In the situation in Kosovo the essential player in 1999 was of course the Serbian portion of Yugoslavia. The Serbian government was in charge of the province of Kosovo at that time. The major player in Yugoslavia was the man who was running the soft dictatorship and had been running it for some 13 years, Slobodan Milosevic. On the ground in Kosovo you had a population of approximately two million people, and about 92 to 93 percent of the population was Albanian, while the remaining population was largely Serb. Although the Serbs were a small proportion of the overall population in Kosovo, they were the majority group of Yugoslavia. For the Serbs the Albanians were a minority inside of Yugoslavia, even though they were a majority inside of Kosovo, and no Serb would ever want to hear that Serbs constituted a minority in Kosovo. This is because they always look at the Kosovo situation as basically an Albanian-minority situation that they have handled appropriately.

I think the record certainly shows there were great difficulties and great mistakes made by Milosevic and his regime in their treatment of the Albanian population. There was a humanitarian problem on the ground. In fact, in the year before NATO launched its attack on Yugoslavia there was an ongoing war between the insurgent Albanians, with their Kosovo Liberation Army on the ground, and the Serbian police and military forces.

Mind you, for a long time, during the war in Bosnia and after, a lot of the Albanian population in Kosovo had followed the passive-resistance strategy. They had decided to follow more or less a Gandhian strategy under their most prominent leader, Ibrahim Rugova. However, gradually after Dayton a lot of younger Albanians in Kosovo became radicalized because their problem was not solved at Dayton. Dayton ended the war in Bosnia and led to this reconstruction strategy for Bosnia, but it didn't deal with the Serb-Albanian problem inside of Kosovo.

This radicalized the younger population and some of them had already linked up with groups that had protested in a radical fashion earlier in the history of Kosovo. It led to the formation of this group, armed with what they could find in the Balkans or smuggle in, called the Kosovo Liberation Army. The Kosovo Liberation Army was determined to exacerbate the struggle to raise the level of violence with the Serbs, even if it would provoke a very radical Serbian response from Milosevic, which it did. The Albanian feeling, by the leaders of the Kosovo Liberation Army, was, if this provokes the Serbs, it will also provoke a humanitarian disaster, then the international community led by the United States will come in on behalf of the Albanians and solve their problem of escaping from Serbian Montenegro. Ultimately that strategy prevailed.

That was another problem with the war, and one reason I disagreed with it. It was very clear that the insurgents, the quite radical Kosovo Liberation Army, were bent upon enlisting us in their cause. Eventually they would enlist us in an even broader cause in Macedonia and make, as I said earlier, the Canadian air force and the American air force their air force. I think we should have guarded against that during the Rambouillet negotiations and been impartial with the two sides, the Serbs and the Albanians. I don't think we maintained that impartiality sufficiently during those negotiations, nor did we take all the steps that we might have taken to end the war through diplomatic negotiations.

The feeling at the end of 1998 that prevailed, certainly in Washington and I think therefore was an alliance-wide feeling, was that the Milosevic regime was the remaining obstacle to democratization in Eastern Europe. It wasn't the last dictatorship; there's one in Belarus and of course some of the former Soviet republics in central Asia have dictatorial regimes as well. But the feeling was that in southeastern Europe, in the south Balkans, the remaining obstacle was Slobodan Milosevic, and he was no longer a part of the solution as he was in Dayton. He no longer could be counted upon to help the international community. So my feeling is the not-so-hidden agenda of the war in Kosovo, the real agenda, wasn't humanitarian. The not-so-hidden agenda was getting rid of Slobodan Milosevic, and he provided a pretext for that by sponsoring a very tough military fight against the KLA during 1998, in which many civilians were casualties of the war and driven from their homes.

But that said, with that humanitarian disaster already happening before the war, as the international community looking at it you have to keep your nerve, maintain your distance and think of the overall goal — who you're helping and what that will imply down the road. That's the difficulty.

Transcending Sovereignty
I think we've reached the point now where we accept the whole question of transcending the sovereignty of countries in order to assist in a humanitarian fashion or to get rid of a leader that's a menace to an area. At this point in the development of international law and the

international community, I think we've accepted the idea that we can't just allow sovereign borders to stand in the way if there's a humanitarian tragedy going down or there's a general menace.

And we're coming back to that same problem. Now we have the international coalition against terror to fight against a remote group of fanatics in remote zones, who happen to be moving around the globe outside of sovereign states, transnational and transborder, and that can bring down two towers in Manhattan.

I think we should not be inhibited in taking action just because we may be violating what used to be a sacrosanct principle of sovereignty between and among countries. We can't get into the dilemma of second-guessing ourselves and questioning our actions in an interdependent globalized world. This is not just a kind of moral imperative. It's a realistic imperative. The world is a dangerous place. Groups inside of other countries, sometimes countries that have lost their ability to maintain order, will take action against states and commit horrendous acts on the world stage, as we've seen in this revolution in international relations after the bombing incidents in New York and Washington.

I would agree with the position put forward by officials who say that just because of certain international norms, we should not be inhibited from taking action. We must have the ability to react in an interdependent world. We have to have the courage of our convictions. In the case of a superpower that has the capability of doing that, we have to try, as members from Canada or other industrialized democratic nations, to influence that superpower to do it in the most thoughtful manner possible so that it doesn't become a cowboy action, but becomes a thoughtful and methodical action to deal with the real problem.

Education

Over the years I've had a lot of young men and women who have taken my courses at Simon Fraser University and who have been veterans of actions in the Balkans and other parts of the world. I hear, almost uniformly, that when they first went over to serve with the Canadian Forces in those particular peacekeeping actions, however successful they ultimately turned out to be, they didn't know very much about the area.

It's hard to keep up with all areas of the world or even to educate our soldiers for every action that we get involved in because they come up so fast on the radar screen: Rwanda, Somalia, Yugoslavia — they're very complicated. But it is an educational process.

It's always been somewhat remarkable to me how much Canada is involved in different ventures around the world, such as peacekeeping and running elections through the OSCE and helping out through various NGOs, and how little is known inside Canada. Many of the stories of those efforts are untold or little-known stories.

I have often attributed the ignorance about these to the fact that Canadians tend to have a real responsibility and involvement around the world without waving the flag much about their involvement. But it certainly would be helpful if more young Canadians in high schools and social studies programs would have an opportunity to really know about how much Canada is involved around the world. That would broaden the general knowledge about international affairs and perhaps prepare each generation a little better to face up to those kinds of obligations. Canada does have a major role in the world through all of these different outlets, an important role, and very often in very dangerous places.

Often, as a specialist on the Balkans, when I lecture to different groups in the university and outside of the university, as I start to go into the complexity of the Balkan zone in a reasonable and sensible way, sometimes even in a simplistic way, I tend to lose the audience because of the complexity of the area. It's hard to know the good guys from the bad guys in history. So much is through the perspective of the various ethnic groups, the members of those groups, or through the perspective of this historian and that historian. Certainly there are books, but when you read them you're not sure exactly who the good guys and the bad guys are, or the message you're supposed to get. That adds to the difficulty of understanding these areas. They have such long histories, so much undigested history and so much historical luggage. It's so different in North America, with our comparatively short history, compared to Europe. There's so much to understand and so much of it is grey.

So many times the bad guys are on all sides, and of course you have to guard against the problem of equivalency, just assuming that everybody's bad. Some groups, some actions are worse than others. You always have to make relative assessments. It takes time, this kind of reflection, and I think that's really the problem of decision making about the Balkans or any complicated zone. Very often, because of the reactive nature of foreign policy making and intervention in these zones precipitated by humanitarian crises, there isn't much time to think it through, to see if what you're doing is ultimately going to cause more problems than you're solving with immediate action.

When we went into Kosovo with the NATO alliance and started bombing Yugoslavia, we definitely had decided that the Serbian side, the Yugoslav side — the Yugoslav government and particularly Slobodan Milosevic — was committing egregious kinds of humanitarian actions and negative brutal actions against the Albanian population. This meant we were the de facto ally of the KLA, the Kosovo Liberation Army, the insurgent Albanian group that was fighting against the Serbs there, and the Belgrade government in particular.

There is a limited but effective learning process going on now in the international community. Only months later, as the KLA began operating among the Albanian population in western Macedonia, we found ourselves part of the NATO alliance trying to maintain the cohesion of Macedonia. We found ourselves trying to obstruct the kind of insurgent activities and violence perpetrated by the Kosovo Liberation Army in order to obtain what they said were more rights from the Macedonian Slav government. The international community saw how the KLA was using and perhaps abusing our trust, so we switched sides, more or less.

Regrettably we've become educated by dealing with the action. In all countries you'll find a large proportion of the public that's ignorant about remote regions of the world such as Kosovo. But everyone was well acquainted with the map as soon as we started the bombing in southeastern Europe. Where's Afghanistan? Not many people got up in the morning asking themselves, "What's going on in Afghanistan?" Now maps are plastered across televisions and the newspapers. But we should have known about the areas before we went in.

JAMES BISSETT

2001 (Post-9/11)

James Bissett was appointed Canadian ambassador to Yugoslavia, Bulgaria and Albania after a long career specializing in immigration and foreign affairs. Prior to his appointment to Belgrade in 1990, he served as high commissioner to Trinidad and Tobago and executive director of the Department of Employment and Immigration. He was recalled from Yugoslavia in the summer of 1992 and retired from the foreign service. He then accepted a job in Moscow helping the Russian government establish a new immigration ministry to implement a settlement program for the thousands of Russians returning from various parts of the former Soviet Union.

I was enjoying my life down in Trinidad and Tobago as the Canadian high commissioner, with the palm trees, the music and the beaches, when I was suddenly called back to head up the Canadian immigration service for four tough years. I was rewarded by being appointed Canadian ambassador to Yugoslavia in 1990. In a sense it was a post that I had chosen — and they were good enough to let me go — because I could see that events in Yugoslavia were leading up to a fairly exciting assignment. I was also during that time accredited to Bulgaria and Albania, so I became the ambassador to Bulgaria and to Albania, which gave me an opportunity to travel frequently and to get a good idea of what was happening in the Balkan area.

I don't think that the government was paying much attention to what was happening there. They had representation there, particularly in Yugoslavia, which was the key country in the Balkans, but from the Canadian government's point of view the Balkans were not a very high priority. It was an ignored part of the world. I think that's true, not only in Canada but also in Western Europe and the United States.

Reports from Yugoslavia
People were beginning to see that Yugoslavia risked falling apart. At the same time you had the collapse of the Soviet Union, you had the Gulf War, so people were focusing on those areas; although they knew there was trouble brewing in Yugoslavia, they weren't paying much diplomatic attention to it. When the fighting started, that was a different story. Foreign policy burbles up when fighting starts.

As an ambassador I was reporting back the situation as I saw it and trying to keep the government fully informed. But you know, in today's world often ambassadors aren't listened to very carefully. Politicians watch CNN before they go to bed at night. The latest line on CNN is the one that is going to have the most public impact and they respond to that probably more than they do to any kind of expert advice or opinion that they might be receiving through diplomatic dispatches. It's sad to say that as an ambassador, but realistically that happened. In terms of Canada's reaction to what was going on there, we, as we always do, followed the American lead and basically did as we were told. Canada got involved because the Americans were involved.

My advice to the government was, "What's happening here is obviously going to result in a civil war. There are no good guys here. There's a lot of bad guys and we should stay out of it and do what we can to try and resolve these problems diplomatically and peacefully." The challenge in the Balkans, when it started to fall apart, was not to jump in on one side with weapons. The challenge there was to try and resolve it and to bring the parties together and negotiate a peaceful settlement.

I think there was great room for that in Yugoslavia. Indeed, the Serbs and the Croats were negotiating among themselves, but once the fighting starts, once the guns go off, once people start getting killed, particularly given the history of the Second World War in the Balkans, bloodshed and violence were inevitable.

And I must say this. I think the Western democracies bear a very heavy responsibility for the ensuing bloodshed and violence. Right from the beginning people were taking sides. The Germans and the Austrians were indeed encouraging Croatia and Slovenia to break away. There is evidence now that they were not only supporting them morally in this, but they were dealing with them in a financial way and giving them weapons.

When the fighting started, an attempt was made to bring the sides together, but there wasn't an objective point of view there. We were siding with the separatists, the Croats and the Slovenes. The Serbs very early in the game were made the demons, the villains in the piece. It was difficult then for the Western Europeans and the Americans to negotiate a peace because they weren't really objective.

The determination of the Germans to recognize Slovenia and Croatia changed the scenario a great deal, so that what was a civil war turned into a war of aggression against these two newly independent countries. Although the British and French resisted the German efforts to do that, the Germans basically bribed the British and the French over Maastricht. They gave them concessions at Maastricht to recognize Croatia and Slovenia, and that changed the whole situation.

The fighting and the massacres and counter-massacres had already started before the Canadian peacekeepers went into Bosnia. Once they got in there it wasn't an easy task. These people were frightened. They had mingled and lived with each other for many years. But they all had memories of massacres that had taken place in the Second World War. There were very few people in Bosnia who had not lost fathers, grandfathers, relatives from either a Muslim massacre of Serbs or a Croatian massacre of Serbs or a Serb massacre of Muslims. So I'm sure the Canadian soldiers had no idea what they were getting into.

And as Lew MacKenzie has said, they weren't properly supported by the United Nations at headquarters. They were pretty well left on their own.

We know that they were alone in the Medak Pocket when the Croatian forces overran the Canadians. It was a situation where they didn't have any friends. They were trying to make peace but they were often looked upon as enemies, so they were in a very, very difficult situation. It's ideal country for guerilla fighting. The ground itself in Bosnia is such that ambushes are easy. And Sarajevo, as MacKenzie has pointed out, was an extremely difficult situation for peacekeepers.

A Short History of Balkan Politics

Balkan politics at its best is complicated. This is part of the problem with the Yugoslav conflict. Covering any kind of a war or civil war through television means that you've got about two minutes to explain an extremely complicated situation. As a result you've got to boil things down to good guys and bad guys. And there's a tendency today, because of television, to exemplify Milosevic as the evil guy who's responsible for everything that happened in the Balkans. The oversimplification of things in the Balkans added to the problems of the Canadian troops on the ground and added to the problems that Canadian politicians and the public had of understanding a very, very complex situation.

You can't understand what happened in Yugoslavia in the 1990s unless you know what happened to Yugoslavia in the Second World War. They lost millions of people. Civil wars within civil wars. Ethnic conflict, religious conflict, occupation by the Nazis, by the Ustashi. Muslims raising an SS division in Bosnia. Albanians raising an SS division. The memories were fresh. The horrors of Yugoslavia had been hidden by Tito when he came to power. He refused to let anybody talk about what had happened in the past, unlike the Germans, who opened up and talked about what had happened and got it off their chests. The ghosts of the Second World War were still waiting in Bosnia to burst forth and cause a lot of bloodshed and violence. We found ourselves in the middle of that and very few people understood it.

The Western point of the view of the Balkans has always been that the Balkans are inhabited by these barbaric savages who periodically go about killing each other. They don't know anything about the culture, the languages, the history of the Balkans. They just see it as a powder keg. Bismarck said, "Balkans are not worth the bones of one Pomeranian soldier." But if you know the history of the Balkans, if you look at it carefully, you realize that pretty well the only time they're killing each other is when, Western or Eastern, some other great power involves itself in the Balkans.

And this is true all the way back to the Congress of Berlin in 1884, when Bosnia was on the table and nobody really knew where it was. These guys around the table decided that Bosnia should be occupied by the Austrian-Hungarian army. They marched in there with their bands playing and thought it would be a 40-day expedition. They never did conquer the Balkans or Bosnia, and you know, it all culminated when Gavrilo Princip assassinated Franz Ferdinand in Sarajevo and started the First World War.

What's happened in Bosnia in the 1990s is much the same. I think if the Yugoslavs had been left alone to resolve their problems through negotiations, through discussion, we would have probably seen Yugoslavia break up, but I doubt very much that we would have seen the terrible violence and the bloodshed. There was a big difference between what happened in Bosnia and Croatia and Slovenia and what subsequently happened in Kosovo. I think the fighting and the bloodshed in Yugoslavia were caused in a sense by diplomatic failure to try and resolve these problems peacefully. Kosovo is a quite different situation. Kosovo was not the result of diplomatic failure. Kosovo was the result of a determined effort, I think, to bring down Slobodan Milosevic.

1999

We now know that long before there was serious trouble in Kosovo the United States and the British intelligence services were arming and equipping Kosovo Albanians and sending them back into Kosovo to assassinate Serbian mayors, to ambush Serbian policemen. The plan was to destabilize Kosovo in such a way that, knowing Milosevic as they did, he would retaliate with tremendous force and Kosovo would be destabilized, and possibly this would be the first step in the overthrow of the "Balkan butcher," as he was called. So Kosovo was different. Kosovo was deliberate.

But this plan didn't achieve any of its stated objectives and it caused humanitarian disaster in Kosovo. The bombing of Kosovo was a disaster and so was NATO's intervention there. I've been opposed to it for a long time and I consider it a disaster and a blunder because NATO did not achieve any of its objectives.

On the contrary, it's probably going to prove to be one of the real turning points in NATO's history, with a far-reaching impact on the way that the overall framework of security and peace in the world is governed. NATO deliberately went in and bombed Yugoslavia, broke international law in doing it, violated the United Nations charter and didn't achieve any of its objectives. They said they were doing it to stabilize the Balkans. Well, look at the Balkans today. Look at Macedonia. Look at southern Serbia. NATO's bombing didn't stabilize the Balkans; it destabilized the Balkans.

They said they were going in there to stop ethnic cleansing, but in fact, prior to the bombing there were not that many refugees from Kosovo. There were some thousand people displaced within Kosovo. After the bombing we had about 800,000 people displaced into Macedonia, into Albania, and many of the Albanians went to find refuge with their relatives in Belgrade. So NATO created a humanitarian disaster. They broke all the rules of international law and they destabilized the Balkans. The total casualties in Kosovo prior to the bombing were about 2,000 killed, including Serbs as well as Albanians. That's not a very nice number. But compared to the killing grounds elsewhere, in Indonesia, in Colombia, in the Turkish massacre of the Kurds, Sierra Leone, and what was happening in Africa, 2,000 people are not a lot of people to decide, "All right, we're going to stop that by bombing a modern European state."

The Bombing

I lived in Belgrade and shopped in Belgrade and got to know the people there. At that time, if you had a dinner party, you would have Croats and Serbs and Muslims. They were all there. They were part of a very strong united country. Belgrade is a modern European city. People are very well educated. They've been around and worked in many countries of Europe and are sophisticated and civilized, with a great culture. They are not the barbarians as portrayed by our media in the West. And I was appalled that we might be raining bombs down on them.

Remember, they bombed Yugoslavia for 78 days. They didn't achieve any of their military objectives. *Newsweek* magazine found a suppressed report from the State Department that showed that they hit 55 of their targets, not 840 or so as they claimed. They did not hit the Yugoslav army in Kosovo. Realizing that, they switched to the civilian infrastructure and that, I think, was not only a violation of the UN Convention and the Geneva Convention, but it was a deliberate attempt to try and bring a modern European state to its knees.

NATO has pretty well destroyed the economic infrastructure of Yugoslavia. All the bridges across the Danube were blown. None of those were military targets. If you look at the geography of Yugoslavia, you see that the Serb army didn't have to cross the Danube to get down into Kosovo. So there was a lot of willful destruction. They smashed Pancevo, a big chemical-industrial city on the Danube, causing tremendous environmental damage there.

They hit the TV towers; they hit the Chinese embassy. They bombed the marketplace in Nis with cluster bombs on a Saturday afternoon. They caused a great deal of damage. I don't think Yugoslavia will be able to recover for many, many years. And they did this for objectives that they never reached. The Yugoslav government claims 10,000, but I think the generally accepted figure for casualties is about 5,000 civilians killed.

There were no allied casualties because they were bombing from 15,000 feet. It was kind of a virtual war, as someone called it. We watched it on CNN and the U.S. television networks every night. But you don't see the impact that the bombs are making. The talking heads were telling us about the tremendous technical prowess of these American F-18 fighters and bombers but nobody showed what happened on the ground when the passenger trains were hit.

This is what really appalled me and made me speak out against the bombing. Because it was quite unnecessary. It was deliberate. I think now everybody recognizes Rambouillet was a deliberate attempt by the Americans to put Milosevic in a position where he couldn't accept that agreement. This would enable the Americans to bomb the country and hopefully bring Milosevic down. Of course it did the opposite: it rallied all the Serbs behind him.

Milosevic
Milosevic and I got to know each other quite well because I didn't leave Belgrade until the summer of 1992, when most of the other Western ambassadors had been pulled out. As a result of that I often used to go and see him and make a démarche with him and confront him with

unpleasant things. He always received me very well. He was always with me alone, no interpreter. He never had any bodyguards around and he usually had a bottle of Chivas Regal on the table.

Milosevic was a shrewd, tough negotiator. He was very similar to all of the leaders in Eastern Europe after the collapse of the Communists. They are Communist apparatchiks. They were all interested in prestige, privilege and power and maintaining those. In the case of Yugoslavia and a lot of other countries in Eastern Europe, when the Communist ideology lapsed, these leaders then turned to whatever else might make them popular. In the case of Milosevic, of Tudjman in Croatia, Kucan from Slovenia, Gligorov from Macedonia and others, these leaders, who were all old Communist apparatchiks, jumped on the ethnic bandwagon. They knew that if they played the ethnic card, they could remain popular.

Milosevic wasn't any better or any worse than most of the others. They all made terrible mistakes and none of them really had any kind of concern for their own people. They were quite prepared to sacrifice their people as long as they could remain in power. Whatever leader, Milosevic or not, had been in Serbia would have had to make the same choices. He could not have abandoned the 12 percent of the Serbs living in Croatia, given the history of their being massacred in the Second World War. People forget Croatia had a big Serbian population for hundreds of years. These were their ancestral lands. When Tudjman came to power in Croatia he used all the old symbols of the first national regime that had slaughtered these Serbians in the Second World War.

By 1990 the Serbs in Croatia were nervous; they were frightened. No one in the Western democracies expressed any degree of concern about them. Nobody was prepared to say, "Look, if Croatia separates, we have to give guarantees of the civil and human rights of these people." And so when Croatia separated, these people rebelled against the Croatians and Milosevic had no choice but to help.

The same in Bosnia. Some 40 percent of the population of Bosnia and Serbia, because of the Turkish occupation during the Ottoman Empire, were Muslim. And because of what happened during the Second World War, no ambassador in Belgrade had any doubt that if Izetbegovic had his referendum and established a Muslim state in Bosnia, the Serbs there would rebel and there would be civil war.

When war breaks out, particularly civil war, there will always be atrocities. There will be criminals who get a gun in their hand and who are prepared to massacre people. If Milosevic is a criminal, and he probably is, we'll have to see some evidence of it. A lot of the charges against him have already been proven to be probably wrong. I mean, the first indictment against him was Racak. Now there seems to be every evidence that Racak was not a massacre. He was accused of plotting to ethnically cleanse Albania long before the bombing, in the so-called Operation Horseshoe. But a German general who's retired now has come out and said that it was a complete farce. Horseshoe was an attempt by the defence minister of Germany to marshal German public support against Milosevic. So if the two major charges against him are shaky, I think it's going to be difficult for The Hague to find him guilty of war crimes, unless they have some kind of electronic information that we don't know about.

Long before the bombing in Kosovo, Milosevic was not a very popular guy. There was a lot of opposition to Milosevic. Had they received any kind of support at that time, those opposition parties might have been able to beat him. But with the bombing, of course all the Serbs then supported him and they supported him fully and actively until the end of the bombing. When the bombing was over, those democratic parties began to get some support from the West and were able to defeat him at the polls. He became an unpopular guy.

After all, Milosevic did bring total disaster to the Serbs and to Serbia, and they all realized that. So his days were numbered and he might have fallen long before the bombing if people had played their cards right. I was in Belgrade in 1991, in March when the whole of Belgrade turned out in a massive demonstration to overthrow Milosevic and almost succeeded in doing it. He wasn't a very popular guy, but he sure became popular after the bombing.

NATO vs. the Serbian Army
NATO had the most powerful military force in the world, with the United States and all of their very sophisticated equipment, aircraft, missiles and intelligence devices. On the other hand the Serbian army was a powerful army, and still is. Before the breakup of Yugoslavia I think it had the third or fourth largest army in Europe. It had good equipment, but by the time the 1990 war started, that didn't compare with the sophistication of the American weaponry.

Nevertheless, they could still have caused tremendous casualties if there had been a ground war because the Yugoslav army was based on total defence. The experience of the Second World War showed them that they could easily be overrun but the fight would continue, so they had massive bunkers in Bosnia. All of their young men were trained and conscripted for military service and they were on a reasonable war footing.

The Serbs are a warrior nation. They have a long tradition of fighting. In the First World War the Canadian army, which had very heavy casualties and fought with a great tradition, had nine percent casualties. The Serbs had 37 percent casualties, more than any other country. So they were prepared for war. They're very good at camouflage, at deception, and they proved that in Kosovo.

NATO bombed Kosovo but they didn't really hit any of the military targets. And when the Serbian army left Kosovo they left with their battle flags flying. They were tough opponents. Looking at the Serb defences, the French general who came into Kosovo from Albania afterward thanked God that they didn't have to try and take them in battle.

We made our major contribution, of course, with our air force. We didn't have the capacity to get the fighters there, but once they were there they did participate in about 10 percent of the bombing. But we don't know what their success rate was. The British fighters, we know, had a very, very low percentage of hits. They were dropping 2,000-pound bombs, but I think they had about a two percent target success.

Even the Americans with their very highly sophisticated weapons weren't able to really detect where the Serb tanks or their artillery were and knock them out. They began to get a little more successful when the KLA got on the ground and were able to report back to the Americans where the artillery was. But the Serbs moved them every night. They had dummy tanks throughout Kosovo and it was difficult to pinpoint where they were to hit them.

Canada and Foreign Affairs
Canadians woke up one morning in March 1999 to find out that we were at war. There had been no declaration of war, there had been no debate or discussion in Parliament. We just suddenly found that we

were at war. Most Canadians hadn't the slightest idea where Kosovo was and they didn't know what the issues were, and suddenly we're at war. This is really an indictment of our political leaders.

And then, what's even worse, once we were in the war we were told by our political leaders a bunch of lies, basically — that we were in there to stop ethnic cleansing, we were in there to stabilize the Balkans. We were in there for a variety of reasons, none of which were really valid. Nobody really said, "Wait a minute, NATO is bombing a sovereign state in Europe that has posed no threat to any other country, that is trying to put down an armed rebellion of separatists who are using terrorist tactics. We're stepping in, not to help them but to bomb them." We didn't gain anything. Unless perhaps we learned that we should be much more demanding of our political leaders before they put Canadian soldiers, airmen and other military people at risk.

I don't think there's very much interest generally in foreign affairs among our parliamentarians. In the last election I don't think foreign affairs were even mentioned by any of the political leaders. There's a tendency in Canada just to assume that we're living next to the United States, the most powerful country in the world, and we can ride with it. As long as we do what they tell us to do we're OK. And we don't have to have a strong military. We don't have to have a defence and we don't have to pay too much attention to foreign affairs because it's going to be looked after for us by our neighbours.

I found it ironic that Lloyd Axworthy, the great humanitarian, the man of peace, our foreign affairs minister, didn't even question the fact. Article 1 of the North Atlantic Treaty Organization, which Canadians had a part in forming, is abundantly clear. It states that NATO will never, ever, even use the threat of force, let alone use force, to settle international disputes. They will only act in accordance with the UN charter. That's Article 1. It was completely ignored by the NATO authorities and our own politicians.

You know, they're embarrassed if you mention Article 1 because NATO is a defensive organization and it will not, in any circumstances, use force to try and resolve international disputes. We broke that deal in Kosovo and we've lost the moral high ground. We no longer can do as our fathers and grandfathers did — say that we are defending rule of law, justice, democracy and so on. We've gone back to the bad old days before the United Nations charter, where the strong nations did what they bloody well wanted to do.

Speaking Out

I'd be the first to admit the UN needs reform and it's not doing its job well. There's no question about that. I can almost feel the frustration of people about the United Nations not doing the job it should be doing. And it's obvious that the United States, the most powerful country in the world, is pretty well ignoring the United Nations. It's already wiped it out, pushed it off to the side. It uses it when it's convenient. The Hague tribunal is an example. The United States completely ignores the UN charter, but says everybody must follow this tribunal that was set up by a subsidiary agency of the United Nations. But the UN also has to take some of the responsibility here.

The fact is that we, the Western democracies, the members of NATO, have violated the first kind of ground rules of our own organization. And that is an appalling thing, one that will haunt us. Because what goes around, comes around, we're seeing that today. If you are a big power and you use force without doing it within the framework of international peace and good order, then you're taking big risks.

NATO's action in Kosovo demonstrated, among other things, that nowadays we no longer declare war. There's no longer a debate in Parliament about whether we should go to war. We go to war because we are part of an international organization. The United States could never have gone to war in Kosovo if they'd gone to their own Congress. Congress would never have allowed it. So they used the framework of NATO to get around that little problem.

The United States have bombed and been aggressive in a long list of countries and they've never gone to Congress to get support for that, and Canada's much the same. I mean, our politicians were off the hook. Chrétien, Axworthy, Eggleton didn't have to explain what we were doing in Kosovo. We were there because we were part of NATO and everybody knows that NATO is a democratic institution, stands for democracy and the rule of law and the United Nations. If NATO's bombing Kosovo, well, you know, we have to go along with it.

And that's part of the problem. Our parliamentarians, our politicians, are not informed. They're not particularly interested in foreign affairs. They don't pay attention to it and they don't really ask the tough questions. With Kosovo you had all of the political parties supporting the bombing. You had all of the major media, you had the Canadian public basically accepting that we should bomb Yugoslavia.

I went to Yugoslavia several months after the bombing. It was in the winter. When I left in a taxi to go out to the Ottawa airport, I noticed children sliding down the snow banks. When I arrived in Belgrade it was the same thing. I was in the outskirts, driving in, and there were snow banks there and children were sliding down the snow banks. The difference struck me because in Canada we don't envisage kids on toboggans sliding down hills when they're being bombed.

Bombing Yugoslavia was a sanitary, antiseptic exercise. It was a virtual war. But it wasn't for the people who were there. Canadians have to realize that war is a nasty business and you don't bomb people lightly and you certainly don't bomb them for humanitarian reasons. You have to do everything you can to resolve these disputes by peaceful means. It's too easy to start using force.

It is almost Orwellian. One of the great sins of our present-day politicians is that they feel that if you can put in a humanitarian objective, then you can do almost anything — it's OK to bomb people if you're doing it for humanitarian reasons. And many Canadians accept that. They think, "Well, we had to go into Kosovo because, look, there was genocide there."

The secretary of defence from the United States was telling us that over 100,000 Albanians were missing, probably killed. Clinton actually said genocide was taking place in Kosovo. Axworthy and Eggleton also said those same things. We found out it wasn't true. If you have politicians who are prepared to lie to you, a media that's prepared to support what they're saying, an apathetic public more interested in the latest millionaire show, a public neither informed nor interested in reading newspapers, then it's easy to get away with what NATO got away with in Kosovo.

There was only one politician, to my knowledge, that stood up in the Canadian House of Commons the day after the bombing and questioned it, and that was David Price, the Conservative Party's defence critic. Very shortly after that he was removed from that position by his leader, Joe Clark, and eventually he crossed the floor of the House. But it's not easy to take on the establishment and it's not easy to criticize your own armed forces and your own government when conflict starts.

But it's the responsibility of people who do know what's happening to speak out. And that's why I've spoken out against the war. I felt I had to do that because I did know what was going on. I did know the history. I did know that there had been a history of duplicity, lying and double-handedness on the part of the Western democracies in dealing with Yugoslavia. The last straw for me was when I actually heard that they were bombing Yugoslavia.

Criticism

Most of the ambassadors of my generation were old cold war warriors like myself. I was a strong defender of NATO. After all, NATO stood for everything I did and what my father had stood for. So they were very reluctant to criticize NATO. And it's not generally acceptable for former ambassadors to criticize the government and to step into the limelight.

We've lost the moral high ground. When Canadians went to war in the First World War, the Second World War and the Korean War, we did so in the full knowledge and conviction that what we were doing was right, and we were right. In Kosovo we were not right and we broke the ground rules. And that's going to haunt us.

We also sent a signal to the rest of the world that these Western democracies that talk so much about the rule of law and the framework of world security don't really mean it. What it boils down to is force. If you're powerful enough, you do what you want. And that, I think, sent a very bad signal to the Russians, to the Chinese and to a lot of other people in the world who said that these ideals the Statue of Liberty stands for don't really mean much because they can be violated whenever the United States wants to.

If you have a true democracy, you have to have some degree of accountability by people who take your country to war. I don't think the accountability was there. I felt by speaking out we'd focus attention on what's really happening and make people conscious that they have to be more demanding of their political leaders. They can't take us to war without telling us why and debating it.

Later I was in Belgrade for a conference. I walked down to the embassy to distribute some gifts to the local staff there. I got into the embassy and was told by one of the officers that I wasn't permitted there, I had to get out, which I did.

Interestingly enough, the guy next to me at the conference was Kostunica, now the president of Yugoslavia. He was appalled and shocked at what had happened to me and said that he could understand that happening in Milosevic's Yugoslavia, but he didn't think it would ever happen in Canada. I think that was a petty thing to do and I don't want to make too much of it, but in a sense it's a reflection of the pettiness of politics.

The Future of NATO

I would like to think that NATO still has Article 1 as the cornerstone of its policy and I would like to see some reaffirmation of that. But I'm afraid we're not going to get it because on its 50th anniversary, in Washington, there was a new doctrine announced for NATO, and that new doctrine basically gives NATO a free hand. In other words, it can go to war whenever it wants to against anybody it wants to.

That's really dangerous. The North Atlantic Treaty is still a treaty. If it's going to be changed, then all of the parliaments of the member countries have got to debate those changes. That has not happened.

Parliament went along with the NATO bombing because most of the members of Parliament haven't got a clue about what was happening in Kosovo. They don't pay that much attention to what's going on in NATO either. The Canadian representative at NATO is a diplomat. He goes to NATO council meetings and he listens to what is told to him by the Americans, who have all the intelligence. The Americans tell the people around the table what they want to tell them.

Canada was not at the table, really. We looked upon that as a part of the world that we didn't have major interests in. We don't have much to do with the Balkans. We don't have much trade with them and we were prepared to sit back and let others take the lead. And this is also true in

Kosovo. We were not members of the contact group, the Russians, the Americans, the French, the British. And we weren't following as closely as we should have been the lead-up to Rambouillet.

I'm quite sure that none of our politicians knew anything about Appendix B of the Rambouillet agreement. That put Milosevic in a position where he had to refuse to accept it. Even the French foreign affairs committee asked for a copy of the Rambouillet agreement, and it was six weeks after the bombing that they were finally presented with it. This was all done by the Americans, clearly staged by Madeleine Albright and Clinton, to bomb Yugoslavia for a variety of reasons, and probably one was to keep NATO going as an institution.

A lot of American critics were saying, "Why have we got this massive military organization in the middle of Europe? The Communist threat is gone, the Warsaw armies have left and gone home, and yet we're spending billions of dollars on this military organization that doesn't have anything to do." Then along came Milosevic. They suddenly said, "Hey, we have something to do now. We can go after this guy. But we can't do it legally because the UN charter would be violated. So we've got to do it illegally and we've got to work up some kind of a system where we're doing it for humanitarian reasons and we can get public support." I don't think Canadian politicians were really on top of it. I think they were simply buying whatever the Americans told us.

Macedonia

Let's take a more recent example. Here we have Macedonia, a very small (population two million), newly independent democratic country, neighbouring Kosovo, which helped the NATO allies during the Kosovo war. It was used as a staging ground and they accepted 800,000 refugees. Bill Clinton went to see them after and praised them for their efforts.

Now what's happened? This KLA, the Albanian terrorist organization which was armed and equipped by NATO countries, mainly the United States, decides that they have learned something from Kosovo. One, if you use force and violence and killing, you'll get your objectives. Second, NATO is not going to easily lose one soldier. They'll bomb from 15,000 feet but they're not going to put the lives of their soldiers at risk. Knowing that, they move into Macedonia and start the same practice again.

They started shooting Macedonian policemen, murdering Macedonian mayors. They were armed and equipped by the U.S. and the whole pattern repeated itself. Now, NATO, instead of standing by this democratic country and saying, "Look, this is a violation of their sovereignty, this is a democracy at risk," doesn't do anything to stop the KLA from going into Macedonia. There are 40,000 NATO troops in Kosovo. They allowed all of these KLA leaders to arm, equip, recruit and send their forces into Macedonia to bring down the government.

In addition to that, when the Macedonian government tried to protect themselves and bought some helicopters from the Ukraine, the U.S. security advisor flies to Kiev and tells the Ukrainians not to give the Macedonian government another dollar's worth of military equipment. Now, how do you figure that? And are Canadian politicians watching that? No, they're not because when they're asked by NATO to switch the Lord Strathcona's Horse from Bosnia to Macedonia, they do it without question. So we've got Canadian troops in Macedonia but they're not quite sure what they're doing there.

As far as I know there's never been a question asked in the House of Commons about this. Nobody's asked why our troops were transferred from Bosnia to Macedonia. No one has asked what Canadian policy is with regard to Macedonia. Why is NATO not doing everything they can to arrest and disarm the KLA and put these people in jail? They're terrorists. They have linkages with bin Laden, we know that. They have mujahideen fighting with them, from Chechnya, from Afghanistan. This is all known to NATO. They're bringing down Macedonia.

They're bringing it down because they're afraid that if they try and disarm their old allies, the KLA, they're going to lose lives. But you can't have double standards when you're fighting terrorists. You can't complain about what happened in New York and allow and support fully terrorists in Kosovo and in Macedonia. The war against terrorism, as they keep telling us, has to be on all fronts.

It is wrong for our politicians to send Canadian troops to war without knowing why they're there. That's happened in Bosnia. It's happened in Kosovo and it's happening today in Macedonia. The troops in Macedonia haven't got a clue what they're there for. Nobody's ever explained to them clearly what they're doing there. They know that there's a fight going on between Albanians and Macedonians and they're in the middle of it. But the moral authority is not with them and that's something we should be ashamed of.

Committees — Canadian, American and Russian

I was surprised that I was asked to go before the parliamentary committee. It certainly wasn't at the request of any of the government members that I was there. I was given 10 minutes and I made a statement. Others who were at the same meeting had given their statements. They all ran over the 10 minutes. When I got to the end of my 10 minutes I was told by the chairman that that was it. Obviously he didn't like what he was hearing. The people around the table, I think, were shocked and surprised that I was criticizing NATO and bringing these things to the table.

What was also interesting was that the man who had replaced me in Belgrade is an old colleague of mine. He was on his way to Sarajevo on a flight when he was suddenly called back to Ottawa because they wanted him to appear to counteract what I had said. He wasn't listed as a witness. After I made my statement the chairman then interjected and said they had a surprise visitor, and "We're going to ask him to come up before the committee and give us his views."

So obviously the government wasn't happy that I was appearing before the committee. I think this is a shame because it seems to me an indication that dissent in opposition is not really welcome. We do live in a country where there's free speech. I'm an example of it. I've had a lot of television coverage and everybody knows I opposed the bombing and I've had a chance to express my views in writing and speaking. But before the parliamentary committee? It wasn't a committee that was interested in hearing a former ambassador's views. It wasn't a committee that seemed really intent on getting at the facts and coping with some of these issues. It was obviously a committee that was nervous about my appearance because I might say something that would embarrass Lloyd Axworthy or Eggleton and the government. So I didn't feel particularly comfortable there.

In contrast, when Washington found out I had these views I was invited by a congressman to come down and express them. I had plenty of time to tell what I thought and they listened carefully and asked questions.

When I left Yugoslavia and retired from the foreign service I went to Moscow, heading an international organization there. One of the first Russian members of the Duma that I went to see (because he was involved in refugee issues) found out that I had been the former Canadian ambassador in Yugoslavia. He asked, "Would you be willing to come before the foreign affairs committee of the Duma and tell us what you think of what's going on in Yugoslavia?" I said, "I will if you understand that I'm not speaking for the Canadian government and I'm not speaking for the international organization I represent, and there'll be no press or media." He said all that would be arranged.

There were about 60 members of the Duma waiting to hear what I had to say about Yugoslavia. They were knowledgeable. They had a lot of good questions. I spent at least two hours with them. I found that a striking contrast because when I came back to Canada from Yugoslavia, nobody was even slightly interested in debriefing me. And I'm sure I would never have appeared before the parliamentary committee had not one of the members decided I might make a good witness.

Parliament Now
I think we all recognize that we've got a Parliament that's basically impotent and the committee system isn't working. When you're preparing the minister to go before a hearing you put the best face on. And it's not what the committee hears. It's what the committee doesn't hear that's often the most important thing because the government is not going to reveal anything that might in the slightest way embarrass the minister. They're public servants, devoted and obedient servants who do what they're told to do. In the last 20 or 30 years there has been a marked change in civil service ethics. I certainly noticed that the primary role was to protect the government from being in any way criticized. As a result, many of the facts that are held in the public service are never revealed. The information doesn't come out because they can't release it.

But the bureaucrats don't withhold information; they couldn't care less. They're told to withhold information. They're told to withhold information by the ministers. It's not the bureaucrats that are afraid of the access to information. They're quite happy to reveal all and often try to do it in devious ways. But generally speaking, it's the culture now of the public servants to work, not necessarily for Canada, but for the minister.

The concept of national interest has been clearly submerged in the interest of the political party in power. Now, maybe we have to live with that, but it's a sad commentary.

Lessons Learned

Kosovo was a turning point. It was in a sense an epiphany. I couldn't believe what had happened there. I had been a devoted, loyal public servant who in my 36 years of service had always believed, basically, that the government was doing the right thing.

I was at the University of Toronto before quite a big crowd shortly after the bombing started, and I was the first speaker. The speaker following me was Ursula Franklin, the world-renowned physicist and humanitarian who had spoken out against the bombing. She got up and looked down at me and said, "Here we have former ambassador Bissett, who for 36 years served his government loyally and devotedly. And all that time Mr. Bissett believed that occasionally the government might be misinformed, but it was never ill intentioned." Then she looked down at me again and said, "Now he knows what I've always known, that governments are always well informed, but seldom well intentioned."

I haven't forgotten that. I just couldn't believe that our country was prepared to toss everything it believed about NATO aside to start bombing people in the middle of Europe over a relatively minor police action that was being carried out by the Yugoslav authorities against these Kosovo rebels and terrorists.

Let's take a look at the truth for a while. We live in the real world. We see what happens. We saw it with the bombing of the Twin Towers. We can expect that to happen more and more often. But we have to get back on the right side. We have to be morally right in what we're doing and we're not at the moment, I'm afraid.

The thing could have been settled diplomatically. The negotiations that were carried out by Holbrooke and Madeleine Albright and all of that lead-up were not negotiations. They were Albright, and Albright going to Milosevic and saying do this and do that, and that's not negotiation. With all of the charges against Milosevic, the one thing that was common throughout his regime, you could negotiate with him. People forget this. He negotiated successfully the Dayton peace accord.

Madeleine Albright called Milosevic "the man of peace." He made deals. He was flexible in many ways. And bear in mind what the two conditions were that he couldn't accept from Rambouillet: the occupation and free access of NATO troops throughout all of Yugoslavia and holding a referendum in Kosovo on autonomy.

What ended the war in Kosovo was when Chernomyrdin and Ahtisaari, the Finnish president, went to negotiate with Milosevic and agreed that NATO would take those two conditions off the table. Milosevic said, "Fine. If those conditions that started the war aren't there, then let's end it." So they could have negotiated with the guy. There wasn't a willingness to do that.

I think Madeleine Albright bears a very heavy responsibility here because basically she said to Colin Powell, "What have we got all this power for if we don't use it? Why negotiate with these guys? Blast them out of the way." But blasting Milosevic out of the way caused tremendous damage and destruction to a lot of innocent people.

Canada's reputation as a middle power around the world has suffered in the last several years. I would suspect that Lloyd Axworthy was very uneasy about Kosovo because he knew that we were breaking international law. Yet he was forced to stand up and defend our actions. We're not tough enough. We followed the lead of the United States on every major issue. We are the greatest friends of the United States. We rely a great deal on them. It would be quite impossible for a Canadian foreign minister to stand up and say, "Look, we're not going to do this."

But you don't let your best friend drive drunk. There are occasions when Canada should stand up to the United States and say, "Wait a minute. If you want us to go along with you for NATO to bomb Yugoslavia, we want to get UN approval."

I doubt if we have many Canadian politicians who have the moral courage to stand up and do that. We're beginning to be seen internationally as a country that preaches human rights but doesn't really stand up at the right moment and make a contribution to ensure that the rule of law is followed, that international law is not violated and that those principles of the founding fathers of the United Nations are still valid.

PLAYING THE OSTRICH

The bombing of Belgrade was a crossroads. It was not supported by a large part of the world. Many saw it as a turning back by the most powerful Western democracies on the rule of law that had been established since the founding of the United Nations. And that, I think, is alarming.

LEWIS MACKENZIE
Major-General (Retired)
2001 (Pre-9/11)

Major-General (Ret) MacKenzie has said that he joined the army one summer so that he could buy a used car. The summer job turned into an impressive career covering the next 33 years. He is a veteran of eight UN or other peacekeeping operations, including tours in Gaza, Egypt, Cyprus and Central America. He became known around the world when he was made the first chief of staff of the United Nations Protection Force in the former Yugoslavia in 1992, just as Bosnia plunged into civil war, an experience he relates in detail in his best-selling autobiography, Peacekeeper: The Road to Sarajevo. *General MacKenzie retired from the Canadian Armed Forces in 1993 and has since run for Parliament and been a journalist and lecturer. He has been active in many charitable causes, such as the Canadian Foundation for Aids Research and the Special Olympics, and is an avid race car driver.*

Recent History in Kosovo

There's a long, miserable history to Kosovo, with a lot of groups vying for control of the province. The problem is that Kosovo was festering, big time, in the late 1980s, but what was going on in Croatia and Bosnia eclipsed it. When the war started there the world took its eyes off of Kosovo. But back in the late 1980s people thought that Kosovo was going to explode.

In 1989 when Milosevic, who was running the Communist party in Serbia, went there, he didn't realize that it was going to launch him into the presidency. He actually stood in front of a crowd, and there were some Serbs being beaten by some Kosovo Albanians in the back of the crowd. He hushed the crowd and said, "Elect me and you will never be beaten again." Big deal, you know, got a cheer, but when he arrived back in Belgrade there were tens of thousands of people on the streets applauding him as the great protector of the Serb nation. He saw that as a platform to launch himself into the presidency, and he succeeded.

While the Bosnian and Croatian wars were going on, the Kosovo Liberation Army started to kidnap Serbian security forces and execute them, or whatever, because they knew that there would be a reaction by Milosevic. They knew that he would, as usual, overreact, and rather than attacking one or two that might be KLA, he would attack an entire village. That would get international attention, particularly from the United States, to focus on Kosovo. And over the hill would come the 7th U.S. Cavalry, with Madeleine Albright in the front with her sword, and they would save them. That was the logic that they used.

That's why they hired U.S.-based public relations firms to make that point for them. The international community wasn't going to get sucked in that quickly — so the Organization for Security and Co-operation in Europe, not NATO, went in there with unarmed observers, a lot of Canadians and Americans and some people still in the military wearing civilian clothes, and they were doing a pretty darn good job. In fact, if you talk to them, wherever they would go the fighting would stop, which is sort of the normal characteristic for an unarmed UN observer.

Then came the Racak "massacre." Whether it was or whether it wasn't, or whether it was a setup, the perception was that about 25 Kosovo-Albanian civilians had been killed by the Serbian security forces and dumped into a ditch. Ambassador Walker, the head of the OSCE monitoring mission — an American who didn't wear an OSCE badge on his vehicle, he actually had an American flag decal on each side — appeared and said, "This is an atrocity. This is genocide."

Meantime they're talking in Rambouillet, in France, about working out an accommodation, a deal that would bring the fighting to a halt and Milosevic would back off. But as soon as this alleged massacre happened, Madeleine Albright rushed into Rambouillet and virtually issued an ultimatum which said to the KLA, "Sign here. Sign up to these modest agreements, and if you agree to that and the Serbs don't, we'll bomb the Serbs!"

Who wouldn't pass up a deal like that? The KLA signed it and the bombing campaign started shortly thereafter. The tragic thing is that the two prerequisites in the agreement that caused Milosevic not to sign in Rambouillet were, one, freedom of movement for NATO forces in Serbia proper. (There's no way Milosevic was going to sign that because he knew he was an indicted war criminal long before it was announced to the international community. The last thing he needed was NATO troops on his back doorstep.) The other prerequisite was a referendum, within about three years in Kosovo, where the will of the people would be taken into consideration.

Considering about 90 percent of the population was Kosovo Albanian, naturally they'd vote for independence, and Milosevic couldn't have that. After the bombing campaign ended, in fact, NATO backed off the two prerequisites. The Russian ambassador and the retired Finnish prime minister brokered that, went to NATO and got them to drop those two prerequisites. So the whole damn thing probably could have been avoided.

Motives and Objectives

The world was really pissed off at Milosevic. They were upset with the way that he'd outfoxed them. We're talking about a guy who's sitting in The Hague waiting to go to trial, but in 1995 he was a contender for the Nobel Peace Prize. Both he and Tudjman of Croatia were on the short list for the Nobel Peace Prize, for God's sake, after the Dayton agreement. The West had anointed Milosevic as a guy to help control Karadzic and Mladic. People liked that. So we, the international community, tend to personalize these wars. Nobody says we hate the Iraqi people. It's Saddam Hussein. We don't hate the Serbian people. We hate Milosevic.

Just once I wish we could fight a war where we hated the people that we're fighting and having to kill, for God's sake. But in this particular case Milosevic had really pissed off a lot of people, and they were going after him and his cronies and they were going to teach him a bloody lesson. Once that momentum started, and once the KLA realized that was the situation and they orchestrated the PR and all of that good stuff, then it became pretty well inevitable. So yeah, like a dog chasing the bus, it's great fun while he's chasing it. But when the dog's caught the bus, now what the hell do we do with it? And that was NATO's problem during the bombing campaign. Because the NATO alliance was very, very fragile during that bombing campaign.

First thing you do when you start planning for a war is to plan how you're going to end it. All of us, from second lieutenant to general, have reacted the same way when we watch Wes Clark, General Clark, the NATO supreme allied commander overseeing Kosovo. On successive days the objective would change. But nobody teaches that you select and maintain your objective, your aim, better than the Americans. I'm a graduate of the U.S. Army War College. I understand that. And we could watch that shifting. So you knew immediately that there was a lot of political input.

When you started seeing the major leaders within NATO in different time zones say exactly the same thing on television, you knew there were briefing points coming out every day from NATO. And the Tony Blairs and the Bill Clintons and the Jean Chrétiens of the world were talking off a script. There was no ad-libbing. The plan went from destroying the Serbian forces, which was proving to be impossible, to stopping a humanitarian disaster. A lot of us argue that in fact NATO had contributed in a significant way to the humanitarian disaster. The massive evacuation, "ethnic cleansing" being the hot term these days, happened concurrent with the start of the bombing campaign.

The propaganda was that there was this tremendous plan for all of this to happen before. Not the case. The propaganda started because bombing campaigns provoke a natural reaction. And as distasteful as ethnic cleansing is, it's a hell of a lot better than genocide. In some of the shots from Pristina where the fog was coming up in the early morning, we saw the Kosovo Albanians being put on trains with their suitcases and their families. They were being sent over the border. And commentators were saying this evoked memories of the Holocaust.

In the Holocaust they were put on the trains and they were taken to the ovens. Don't insult the victims of the Holocaust. This is purging the population, which happens in every war. It's distasteful, it's immoral, it's unethical, it's terrible. But the fact is, it happens. When military forces roll forward, civilian populations are killed or pushed out of the way.

So there was to the very end a distinct lack of focus on what the objective was. If the military guys and gals had been in charge, that wouldn't have been the case. But don't forget, NATO is very much a political organization too. There were a lot of balls to juggle, not the least of which were the Italians, the Greeks and other people who were very uncomfortable with being there. I think Canada might have been in that latter category.

NATO's first and only operational campaign could well be a case study on how not to conduct a military operation. When you throw 19 ambassadors in a room and you've got to come up with the lowest common denominator, this is what happens. What was the outcome for NATO out of all this? The hope was that NATO would escape some of the debilitating compromises that plague the UN.

If you look at the key decision-making UN committees, there are 15 in the Security Council in the UN, of which only five have the veto. So the permanent five, China, Russia, France, the U.K. and the United States — a fairly tight, select group — represents the world in 1945. But nevertheless, that's what it is.

In NATO — where we all talk about having equal influence — B.S.! — but nevertheless, that's the perception — you're talking 19. So it's an even larger committee that you're dealing with. It's complicated. In addition, within the UN you have very, very little military-efficient staff planning capability. There's no military headquarters. Far from it. And the UN would never permit it to have one.

Whereas in NATO they've been doing this since 1948. It's the most integrated, effective military headquarters in the world. All of a sudden it was turned loose on the Kosovo problem. I'd imagine in the very early hours of the first day they realized that they had to play the political game too, particularly General Clark. He was responding multiple times every day to the political imperatives. Solana, the secretary-general, would show up on television as much as Clark did, if not more. In the United Nations you would never see a UN military officer making any comment. Maybe the undersecretary-general for peacekeeping or the secretary-general, but not a military officer.

In the old days before the cold war ended, if the Soviets had come across the East German border and were attacking toward the Channel, the objective would have been obvious. The military had their plans ready and the politicians wouldn't be trying to second-guess. But in the case of the Kosovo operation, the Greek ambassador, for example, is dealing with his leadership back in Greece, wondering whether what they're doing — because it's so unpopular — is going to cause their government to fall, even before the next election. Those are the issues that they had to deal with. The Italians, who could hear not only the planes taking off, but in some cases the bombs landing on the other side of the Adriatic, had serious challenges that they were facing too. That wouldn't be the case if your way of life were threatened. If you were attacked and you were fighting for survival and sacrificing your young men, a common, homogeneous NATO objective would have been easy. But Kosovo wasn't easy.

A Journalist in Serbia
When I blamed the Bosnian Serbs in one interview for only 65 percent of what was going on in Bosnia when I was there, I became their national hero, for God's sake! So it was suggested I might be able to negotiate the release of the three Americans taken hostage. An excellent cover came from CTV, suggesting that because Tom Clark and I had previously worked together over there, how about going into Belgrade? So we got clearance for our entire team and I think we were the only international television crew that was permitted access. When we got in we didn't have anywhere near the control put on us that the other news media had. I had access to the various ministers and ministries, and did a lot of interviews there and tried to find out what the hell was going on. It really disturbed me that some people suggested we were reporting from the Serbian point of view. That pissed me off. I even wrote a piece in defence of John Simpson of the BBC because he was accused of the same thing in the British Parliament.

My argument, as a pseudo-amateur journalist, was that the whole reporting of war changed when Peter Arnett went into Baghdad. All of a sudden there you were, on the ground reporting what was happening, and you were a citizen of the country doing the bombing. Now, can you imagine sending Canadians and Brits and Americans into Berlin or Dresden when it was being firebombed?

My argument was, "Sorry, this is the new technology. We're reporting from Belgrade. We're showing what's happening in Belgrade, and we're really sorry if you're uncomfortable with that because now you're seeing that people are suffering on both sides." I think it's great, quite frankly. If we had had television, World War I would have probably lasted for about two months, maybe.

So it's no bad thing. But there were a lot of people that were very uncomfortable. "Gee, the Western reporters are in Belgrade and they're showing this grandmother standing there, with her headless grandchild in her arms, having defecated all over when she was killed." I mean, that's a pretty gruesome scene, no matter whose side you're on. Maybe it's not so bad that it's shown to the international community.

After nine years in NATO serving in Germany, and having served for 33 years in an army that's part of NATO, it was a little bit bizarre to be on the other end of things. On one particular occasion when I was doing a report, I stopped 15 kids on their way to school on bicycles. Thirteen of them didn't know Canada was in NATO. We go around saying we delivered 10 percent of the strikes. And my article was, "Even when we bomb them, we don't get no respect."

Very seriously, though, what was disturbing to me was that for the first time in my life I heard propaganda coming from my own side. And I knew it was propaganda. In one particular case an apartment building had just been absolutely flattened and there were a lot of dead around. There were cluster bombs all over the place. And naturally they were saying that cluster bombs were never used against anything but purely military targets. Well, there wasn't a military target within 20 kilometres of this place, and even that had been abandoned about three years earlier.

So was it a mistake? Was it intentional? I don't know. But I didn't like hearing the propaganda. I'd be sitting there watching the NATO briefings in Belgrade in my hotel, and they're saying that the Serbian people are victim to all Milosevic's propaganda because they don't have access to television. Well, I had more international news available to me in Belgrade than I do here in Bracebridge or in Toronto. I had ATV. I had BBC ONE, BBC TWO. I had CBS and ABC, NBC. I had both CNN channels, Sky, and on and on. I watched everything.

I saw the Canadian briefings, the American briefings, the NATO briefings and all the questions being asked. And I'm sitting there in Belgrade, for God's sake. It was such a stupid thing to take out the television studio with a missile attack. It killed a bunch of people that were helping us during our interviews.

It was so stupid. The Serbian people were laughing at their own bad propaganda. Like it would be reported that 500 American soldiers threw down their arms in Macedonia and escaped over the border into Greece because they refused to attack Kosovo. That type of B.S. It was just so silly.

Most of the attacks were at night. We knew where most of the attacks were going to come in because they were strategic targets, oil refineries or whatever. So there was this mad rush at last light with people screaming through town at 90 miles an hour to get back to their hotel, get to the bar. When you saw the cities during the day, Novi Sad or Belgrade or whatever, they were pretty normal.

We'd go out the next day and check out the damage. I kept an eye on the Russians because I figured they had an inside track on some of the information. I also figured if the Russians were going in to report from the television studio, then the chances were it wasn't going to be blown up that night.

When you bomb somebody it tends to bring them together. Because let's face it, not a lot of them were Milosevic fans at that stage. But unfortunately, paradoxically, the bombing drove them together to support the government.

What did the bombing accomplish? Oust Milosevic? Destroy the Yugoslav military? Stop the ethnic cleansing? None of the above. But very successful in destroying the infrastructure of the country. The heating plants and the electrical supply. The bridges. Not only the traffic on the Danube within Serbia, but more importantly from the heart of Europe, in Austria, all coming down the Danube. The bridges were knocked down so ships weren't coming through. It was devastating to the economy, there's certainly no doubt about that. As far as the Serb military goes, it's too easy to hide. Yugoslavia's been paranoid ever since it's been a nonaligned middle power. It assumed it was going to get attacked by the Soviet Union and by NATO, so it's got hiding places everywhere.

In Sarajevo when we were there in the peace operation, we went into an elevator and went down 16 levels into solid stone, which is where the Serb military was going to escape to. Every government building by law has a bomb shelter in the basement. Lots of tunnels because it's very mountainous terrain, and as a result you can drive your entire regiment of tanks into a tunnel and sit there. And nobody, no guided missile, is going to do a thing to it. They even had inflatable tanks. They had inflatable aircraft. They had dummy armoured personnel carriers made out of plywood. And NATO was zapping them and wiping them off the face of the earth. But they weren't hitting the real equipment. Stopping the ethnic cleansing? No, because ethnic cleansing is done by a guy with a knife or an AK-47. And a lot of ethnic cleansing is done by intimidation and rumour.

Even in Bosnia with the infamous Arkan — who's now departed, fortunately — they would go in and maybe cut three or four throats. That's all you had to do before the entire town hears about it and starts to move. When they arrive at the next town they say, "Hey, be careful. These guys behind us, they just slaughtered 200." It might have been four or five, but the rumour spreads and the population moves. The Kosovo Albanians were flooding up against the border with Macedonia and Albania. Did the bombing stop that? No, it increased it. As the first bomb fell, naturally the Serbs said, "Those bastards are the cause of us being bombed. So let's get rid of them." When I say "naturally," that doesn't mean it's a good thing. It doesn't mean I agree with it. That's the way the story unfolds.

You have no idea the accuracy of these modern weapon systems. I was taken on a tour by the general manager of the Novi Sad refinery, one of the biggest refineries in Yugoslavia, which covers I don't know how many square miles.

We went around to the towers where the actual work is done. This guy had been trained in Houston and he said that Texaco had put these in, which was sort of funny too, I suppose. The only important part of this whole process is contained in something the size of two 40-gallon oil drums in the centre of the tower. And he showed me where the missile came straight down the chimney right into those two tubes and exploded them. And those things were fired from 50 miles away.

The amount of collateral damage was relatively minuscule, but not very minuscule for the 3,000, 4,000, 5,000 people that were killed. But considering the phenomenal amount of damage that was done to infrastructure, it really was very, very precise bombing. Once again, though, that's for hitting the static targets. That's not for stopping ethnic cleansing or hitting tanks on the move.

Inside Kosovo
Certainly within Kosovo itself the players were the Serbian security forces, not the army at all. It's the MUP, the internal security forces, vicious, nasty SOBs. They were the heavy-handed security people in Kosovo. The military, which is a much more disciplined organization, came in to reinforce them as the war and the possibility of invasion ensued. The Kosovo Liberation Army started with 10 or 20, 15 years ago, but grew to some 6,000. New York City got a lot of publicity when Albanians went home to fight with the KLA, but it was a fairly ill-disciplined organization. But like any guerrilla army, very, very effective. With a big, structured army and security force, it's more difficult to react quickly.

Kosovo is on the crossroads of the drug trade and, to this day, the trade in child sex slaves, prostitution, selling women. And that was part of the counterattack against the KLA.

Where did the weapons come from? Well, remember the big pyramid scheme that collapsed in Albania? They raided the arms depots and tens of thousands of weapons were stolen. A lot of them ended up in Kosovo just over the border. That was the favourite mule-train route, over the border from Albania into Kosovo

The OSCE was a key player and I think a missed opportunity. But Rambouillet trumped them when Madeleine Albright, at the head of the parade, decided that NATO was going to get involved. Questionable whether it was legal. It's an interesting legal debate internationally because there was a UN resolution that permitted air strikes in the event of X, Y and Z. But did X, Y and Z exist when the air strike started? There's a strong argument made by many that this did not have UN Security Council approval.

If it had gone to the Security Council for approval, obviously it would not have passed because Russia and/or China, and maybe France, could have vetoed it and would have. This was an action taken by an international organization, NATO, which by constitution and charter is a defensive alliance, taking on an offensive action against a sovereign nation. So it's a good thing they won. Because if they had lost, then they'd probably have some people sitting in the dock in The Hague. That's the way it works. You've got to win in order not to be tried.

I had a long chat with General Clark, the supreme allied commander, shortly after the war was over. He told me a wonderful story about the Greek ambassador, who came up to him in Clark's operation centre during the war. General Clark, trying to be courteous, said, "This is really difficult for you because there's a lot of controversy about this air-strike campaign against Kosovo." And the Greek ambassador said, "There's no controversy at all in Greece about this. We're all against it. But we're here because we're members of NATO." Well, sometimes I think maybe Canada fits into that same category. It was uncomfortable for us.

This is not a commercial. We have let our military be reduced to such an extent that we need coalition support in the event that we ever get ourselves in trouble. And as a result we have to maintain good relations with our alliances. And NATO is our key alliance. We couldn't say, "No, no, we're not coming. We're not going to play." So we made a significant contribution.

Maybe I'm one of those few people that could compliment the Canadian pilots on what they did and at the same time criticize the government for putting them in a position where they had to do that. These guys did their work well. They came home and they were called aces. I got upset about that because, you know, an "ace" means shooting down X number of enemy aircraft. I think some of our pilots would have been embarrassed at being called aces. I mean, 15,000 feet and firing precision munitions and operating under intense situations and anti-aircraft and all that, God bless them. But unless the definition of ace has changed, let's not make this thing bigger than it was.

Canada and Kosovo

They had just put the contact group together, back in 1994, 1995, for Bosnia, and the contact group was Italy, a bordering country, the United States, France and the United Kingdom, who had big contingents there. During the filming of a documentary I said to the prime minister, "Why the hell aren't we part of the contact group? Per capita we've left more blood on the ground in Bosnia than any other nation." The highest number is France, who had more killed than we had, but per capita we've had twice as many killed and we've had over 100 guys seriously injured.

So I asked, "Why the hell aren't we part of the contact group?" And the prime minister looked me in the eye and said, "They didn't ask us."

You don't wait to be asked. You insist. The same thing with Kosovo. You should insist, and if you don't get invited to the meeting, you should be standing outside the bloody door when the meeting starts. We make significant contributions, relative to our ability to do so and our population. And yet we don't insist on a seat at the table. We wait for someone to pull it out for us. I was really shocked at the PM's tremendous honesty. I mean, it wasn't a glib response. He was serious. He just said, "They didn't ask us." Well, we earned our right to be there.

There's a characteristic that evolves when an operation is being run by either the superpower, the United States, or within the UN by a member of the Security Council, the permanent five. Don't forget that in the long history of peacekeeping operations, the French and the British and the Americans never participate. The U.K. was a small exception to that rule in Cyprus because they had two major sovereign bases on the island. So they participated. But the theory was that those five permanent members stay out of peace operations.

When I ran the operation in Sarajevo I had one phone call from the government in six months. It was Barbara McDougall saying, "How are things going?" She was at External Affairs at this time. "Things look pretty good from this side, thank you very much." When Morillon followed me, from France, there were probably three or four calls a day from the Elysée Palace. And when Rose followed Morillon there were lots of calls from MOD, London, and lots of calls from 10 Downing Street. Because there you've got two masters: your own significant national political master and the institution, the UN or NATO.

So Canada didn't have much say in Kosovo. When it came time to suggest we should have a ground invasion in order to get Milosevic to change his mind, it was too late for us to participate. But when the follow-on force went in there we sent new equipment in, not necessarily what the coalition commander wanted on the ground, but we said, "Hey, we've got some of this new stuff and we're going to send it over. See if you can use it somewhere." He did and it worked very well.

Thank God we didn't have to fight, though, because there was just a tiny little packet of Canadians attached to somebody else. I thought we spent the previous century lobbying to make sure we fought under our own command at a fairly significant level. That doesn't seem to be the case now. We just plug bits and pieces into other people's commands. I don't like that.

The Outcome

As usual the civilians, particularly the Kosovo Albanian population, are always the victims. Since the end of the cold war 90 percent of the victims in most wars are civilians. In this particular case they got booted out and lost their homes and then were brought back in. No matter who was right or wrong, they were big victims.

The minority Serb population that remains in Kosovo, maybe five percent of the overall population, are victims. They're only staying because they're stubborn. They certainly don't have any quality of life there anymore. The KLA have changed their spots and joined a legitimate sort of government, but haven't changed their character.

The Serb military has left, but paradoxically has been invited back because NATO doesn't want anybody to get hurt. So in some of these dangerous areas, in the buffer zones, it's better to put the Yugoslavian National Army special forces in.

What's happened in Serbia is only partially related to the air strikes. NATO would very much like us to think otherwise, but I'm not sure that's the case. The infusion of a tremendous amount of capital and organization from the West to Kostunica and the opposition parties in Yugoslavia had a tremendous impact on bringing down Milosevic. People were getting sick and tired of Milosevic, and speaking quite openly too. Sure, a handful were killed, influential people, editors and lawyers, but in the street people were not.

It wasn't like the old Communist state. They didn't mind speaking out against Milosevic at all. So there's been a tremendous moment of opportunity, more for Serbia than Kosovo. As much as we all believe that Kosovo was the Jerusalem of the Serbs, and that they would never give it up, the conversations I've heard say, "The hell with it. It's not worthwhile. As long as we can keep the northern little bit of the northern chunk — where the famous battlefield of the Blackbirds is and some of the monasteries are — but the rest of it, it's not worth it." Hopefully Serbia might be on the road to recovery.

NATO

It's important to recognize that NATO's credibility was threatened close to the end of the conflict. A large number of nations didn't want the air strikes to continue. They saw it as punitive against Serbia rather than stopping the humanitarian disaster in Kosovo. Therefore, and Wes Clark will admit this publicly, it was becoming very difficult to keep that political cohesion together. And if it had split, if it had broken, they would have had to stop bombing.

Not because they felt they had achieved their objective, but because nations were saying, "We will not go along with this anymore." That would have been rough on NATO and NATO's continued existence. Even though I'm not a fan of NATO expansion, some people are wedded to it and see it as a way of stabilizing the entire European continent. That wouldn't have been possible, obviously, if the alliance had fallen apart.

NATO is moving farther and farther away from the U.S. The reason the Americans are in NATO in Europe is because the Europeans want them there. Why? Because if the Yanks weren't there, the Brits, the French and the Germans would be at each others throats again, deciding who's going to run the continent. Now, I don't mean that they're going to go to war, but I do mean that it would cause a lot of tension, in a large number of institutions, about who's the lead country.

Canada's Position

We're in danger of becoming an orphan. When I was at the United States Army War College they had a week on NATO and a week on the United States, and Canada didn't get mentioned in either of them. So I put up my hand as the lone Canadian and said, "What about us, you know? We're a member of NATO too." "Oh well, we always sort of take you for granted."

It's expensive maintaining forces like that overseas. So the U.S. pulls back. And we are very, very much in danger of becoming a little pimple, militarily, on the American forces. I'm not sure that would be good for us.

I think the critics are correct. We're much more comfortable as a full-fledged member of NATO or as a significant — as we used to be, but no longer are — contributor to the UN. We're still pumping propaganda saying that we're still a big player in the UN. Give me a break. Ten of the 13 UN missions we're in are in single digits personnel-wise, for God's sake. Some of them are one person, like in Cyprus. Maybe it's up to two now, but it goes between two and one.

So we are no longer a significant player in UN peacekeeping. And for people to say, "Well, we'll provide our expertise because we have all this background," is arrogance to the extreme. You lose your expertise very, very quickly as the world evolves. The rules that we applied in Cyprus didn't apply in Bosnia. And the rules we applied in Bosnia didn't apply in Eritrea or Ethiopia. So forget our expertise. Other people are learning much more quickly than we are right now.

We have about 1,500 personnel in Europe with NATO, 1,300 or whatever in Bosnia. Why? You don't need that many troops in Bosnia to keep the peace. The Bosnian army isn't going to launch an attack into Serbia or Croatia to re-establish borders. Every time that the mandate comes up for renewal, sure there's some tension. That happens in every mission because they want the force to stay. Why? Because it's a floodgate of funds, of money coming into the area. The force in Bosnia, you could do what you have to do there with a modest observer group of a couple of thousand folks. "Oh, but when the refugees come back, they're getting beaten up."

Fine. You have to have law and order within your own country. You have to establish your own police force. Train their police forces. Establish a judiciary. They've done all of that in Bosnia, but we don't need 16,000 NATO troops parked in Bosnia like we Canadians were parked in Cyprus from 1964 to 1992. The UN's still there with the Argentines and the Brits. It's just madness to maintain this presence for so long.

I've spent time in other countries, particularly the United States, discussing these issues and they're all searching for criteria, particularly the U.S. Congress, searching for criteria for deployment and criteria for pulling out. And I keep saying, "Don't waste your time." We have criteria in Canada and we've defied every one of them every time. Why? Because there will always be a demand to do something.

I was begging for Canadian troops to come into Sarajevo. I had no identifiable end state. I didn't know when the end state was going to be. What was the acceptable degree of risk? What's the proper structure and organization and confidence in the chain of command?

You defy them all the time because the government says — which is their right — "We think we should go there and do that." And even the prime minister has said a couple of times, "I don't like what I've seen on TV. I think we should go and try to help." Those are honourable undertakings, but they're not precise criteria with an identifiable end state.

Soft Power

I've been a little facetious and unkind on soft power. I said a couple of times from the stage that Lloyd Axworthy thought when there was a conflict we would go in as Canadians with insightful thoughts, and then get the other people to do the dirty work.

Sorry, but it doesn't work that way. If you're not prepared to do the dirty work, you don't get any credibility for your insightful thought. You know, walk tall and you occasionally have to carry a stick, and we have less and less ability to do that.

Our American friends as usual are very kind to us in public but behind closed doors ... But then I explain the size of our military to American general officers when I lecture down there, and they keep waiting for the punch line after I finish. They think I'm joking. They actually think I'm joking with them.

When I tell them our army is less than 20,000 and the deployable is somewhere around 14,000 on a good day, they just think it's a joke. Unfortunately it's not. "Well, we see you guys on quite a few missions around the world." Yeah. One or two guys here. Two or three there.

You see a lot of us in Bosnia and that's our only location. That's now become fairly comfortable and very safe, relatively. Unfortunately, occasionally you have to put your neck out. "Early in and early out," as the minister said. Fine. I don't mind that as long as it's not an excuse for doing less. Don't forget "early in and early out" means the ability to get there and get out and accept the risk. There's always risk. The earlier you're there, the more dangerous it is.

Speaking Out

When I came out of Sarajevo in August of 1992 it seemed everybody in the Western world, all the leaders, wanted to figure out, "What should we do in Bosnia?" And rather than doing a thorough analysis, which probably they should have done and studied what was going on, Bush was saying, "No way. We're not going to get involved in that." I was having lunch with the prime minister. The obligatory and appreciated lunch when you come out of an operational theatre with a high profile, I guess, and the phone rang. Arrangements were made that I would go and appear in front of the U.S. Congress, the first time a Canadian officer had ever done that.

"What do you think we should do?" And my response in a nutshell was, "Nothing, stay out of it. Don't touch it with a 10-foot pole." Well, because that was the Bush administration's philosophy at the time, I got invited back by the Senate.

"What will be the end of our mission?" And I said, "Your grandchildren." Senator Sam Nunn said to me, "What would you advise President Bush to do?" (Bush, Sr., that was.) And I said, "Absolutely nothing, Senator. I'm a Canadian." And the senator said, "Well, consider yourself an American for 10 minutes and tell us what you'd say." So I went through a long brouhaha on why America shouldn't get involved in the Bosnian situation, which really endeared me to the Bosnian government.

137

They've hated my guts ever since I said it. But nevertheless, at the end of it I said, "If you do go in, you better start training your grandchildren as peacekeepers." They said their end state, their exit strategy, would be one year. Clinton said, "Absolutely max, we'll be home by Christmas 1995. I guarantee it." Well, they're still there six years later.

When I got back to Ottawa I had a strip torn off me for discussing what was deemed to be my personal opinion. Well, I could live with that, but then our own parliamentary committee wanted to talk to me about Yugoslavia and peacekeeping in general and the military.

I found it bizarre that when I appeared in front of the U.S. Senate I was told by Ottawa, "Give them your own personal opinion." When I appeared in front of Parliament it was, "Here's the party line." I was told, "Don't stray from this, and do not criticize government policy." Well, if I'm not going to criticize government policy, then why the hell do you have to ask me? Because if I'm just going to spout government policy, then it's no use interviewing me. Bizarre.

I went in front of the U.K.'s parliamentary committee and once again was told, "Offer your personal opinion." I actually had dinner with 14 of the NATO ambassadors at Raymond Chrétien's house when he was the ambassador to NATO. The same thing, "Just give them your personal opinion." But in front of my own parliamentary committee, "Here's the party line."

The congressmen and the senators that I dealt with were very knowledgeable. They could take any general on in the American forces, one on one, and talk geopolitics and strategy. In Canada when we have debates on serious issues, whether it's conversion from UN to NATO mandate in Bosnia, the Gulf War or Kosovo, each party nominates a representative to read a prepared statement in the House for the record. I've even seen parliamentarians confuse UN and NATO in the same sentence. It's so disappointing to see the lack of sophistication in the capability of the military, what it contributes to foreign policy. To be honest, foreign policy has to be locked in stone before you start talking defence policy, and that hasn't been clearly defined for a long time either.

The committees I've witnessed, to give them great credit, come up with some tremendous recommendations, whether it's in the structure of the military, the funding, the employment of the military. I've never seen those recommendations implemented. Even when I go and contribute to a particular report as a witness, and I read the report and say, "That's great, you know. We got our message across," nothing happens. I've given up hope.

I took an early release. You don't have to fall on your sword; you don't have to go that far to make your point. You can just go and put your toes over the edge of the precipice. The troops will respect you for doing that. For being honest and being up front. But you don't have to stand 20 feet back from the edge and play it that safe.

Losing Credibility

The problem is, Mr. Trudeau, rest his soul, was very ingenious in wanting to usurp, or at least remove, the military as a key player in the decision-making process. Defence Minister Macdonald integrated the headquarters and put the civilian bureaucrats and the military cheek by jowl as co-equals — his horrible term — rather than maintaining total civilian control. The military does what it's told. The government controls the military.

When Trudeau did that our senior people became part of a collegial political team, small "p." As a result even good military friends of mine within that process had their minds changed over a couple of years. Once they were inside the process they actually believed that they were more effective inside the process.

Now, if these people were good at small "p" politics in the military, guess how they were rewarded? We left them in Ottawa, and the more we left them there, the less credibility they had in the field. The regular troops look up and say, "He's got to be political. That guy's been in Ottawa for six years. And he keeps getting promoted, so he can't be thinking about us."

Now, that's not the truth, but that's the perception. Someone like General Boyle, who was a good commander of air force overseas, went to Ottawa as a brigadier-general. He left as a four-star general having never gone back to the field. You could be Gandhi, for God's sake, you could walk on water, and if you went to Ottawa as a one-star and left as a four-star, never having gone back to the field — none of those people could maintain credibility with the soldiers. It's just the perception that's created.

We're so small now, there's not a lot of command left out in the field. Even the commanders of the army, navy, and air force are located in Ottawa, so they're seen as staff officers. They won't even call them commanders anymore. Say there's a bunch of the enemy on a hill, and you're going to go out and attack the hill and you're going to lose half your troops there. Do you want the chief of the land staff to be leading you up the hill? Or would you rather have the commander of the army?

Some of my colleagues who are currently in uniform see those of us who criticize defence policy as the enemy. We are not the enemy. We are sworn, we have a lifetime love affair with the profession of arms and we don't like some aspects of what we're seeing. So we're exposing this to the public in an attempt to assist our colleagues in uniform.

But the take is, "Gee, as soon as we get out, then we start criticizing." I got out because I was criticized for criticizing. I was given a formal reproof for criticizing the United Nations when I said that they weren't capable of running a military operation. People had been saying that for the 40 years before I said it, but I had this fluke of profile so I owed it to my soldiers to say it.

At least the UN decided to get their staff around to a 24/7 operation rather than nine to five, as far as peacekeeping went. The fact is that you have to stand up and be counted occasionally, and a lot of my colleagues have done that. Then a politician says, "You're all yes-men until you retire." Sure, there are some of those, particularly those who are looking forward to a deputy minister's position.

If our country has a habit of offering post-military employment within the government, then naturally a person isn't going to be an outspoken critic of the government. I think in your last six months you're bulletproof, you are absolutely fireproof. You can say anything you want. By the time they fire you the six months is up. General Zinni, an outstanding four-star general of the United States, hammered his profession and what the American political leadership was doing to the military, in particular the Marine Corps, in the last few months of his service. The guy had tremendous credibility with his marines. And with politicians too.

He got to say farewell and to make speeches and he hammered them. And when asked what he hoped his son, who's a second lieutenant in the

Marine Corps, would achieve, the quote was something like, "I hope he has the *cajones* to stand up and say it the way it is for his entire career." That's the way it should be. But that type of outspoken criticism — objective, I hope — is not encouraged by the structure that we have at the top of the Canadian Forces.

When I made my comment that the army of today is not as operationally capable as the army of 10 years ago by virtue of numbers, I was expecting to be hammered. But I found the politicians' questions quite sympathetic, leading me to elaborate. That doesn't mean they necessarily believed me. I found that after those comments the military leadership started to fine-tune its comments. "We are more operationally capable than we were 10 years ago in some selected areas." I can buy that. The air force in particular has precision-guided munitions as opposed to dumb bombs, and the navy has some really nice sophisticated seagoing vessels. But the army? A modest infusion of new equipment doesn't create a better army, particularly when it's half the size. It's more operationally deployable than it was 10 years ago because it's half the size. But the fact is that it's not more operationally capable in fighting at formation level. There hasn't even been a formation comprising 6,000 or 7,000 people in a brigade group. There hasn't been an exercise in eight years.

The spin is politically correct. Simple as that. "Some money is being found." The Defence Department contributed more than any other department in government over the last eight years to fighting the deficit, 23 percent of its budget. Billions and billions of dollars, and now some modest amount is trickling back in. But it can't stop the hemorrhaging. But naturally the political spin is we're doing better than we were 10 years ago. You can show a video about precision-guided munitions; you can show a new ship. But the Gulf War, land side, only lasted a week. I don't see anybody guaranteeing that's going to be the case in the future, and with an army of about 14,000 deployable regulars, it would be chewed up pretty darn fast.

Quick Response
If diplomats have taught me anything over the years, and I attended one course at NATO Defence College which was 50 percent diplomats, it's that the military jumps too fast. These things take time to study. Zaire was an attempt to go in and deliver food and medicine and rescue

people who were being subjected to genocide. And boy, if there was ever an example of something that should've taken some time, it was the Zaire operation. First, you didn't know where the enemy was. You were going in right at the historical junction point of the old empires, between the U.K. and France.

All of a sudden there we are, just dumping our people. I lay no blame at the foot of the military folks who were sent over there, the ones that got there. But you're just dumping them into the middle of the jungle with the international media paying a lot of attention.

My greatest criticism was, "We're there to do what?" Were you going to set up food stations and then go to the edge of the jungle and say, "If there's anybody in there, come out and get it?" It was one of those horrible examples of wanting to do something — anything — so let's get on the ground and have the appearance of doing something. As Roméo Dallaire will describe over and over about the Rwanda operations, a lot of it was timed to hit the news at the right time.

Coverage first. Wait till the cameras arrive. Why? To help the mission? No. To give the impression back home that something's being done. It was disturbing, too fast, too quick, and it certainly wasn't well thought out. We have to reorganize oversight to get enough horsepower focusing on a particular problem to come up with a proper plan. And we sure as hell didn't give them very much.

I remember that with Somalia. Somalia was done very, very quickly. There was a lot of horsepower expended in a very short period of time. And then, guess what? The mission changed halfway through the planning process. "Oh, forget peacekeeping. We're going to have to go in and fight. It's a Chapter VII operation now, under the leadership of the Yanks."

Reflections

It's really interesting in Canada. Opinion about the military is an onion: you just keep peeling away different layers of it. My own feeling is that one of the significant factors is that Canada is one of the most multiethnic countries in the world. Tremendous new numbers of new Canadians are always coming in.

We were very concerned back in the late 1980s that the Forces weren't getting the representation from the ethnic communities. It's not something they line up to do when they get here. I went around Toronto, where you've got more ethnic communities than anywhere else, listening, and the answer was always the same. "General, you have to understand, most of us left countries to get away from the military. Most of us left countries where the military were not looked upon as role models. Give us a generation or two and then we will start to see our kids and our grandkids joining the military."

Peacekeeping — even though it's a myth, and now it's an oxymoron, there is really no peace to keep — if it's not dangerous, it's not necessarily respected by the population. They don't automatically say, "Gee, these guys are doing tremendous work." Even the significant amount of post-traumatic stress doesn't impress the civilian audience.

If you go in and attack, and you have two or three people killed, your reputation is up there for the next two years. I'm not saying you should be doing that, but the perception is that peacekeeping's pretty safe. Relatively safe, relatively touchy-feely. They don't understand peacekeeping is putting bits and pieces in a body bag and reuniting a kid that's had her arm blown off with her uncle because her father was slaughtered, his throat was cut. All that nasty stuff. We don't talk about those realities much back here in Canada.

In the United States you can have famous regiments rape, murder, mass-murder, in one particular case, three people killed in one particular camp, and it's not a cause célèbre for the next 10 years. It doesn't destroy the military's reputation. That unit is still an outstanding unit that's still serving valiantly.

On the other hand, the Canadian army had one despicable act of torture and murder in Somalia. You'd think it was a trend. The military's average size from World War II to today is 96,000. And that's the population of Sudbury. If Sudbury had one despicable act of torture and murder in 100 years, it wouldn't be a trend.

I'm the only Canadian that I'm aware of on the media side that's been back to Belet Huen in Somalia, to the scene of the crime, three times since the Airborne was there. And I was mobbed each time I went back by the people, saying, "Send back the Airborne." They'd had the Germans, the Bangladeshis and the Italians, all of whom did good work, don't get me wrong. They did their job and whatever it was, nine to five. But they didn't purify the water, they didn't build schools, they didn't put in bridges.

At that time the local police were not allowed by law, such as it was, to be armed. So our guys would walk behind them and provide security. People said, "Send back Airborne. Send back Airborne." Yet in Canada it's seen as the great dark day.

It was terrible. It was an act of murder. It was awful. But the fact is, it wasn't representative of the military. And if we have recruiting problems, it's as much a criticism of senior leadership as criticism of our soldiers in Somalia.

Yet when the Brits have someone killed in Northern Ireland, next day there's a spike in recruiting because it's part of the macho thing too. But that's not the motivation. It's dedication. It's nationalism. It's patriotism. It's all that stuff. Those are the types of guys and gals you want to come in. You don't want a bunch of wussies lining up to join, looking for skills to apply on Civvie Street when they get out.

Now, I know every generation that retires says, "It's all going to hell in a handbasket." That's not the case. But the fact is, even the prime minister calls us Boy Scouts. Like good Boy Scouts, we go where we're needed. Well, that's an insult to the Boy Scouts, as far as I'm concerned, and an insult to the military. We go where we're needed, yeah, where there's tough work to be done, and where sometimes you have to kick ass.

Soldiers over the last 10 years have felt abandoned on frequent occasions.

We didn't have a lot of people being killed or seriously injured during the glory days of peacekeeping, up until the end of the cold war in the late 1980s. All of a sudden everybody was on a fast learning incline when we started taking casualties and fatalities and, even more difficult, dealing with serious handicaps.

Now, when you start dealing with a bureaucracy you run into frustration. The fact was, whether it was Veterans Affairs or the military, there was only one person that was responsible for a soldier, and that was his commanding officer.

The commanding officer first of all knew the soldier. He knew his soldiers and he had the responsibility. Commanders still know their soldiers, but they don't have the responsibility for the medical side, the social side, the welfare side and all of that. For that there are all of these so-called experts around the base system, looking after the soldier. So if he or she is hurt and gets punched into the system, there's no friendly face that shows up every day, no fellow rank that's assigned to go and check on the individual.

When they're released it's even worse because now they've entered a new and even bigger bureaucratic jungle that they have to work their way through, whether it's getting a wheelchair, getting access to a building, getting a pension or getting rebates or whatever, and it's taken awhile for the military to respond to that.

These weren't a bunch of bad people making bad decisions in a padded room. The system just wasn't tuned for operations. You see, that's the point. That's all we're about. Without operations we're nothing, we contribute nothing — we, the professionals, the arms in the military. Yet it's been so comfortable in this long period of peace with touchy-feely peacekeeping — when there was peace to keep — that we became incapable of dealing with serious personnel problems. That's changing, but some guys got caught between the cracks. And we all know who they are.

PART THREE

Views from the Inside

DOUGLAS BLAND
Lieutenant-Colonel (Retired)
2000/2001

A respected author and lecturer, Douglas Bland holds the chair *in defence management studies in the School of Policy Studies at Queen's University. Dr. Bland is a graduate of the army staff college in Kingston, Ontario, the NATO Defence College at Rome, and he holds a doctorate in public administration from Queen's University. Since 1990 Dr. Bland has been a consultant for the federal government's Advanced Management Program and has completed reports on defence policy, organization and civil-military relations for the Office of the Auditor General of Canada, the Department of National Defence, the Department of Foreign Affairs and other departments and agencies in Canada. His published works include* The Administration of Defence Policy in Canada 1947–84 *(1987) and* Canada's National Defence, Volume 1: Defence Policy *and* Volume 2: Defence Organization *(1997–98). In 2000 he edited* Backbone of the Army: Non-Commissioned Officers in the Future Army.

Paul Hellyer

Paul Hellyer was a singular defence minister, one of those few Canadian politicians who spent a great deal of time understanding national defence issues. When he became defence minister in 1963 it was in the context of the immediate aftermath of the Cuban missile crisis, when Canada suffered a civil-military relations crisis of a sort. The military had begun to react, in the Cuban missile crisis period, to allied signals, orders and intentions, and the government of John Diefenbaker was either befuddled or indecisive, not sure what it ought to do, mainly because it wasn't aware of the consequences of its own defence policies. When the Liberals took over the government following the defeat of Diefenbaker, Lester Pearson made a particular statement to his new defence minister. He said, "Don't let the military do to us what they did to Diefenbaker." In other words, he wanted strong political direction of the Armed Forces.

Paul Hellyer went into the department to bring that strong direction to the Defence Department and to the Armed Forces, but what he found, to his horror, as many ministers had before him, was that there wasn't one military, there were three: army, navy, air force. There were three sets of war plans, three intelligence estimates and a great deal of confusion. These forces had been built up to work within an allied framework, not a national framework, and he set out to make that right. His principal notion was that there would be one national strategy, one war plan, one Armed Forces directorate and a chief of the defence staff to run the whole machinery. He took that notion to the Liberal Cabinet, but to implement it the government would have had to substantially change our arrangements with our allies in NATO, in NORAD, and to a certain extent with the United Nations.

But in Canada prime ministers, including Lester Pearson, are not interested in radical changes to military policies. That's not our style. That's not what we do. And Pearson said to Paul Hellyer, "Now, Paul, we don't need to change anything. Let's just keep doing what we've always been doing," and that was the end of Paul Hellyer's strategy for a unified national command and a unified war plan and a unified anything. Then outside Cabinet he had to fall back on the idea that the reason for unification, which he was going to push through anyway, was administrative and resource based. And he tried that, but the lack of a real understanding and a real rationale for unification has caused 30 years of anguish and confusion in the Armed Forces.

When we think of the Paul Hellyer era, he was facing one of the perpetual problems defence ministers face everywhere. You need money to pay for personnel and ongoing operations. You also need money to renew, to recapitalize, to buy new equipment, to renew old capabilities. But he wasn't going to get any money. Lester Pearson made that plain when he took office. Therefore he was in a commitment-capability crunch, and he hoped that by reorganizing the Armed Forces he would be able to free up 25 percent of the defence budget for new equipment. It's a dream that ministers since then have had as well.

The other thing that's interesting about the Hellyer period is how applicable it is to this period. In other words, perhaps Paul, the reformer, was many years ahead of his time because when he tried to build a national strategy for Canada with its own command structure built on national interests within the facts of national life, he was overpowered by alliancemanship, by the power of the alliance strategy. Today when we're "home alone" and there is no strategy in NATO that we can use, when the United Nations fails as a command structure, we have to develop these things, a national unity in command, control, organization, deployment, strategy in the Armed Forces. And Paul Hellyer's scheme of unification is part of the answer to getting to that position.

Government and the Military
Maintaining stable civil-military relations in a democracy requires the sharing of responsibilities between the government and the military. The government says the policy provides the resources and so on, and the military then turns that declared policy and those resources into actual policy and capabilities. Where there is a consensus — on missions, on how many resources are needed and what kind of organization you need in the Armed Forces, on the areas of operation and the capabilities the Armed Forces is going to have — you'll have stable, if not always pleasant, civil-military relations.

The defence of Canada isn't the responsibility of the Canadian Armed Forces. They're the instrument of Parliament, and Parliament is acting as the representative of the people. And therefore Canadians are responsible for the defence of Canada. They will decide through their voting patterns and so on how much will be spent, where we will be deployed, what people will do. And they will take the risks, the real risks and the implied risks, of those kinds of decisions. It's important, though, for the members of Parliament to be well informed about these risks and the decisions that are being taken.

Therefore it's important that members of Parliament be well informed on the policies of the government and on the consequences those policies hold for national defence and for the Armed Forces. This is perhaps the most particularly important job members of Parliament can do for national defence: act as the check and the balance on government policies, act as overseers of the military to make sure that the military is acting in accordance with the law and with regulations in the design and execution of operational plans.

I would think that Parliament has been particularly weak in this area for a very long time in our history. Most members don't seem to understand their requirement to oversee the government and the government's policies and the Armed Forces and the actions and decisions of senior leaders of the Armed Forces. They are not particularly well informed about the details of national defence.

They don't need to know all the technical aspects of how an armed force functions, but they do need to understand the relationship between budgets, missions, procurement, personnel policies and particularly the rules of engagement of the Armed Forces when they go overseas and so on. And Canadian members of Parliament have been particularly weak in all those areas.

You may recall that the Somalia inquiry made a significant point of asking for a vigilant Parliament. This was in the context of the Somalia deployment. And what they were asking for, in essence, was that Parliament make an investigation of deployment before people go overseas, not after they come back, so that when the Canadian Forces are deployed on missions from now on, we'll know that the commander has the right mission, the right resources, the right plans and the right laws to enable him to accomplish his mission.

But since the Somalia inquiry this hasn't happened. There have been no parliamentary interviews with commanders going overseas, even in very serious operations like the Kosovo air war.

Problems with Defence Planning

In the 1994 special joint committee of the House and the Senate, members tried very hard to get at the details of national defence planning and in many regards were successful, but it was a struggle, and it's a struggle for two reasons. One, members of Parliament, then and now, have very few resources to allow them to research complex problems. Not just in national defence and security but in most other areas. And our committee system of the House leaves members pretty well on their own with a very small staff to address these complex matters. And that should be changed.

The second problem rests with the bureaucracy, which is not always as co-operative with members, ordinary members of Parliament, as they should be. When members ask for detailed examinations of operations and plans, these are often very slow to come forward, if they come forward at all. Both these factors hinder members' ability to oppose, oversee and challenge policies of the government, or to oversee the actions and decisions of senior leaders of the Armed Forces.

Parliament has a traditional responsibility. It originated as a body to check the Crown and the Crown's ministers and the bureaucracy, the government, if you will, in its duties. And it was the responsibility of every member of Parliament to undertake that duty. This traditional responsibility has withered away over time, not because Parliament has changed, not because Parliament doesn't have the responsibility or the powers to subpoena witnesses to ask for testimony, to demand accountability of ministers and so on. But it's withered away mainly because the party politics, the politics of Parliament, have got in the way of the business of Parliament.

It's in that area where we face our greatest challenge — not in inventing a new system of Parliament that will allow ministers to be held accountable, but to reinforce the traditional way that Parliament is supposed to operate. And that can only happen if members of Parliament decide themselves to make these kinds of changes to reinforce and enhance their traditional responsibilities.

You can harangue members of Parliament and tell them why they ought to be involved in defence planning and national security planning, but you won't convince every member that it ought to be his or her prime responsibility, and that is entirely understandable. But some members ought to be involved in this business. They need to be involved in this business because we're expending a great deal of money. We are talking about the nation's safety. Besides, government policies for national defence and security involve spending people's lives to achieve the government's objectives.

If that won't motivate members of Parliament to take an interest in what's going on, perhaps the only thing that will is the sudden crisis that falls upon the country and we find that we are unarmed, improperly armed, inappropriately organized, and we make the country vulnerable. The other thing that seems, sadly, to be the only motivator is a great deal of political scandal in the way we spend the money or the way we organize forces or the way forces actually conduct themselves in the field.

The Somalia affair was a prime example of defence going to the front-burner issue in Parliament and in the media, not because of problems with national security policy per se, but simply because the government had a scandal on its hands.

The Committee System

One of the weaknesses in the House of Commons committee system, and the House of Commons as an opposition and as an overseer of civil-military relations, is the fact that members aren't around for a very long time. Very, very few of them have a chance to develop experience and knowledge in the field. And for many of them it seems like a very complex business and thus they avoid it.

On the other hand, we have to understand that Parliament is made up of not just the House of Commons but also the Senate and the Senate offers many possibilities to redress some of the weaknesses that are in the House of Commons.

In the first place senators tend to be around for a long time and they can develop a body of expertise. Secondly they have time to work on many of these issues. They are not consumed by constituent affairs like ordinary members might be. The Senate can be a very important instrument for building knowledge, reporting, overseeing and building awareness in the country about national defence issues.

In the 1980s the Senate performed these duties very well through a dedicated defence committee of the Senate. That body fell apart, disappeared and has not been resurrected until just recently. This year, I believe, a new Senate committee on defence is going to be formed. We can hope that they will perform some of these duties in co-operation with the House of Commons.

The effects of the Somali inquiry — not just the recommendations, but the exposure of the conversations and the testimony of witnesses — has had an enormous effect on the Armed Forces. Not perhaps at the level of the general officers who were involved in the business or who were in positions of responsibility at the time. But it has had an enormous effect, in my experience, on the younger officers and personnel of the Armed Forces.

Many of them have said to me at staff colleges and other places, "Never again. We're not going to get ourselves into these kinds of situations again. We're going to make sure that we follow the rules and the doctrine and the experiences for Armed Forces planning. We will command our units properly and we'll maintain discipline and we will be held responsible and accountable for what we do." I think it's very encouraging.

The change in the Armed Forces comes about not simply by a change in rules and regulations, by changing the names on doors and reorganizing staff. It comes about in the hearts and minds of the members of the Armed Forces themselves, and especially in the intellect of the officer corps. When the officer corps changes its attitude from the way it has been behaving then you'll see an enormous change in the Armed Forces. This is the lesson that is developing now in Canada, where younger people in the Armed Forces see themselves and their profession in a different light with a different set of responsibilities, and they are changing for the better.

One of the things that some military officers have come to understand is that they have to design plans, forces, force development plans and operations, and the rules and regulations for the Armed Forces to match the expectations of the society they're living in — Canadian society, how it operates. What that means in many respects is that they can't expect to be front and centre in every issue. They can't expect to control the debate over national security issues. They have to become much more aware of politics and how policy is made in Ottawa and across the country.

People have criticized the former chief of the defence staff and other senior officers for not speaking out more strongly about the declining capabilities of the Canadian Forces. Assuming that the former chief of the defence staff believes that the Canadian Forces capabilities are declining, one explanation for the institutional silence is that it's easier to advance the military cause and the national defence cause by being co-operative with the government rather than being in opposition. And they found various ways to do that. The institutional people will argue that that has been successful and brought more money and a better understanding into defence matters.

Other people would disagree and say that the military ought to be in opposition to the government, as happens occasionally in the United States. But the position for military politics in Canada is entirely different than in the United States, and that's not the way that anyone is going to advance the Armed Forces' interests in this country.

The danger in the attitude of "go along to get along" is that you confuse Canadians about the capabilities of the Canadian Armed Forces. You might build a certain degree of cynicism within the ranks when they look at things from a different point of view. Even more dangerous is the possibility that you could confuse the government as to the capabilities of the Canadian Armed Forces. Some people will say that is exactly what happened when we undertook the Zaire operation, that the prime minister and senior Cabinet ministers weren't fully aware of the limitations in the Canadian Armed Forces.

However, this danger can be redressed to some degree by the close co-operation of the chief of the defence staff and his senior members with the minister, with the deputy minister. And that's why the relationship between the chief of defence staff and the minister of national defence is so important. Of anyone in Cabinet, the minister of national defence should be able to explain very carefully and confidentially to the prime minister the actual state of the Armed Forces. It is a link that didn't perhaps work very well in the past.

The relationship between the defence minister, other senior Cabinet members and the prime minister is critically important in these matters. If the defence minister can carry his arguments well in Cabinet, then it will benefit the Armed Forces, and the Department of National

Defence of course. The relationship between defence ministers and prime ministers over the years varies. In Trudeau's time, with Donald Macdonald as defence minister, this was a very strong relationship. The personalities influence how this happens, how the relationship develops and what issues are addressed.

But perhaps the most important factor in the relationship is the situation, the national defence situation at the particular moment. If there is no crisis, if there are simply routine operations going on, then quite understandably the prime minister and the defence minister aren't going to meet every day to talk about things. However, experience suggests — and conversation with people who have been in these positions recently suggests — that in crises, during the Kosovo war, for instance, the defence minister and the chief of the defence staff met with the prime minister very often. And in many cases, as some people report, the defence minister held the conversation over the foreign minister.

And after the war was over business returned to normal. And defence slipped from the Cabinet table to another position and the prime minister went on to different matters. But it's a very dynamic relationship and is significantly dependent upon the capabilities of particular defence ministers.

Although the government makes policy and public servants, military officers in this case, administer that policy, everyone understands that in fact the distance between the policy makers and the administrators is blurred. It's a grey zone. Governments do make policy and bureaucrats change that policy into fact. But at the same time governments get involved in detailed administration of their own policies in the situating of bases, details of contracting, and who will get what out of the pork barrel.

At the same time senior members of the bureaucracy and the Armed Forces get involved in policy making. They have tremendous discretion to spend the money in ways that they think will bring the government's policies into effect, and they can't help when they're doing that to bring their own ideas and attitudes, interests and opinions, into the policy-making world. That happens all the time. It's a fact of life in bureaucracies.

The only way you can guard against this becoming unbalanced — so that we have bureaucratic politics and not government politics or policies — is for Parliament and members of the Cabinet to very closely supervise the actions and decisions of the members of the Armed Forces and the bureaucracy so that they all do what they're told to do. In many respects in Canada, that overseeing responsibility has been particularly weak.

There's a continuing debate, both in reality and in the academic world, about the responsibility of public servants. On the one hand people will say, "As a responsible public servant my duty is to do whatever the government says. If the government says black today and white tomorrow, then I without question take that action."

An older tradition in Canadian public service is that public servants, senior public servants especially, have a responsibility not only to the government but to the people, to guard funds, to guard programs, to act in the national interest as the public service sees it. This does not mean that they will stage a coup on the government.

What it does mean is that they won't be captured by the "Yes, Minister syndrome." That they will very forcefully and directly make their point to the government and then the bureaucrats will decide for themselves individually where they stand, once the government's made a decision. That is, can they stand the policy or must they leave? Or will they try to argue the policy in some other direction? It's a critical and difficult area to work in, but it is the nature of our kind of government. The original parliamentary concept did situate two separate entities, Parliament and the Crown and the ministers of the Crown.

But as times have changed and democracy has matured, the government is in fact already in the Parliament and the Parliament and the government are in some respects one entity. But in fact the government is represented now by the prime minister and his Cabinet, and they are more or less backed by their party and opposed by everyone else.

The only way to change the system, to have Parliament make the Cabinet more distinctive, would be to change the rules and regulations governing how individual members of Parliament act, that is, by giving them more free votes, by opening up debates, by not requiring party discipline on all issues before the House, by hoping that in certain very critical areas, such as the defence of the country, Parliament could develop a non-partisan viewpoint.

Now, it may not seem feasible to some people that you could ever have a non-partisan policy in such an area. But once you take away the rhetoric from the various parties over time, old parties, new parties and so on, their prescriptions for how to defend Canada have almost always been the same, their recommendations are almost always the same. So the basis for a non-partisan defence policy is there, but it is a huge intellectual leap for most members of Parliament and most people who talk about Parliament.

Checks and Balances

There are no checks and balances in the Canadian parliamentary system as one can see in the American system. There are no rules built into the process that separate the Cabinet and decision makers from policy making. That's one in the same thing. People will say that we need to get more power to committees such as the defence committee of the House. But in essence that is a kind of power that will come not from regulations, but from change of attitude and from permission of the political system — that they would allow committees to be more influential in shaping policy.

To do that we need these committees to build up their research capabilities again, their access to the media. We need to get the media to pay more attention to the committees, and these committees need to produce a continuous stream of information, reports and so on, many of which need not be controversial, simply to build up the interest and the information in society.

The defence committees could, with the aid of the governing parties and without too much interference, inform the public regarding civil and military relations, the nature of command and control of the Armed Forces, the nature of the duties of the chief of the defence staff. And on some occasions Cabinet committees have done that, such as the deliberations over the quality-of-life issue in the Armed Forces.

Too often people jump to the conclusion that giving more power to parliamentary committees, or committees of the House, will put them in conflict with the government. But actually you can give more responsibility to these types of committees without challenging the government.

Parliament has, in its overall responsibility for national defence in the name of the people, as representatives of the people, to ensure that operations of the Armed Forces are efficient and effective. They also have a responsibility to safeguard the blood and treasure of the nation, the moneys that we expend on these kinds of operations, which can be enormous, and the lives, of course, of all the people involved.

Parliament needs to be involved in the debates and discussions about when and where the Canadian Forces will be employed, especially in overseas operations, whether they are peacekeeping operations, humanitarian operations, near-combat operations or real-war operations. It's only a tradition that Parliament is to be consulted when the government takes a decision to employ the Canadian Forces, but that prerogative ought to be strengthened — not to challenge the government, but to involve all Canadian people, through their representatives, in these kinds of decisions.

It would be most beneficial to have inquiries into Canadian Forces operations overseas before they go on operations, not after they come back. Or while they're involved in the operation. If Parliament is going to mature into the next stage of handling national defence and national security issues, then they need to develop, in individual members and in parties and in committee structures, the capability to address the right questions, the most relevant questions, appropriately. That's going to take time.

Lessons Learned

From Somalia, from the operation in Zaire, from the Kosovo operation, in the sense of being a more diligent overseer of these kinds of operations, it doesn't appear we've learned much. That may be explained because members of Parliament tend, and other Canadians tend, to see these things as events. A one-off event, unrelated one to the other. Perhaps because they're in different parts of the world or perhaps because the type of operation varies, but for one reason or another they don't seem to have made the link between the fundamentals of defence decision making: command and control, resources, personnel, rules of engagement.

There are only a few simple questions that members of Parliament need to ask of the government and of the bureaucracy and of the senior commanders before we deploy people overseas. Are they properly commanded? Are they properly organized? Do they have the resources for the job as we understand it at the moment? Is the mission clear? Do we know how we are going to support and supply and safeguard our people overseas? These are very simple questions. Difficult in the answer, perhaps. But these aren't questions that should be hard to ask.

People just don't seem to understand that those basic questions apply to all kinds of operations, not just one here, one there. And people don't need to develop a great understanding of the complexities of African security policy or NATO security policy or American security policy. All they need to do is understand these basic questions. And if they ask those questions, they'll greatly improve Parliament's ability to oversee the Armed Forces, the bureaucracy and the government, and will also reassure Canadians that members of Parliament are taking their duties responsibly.

It often seems that members of Parliament, commentators in the media and ordinary citizens become confused about two sets of responsibilities that arise when we become involved in a serious operation, as in the air campaign in Kosovo. The first set of conditions is the allied politics of going to war, making a decision, acting united and so on, in the context of how lesser powers operate with major powers in a coalition.

People often just throw up their hands and say, "Nothing can be done. We are too small and insignificant, maybe even irrelevant. We can't get involved in these kinds of issues." The result is that they might not even try to ask the right questions.

But there is another set of circumstances embedded in all these operations and that is the condition and operating circumstances of the Canadian Armed Forces and other members of Canadian government in these operations. While members of Parliament might not feel particularly effective in challenging the government's relationships with the U.S., NATO and with the UN, they ought to feel very comfortable and responsible about asking detailed questions about how Canada is going to operate in these kinds of situations.

What are our command relationships? Who is going to guard the Canadian soldiers? What kind of support do they have? Do they have the proper weapons and equipment? These are questions inside these missions that ought to be very easy for members of Parliament, members of the media and other people to worry about.

The Ad Hoc Approach

How does national defence, and to a greater extent national security, which is a much broader concept, function within the framework of departmental organizations and other agencies like the Privy Council Office and various semi-independent intelligence organizations?

There is no minister responsible and accountable for national security and the responsibilities are divided between the minister of national defence on the one hand, the solicitor general and the RCMP on the other hand, the CSIS organizations and so on.

When a crisis occurs in Canada or involves Canada — as in Zaire, in Somalia and Kosovo, and further back to the FLQ crisis — the response in Ottawa is to form an ad hoc committee. To bring officials together hastily to try and cobble together a national strategy, a way to handle that event. Once the event is over the committees disperse back to their departments and it's business as usual.

There is no continuing national view of what our national security problems are and how they might be addressed. There is no continuing staff to work on these kinds of issues. There is no national operations centre to co-ordinate operations when they are in progress. While some people might have said this was fine during the cold war when things seemed to be more stable, it is evidently not fine now.

Even when you look at simple problems like the arrival of a boat full of illegal refugees off Canada's shore, the management of that problem involves intelligence agencies. The RCMP, the Coast Guard, the Canadian Forces, immigration services, provincial police, provincial resources, detention centres and so on. All of these agencies are brought together for that one event in some kind of ad hoc way. If national security is now defined as a broad area with seamless issues that go on continuously, then it is high time that we had the machinery of government reorganize to address that thing in a coherent way. And we are nowhere near doing that kind of thing.

If the government is going to redress these difficulties, it is going to have to go into a long process of rebuilding capabilities in the Armed Forces, in the diplomatic service, in the RCMP, in the intelligence units, and it is going to have to do it all at the same time. And that's our comeuppance. Because we're going to have to pay now for what we haven't paid for in the past.

And here we come back to Parliament. One of the responsibilities of Parliament, one thing that is not very difficult for members of Parliament to do, one would think, is to keep abreast of this situation to understand the kind of world we're living in. That takes in the consequences for policy, the consequences when goals and means are mismatched.

And then to bring that to the attention of the government, of the media and of the people in the country. This is, of all the criticisms, one that you might lay on members of Parliament: it's not that they aren't technically competent, that they aren't involved all the time, it's that they don't even have a broad overview of Canada's national security problem and the consequences for our policy in the future.

One of the most serious problems facing the Armed Forces has to do with its implosion, its continuing collapse as an institution, a professional institution. That doesn't mean that people aren't dedicated, aren't working hard, that they aren't clever, but as the Armed Forces becomes smaller, as they have fewer and fewer capabilities, the chance to maintain a professional stance, a professional competence, drops away. And here we're not talking just about the fact that ships and planes might be rusting out.

In my view those capabilities are hardly the most important ones. What we're talking about is the shrinkage of the officer corps. The smaller the pool gets, logically, the less chance you have of finding those few brilliant people who can lead the Armed Forces in new experiences. The smaller the operational branches of the Armed Forces become, the fewer opportunities we have to send people overseas to gain experience. Armies learn by doing things.

As the Armed Forces become smaller, as the personnel, the profession, becomes smaller and smaller, the capability for improving the force, for maturing the force over time in new circumstances, becomes very difficult.

People will complain now that we have shrunk the officer corps, so everybody is involved in the work of the day and nobody has any time to put their feet up on the desk to think about what our future security problems might be.

That's a real difficulty, and all these problems will come to a head as the Armed Forces becomes smaller, older and less well equipped, until it just may, like the old soldier, fade away.

That's the big danger Canada faces now. And it can only be turned around over a long period of time. A government decree tomorrow to increase the size of the Armed Forces and to buy all sorts of new equipment and so on will have no effect for three or four or five years, as these people and machinery and so on are brought into operation. So the prospects for the Canadian Forces in this year is that they are going to continue to lose capabilities and confidence for the next three or four years. And it will continue to lose unless the government makes some very radical and expensive decisions right now.

The end result technically used to be called "structural disarmament." If you keep the pot of money the same and the cost of people and equipment increases, you necessarily have less and less and less until you are down to one ship, one airplane and a couple of people standing on the runway. And you're still spending all that money. You, the country, will become disarmed, unarmed through neglect, through lack, loss of confidence and capability, intellectual capability in the Armed Forces, through the rust out of equipment, through the scarcity of money and resources, and from just lack of interest of people. The institution will just fade away.

Rules of Engagement
Rules of engagement can be viewed from two points of view. One, it is a standard, normal, tactical aspect of military operations. Commanders always impose rules of engagement on their soldiers about what kind of targets they can fire at, when they can fire at them, how much ammunition they can use and so on. This is a standard military concept.

But rules of engagement also have a political and, more importantly, a legal context. They are the directions from the government, in law, about in what circumstances the use of force will be permitted to members of the Canadian Forces. Even the government doesn't have free rein to decide what those rules of engagement might be. When we are talking about rules of engagement and situations that involve the use of deadly force, members of the Canadian Forces must be guided by the laws of Canada. And members of the Canadian Forces, whether employed in Canada or abroad, are subject to the code of criminal justice.

The basis for rules of engagement for Canadian troops deployed overseas are Canadian standards. Some people have suggested that in multilateral operations there ought to be harmonized rules of engagement. The question is, whose laws, whose standards are going to be used as a basis for harmonizing rules of engagement? Are we going to allow our soldiers to be directed by rules of engagement that are based in American law? Are we going to allow our soldiers to use rules of engagement based in Russian law, or Russian concepts of the use of force?

Probably not. What we need to do is ensure that our soldiers understand the concepts of rules of engagement, that our commanders understand the basis for rules of engagement and that we put them in situations that are appropriate to our circumstances and to our laws. As coalitions build around the world that involve people from very diverse backgrounds, cultures, laws and political situations, we need to pay much more attention to the rules of engagement we apply to our soldiers.

Responsibility
There is some complaint and some contradiction in the way we are building the machinery of government in Ottawa. Parliament has created all sorts of independent commissioners, privacy commissioner, language commissioner and so on, and oversight committees looking at the Armed Forces. Some people see these as a danger from two points of view. One is that they provide an excuse for members of Parliament not getting involved in issues. "Don't ask me about these things, go see the privacy commissioner."

The second danger is that these agencies might develop their own agendas and their own criteria of what is right and proper for the Armed Forces. They will then impose their views on the Canadian Forces. But not accountably.

In both of these aspects, the distancing of members of Parliament from their basic responsibilities and the fact that commissioners and ombudsmen are imposing their own view of the world on the Armed Forces might be a danger to the Armed Forces and to international defence.

Lack of attention by members of Parliament means their duties might fall to someone else. The obvious place is to Cabinet, but Cabinet obviously isn't in a position all the time to be actively supervising the Armed Forces. The next obvious organization that will do this is perhaps the federal public service. In other words, civil control of the military will pass from Parliament to civilians. There is no reason to believe that that will be effective.

This was perhaps the chief characteristic of the national defence situation in Canada in the 1970s and the 1980s. Then many parliamentarians and even some ministers dismissed their responsibility for civil control of the Armed Forces and passed that to deputy ministers and senior public servants and to the Privy Council and other individuals. In some cases the public service simply decided they had to take over these responsibilities because no one else was doing it.

They exercised their responsibility by changing defence budgets, by allocating resources in different ways, by changing the structure of National Defence Headquarters, by changing the relationship between the minister and the chief of the defence staff and the organization of military staffs in the headquarters. That brought about, in the view of many, such things as the disaster in Somalia. When military planning, civil control of the Armed Forces, fell completely into the hands of certain elements of the public service, that brought us a catastrophe.

When members of Parliament are not involved in decision-making processes, they can't bring to bear their political experiences and they have no say in what is happening. Responsibility then falls to the bureaucracy as the advisor, the political, the military, the intelligence and the international advisor to the government, and they tend to take a bureaucratic view of these sorts of situations. Often they simply end up in a large quarrel with each other about what is to be accomplished and how it's to be accomplished.

General Baril, when he was reporting after the Zaire mission, stated that the only national strategy he had to follow was what he could infer from the United Nations resolution to deploy force into the area. Other than that he was on his own. There was no one at home for General Baril to report to, except various departments or ad hoc committees. There is no national security agency, no staff, no co-ordinating body to help our national commanders overseas accomplish their missions.

There is some notion abroad that because we are supposedly a peaceful country, involved in peacekeeping missions and operations around the world, we are simply a new type of missionary, we can do these things without any cost in blood and treasure. We're finding out this isn't true. And there was a great concern in political and bureaucratic circles that Canadians would respond by refusing to go into any more of these kinds of operations because it's too costly. But the facts seem otherwise.

Most surveys that I've seen that have been conducted with members of Parliament, the members of Parliament split on the question when they were asked, "Would your constituents accept casualties in operations for a worthy cause in a faraway place?" They responded almost 50/50 that they would accept these kinds of casualties. And that is a different attitude than the received wisdom on these ideas, that the body-bag factor is a big decision-making thing.

I think that what would really concern Canadians, what has always concerned Canadians when we use Canadian troops overseas, is the efficiency of the operation. If they believe that we have sent Canadians into an operation without the proper equipment, without the proper support, without the proper command structure on a mission that causes casualties, that places the troops in an unfair situation, then they will respond with anger and concern.

Parliament's responsibility is for its own good, for politicians' own benefit, to make sure that they don't cause a domestic crisis by allowing our Armed Forces to be deployed in situations that they're not prepared for.

There's a tendency to see national defence and the employment of the Armed Forces as a bureaucratic undertaking. It was just a matter of assembling the troops, getting them overseas, employing them, bringing them back. And to do so without bothering the members of Parliament, the government, the treasury or the Canadian people. These were far-away things. The army could be at war but Canada was at peace.

The problem, of course, is that the bureaucracy, made up of all sorts of well-meaning people, tends to focus its attention on the political needs of the government of the day, keeping the event under control so that it doesn't force extra spending from the treasury. More and more they concentrate on the domestic aspects of overseas operations. The tendency is to forget the needs of the soldier on the frontline. In fact, in some circumstances they might even think that the soldier on the frontline is a complaining, worrisome and bothersome person who should just do his job and leave the politics and everything else to the centre in Ottawa.

Of course the difficulty with that is that it's not only unethical, it's inefficient. This kind of non-oversight leads to all sorts of difficulties in theatre, maybe even to discipline problems and the falling apart of units and so on. But more than that, it will eventually rebound on the bureaucracy and the high commander of the Armed Forces and the government when the people start to ask the question — as they did during the Balkans operations and in Somalia — "What happened to our people? Where is my son? How was he killed?"

When the bureaucracy responds by saying, "We don't know," or they lie about it, or they try to muffle the question and the answer, they are inviting a response from the population and a domestic crisis. And arguably that's the story of the Somalia affair.

PAUL HELLYER

2000

Paul Hellyer was elected to the House of Commons in 1949. After serving in Opposition as the defence critic during the Diefenbaker government, Mr. Hellyer became minister of defence in the Liberal government of Lester B. Pearson. His white paper in 1964 led to the unification of the Armed Forces. He resigned from the Trudeau government on a question of principle when he was deputy prime minister and chair of the Task Force on Housing and Urban Development. In 1995, concerned about the future of Canadian sovereignty, he started the Canadian Action Party to fight for an independent Canada. He has twice stood for election as its leader.

When I became minister of defence in 1963 I think it was considered one of the four top portfolios. Starting with the prime minister and the minister of finance, the minister for external affairs, and below that the minister of defence and probably either transport or justice. Those would be the top portfolios in the government. Defence had a very large proportion of total government expenditures in those days, before the social security system had been set up. It was considered, well, I guess a plum in a sense, to be offered that portfolio. It's been downgraded very, very substantially. I doubt if it's considered in the top, I was going to say 12, but it's certainly not considered one of the top portfolios anymore, and certainly not in expenditures. Defence expenditures have been downgraded, other expenditures have increased: social security and especially the interest on the federal debt.

So the Department of Finance has become even more important than it was. Defence has been given short shrift and part of that has been because of the constant rotation of ministers. They just get there for a few months or a year or two, which is barely enough time to learn which way the corridors lead, when they're moved.

I guess the reason I had some success in the early days was because I had been parliamentary secretary to Ralph Campney, who succeeded Brooke Claxton as minister of defence years before, at the end of the St. Laurent administration, and I had been associate defence minister just before the election in 1957. I had some background in aeronautical engineering and I had acted as defence critic for a number of years, so I had, I suppose, a leg up in starting out. But even then I thought it was just terribly important right at the beginning not to sign anything for 30 days, until I knew what was going on, and then to do a thorough review of the department's policies and practices.

The military had pushed for the nuclear option and this contributed to the controversy over whether Canada should or should not accept nuclear weapons. Ultimately it split the Cabinet and led to the downfall of the Diefenbaker government. Diefenbaker probably thought that the senior officers had some part in that, perhaps with a little encouragement from Washington.

But on the other side, the senior officers in the Department of External Affairs were pushing equally hard in the opposite direction. So you would have to say that the senior officers on both sides were contributing to this public fight over whether Canada should or should not live up to its obligations and accept nuclear warheads, which were implicit in the acceptance of several weapons systems that required them. I had no intention of letting them do that to Pearson or to me, but was resolutely determined that the department would be run by the minister and by the government, and that we would set policy and let the military know what we expected of them.

I think the appreciation of the military has gone down dramatically and I think this is a shame. They're underpaid, their morale is not good and they feel they're not appreciated. It's easy for them to get that impression. All they have to do is read the newspapers. Every time they do something wrong it's played up in the newspapers, but the newspapers don't pay the same attention when they do something right and perform admirably for Canadian citizens.

Since the end of the cold war people expect a peace dividend. They expect something good to happen as a result of the reduction of tensions in the world. What they don't realize, of course, is that there have been continuous wars, one after another, ever since World War II. There have been wars everywhere, dozens of United Nations operations, and Canada has participated in many of them. So we're still required to do things all around the world, but without Canadians really appreciating the fact that there is this constant demand for services and assistance and not much attention being paid as to how to fulfill those adequately.

Unification
The Forces, in my opinion, were in good shape when I left. Their operational capability was high, they had lots of new equipment coming down the pike and everything was going well. Sure, there were a few disgruntled senior officers that didn't like what had been done, but by and large they were in excellent shape, the best they had been, probably, since the Korean War and maybe even since the Second World War. Four years after I left they amalgamated the civil headquarters and the military headquarters. This was a terrible mistake in my opinion. It was not part of my plan. I would never have condoned it, I would never have gone along with it, and it shouldn't have been done.

This is really the source of what the military calls "the civilianization of the military," and of course the Forces didn't like it. They began to establish army, navy and air force headquarters outside Ottawa in order to ignore the Ottawa headquarters. Consequently they put back in place much of the inefficiency, the duplication, the triplication that existed before I came along, and with that came the bickering over budgets and the breakdown of the command-and-control structure that I had put in place. I'm convinced that this was something that was avoidable. It still should be remedied. It is not a good system, and I think that Canada has paid dearly, and so have the Forces, because I don't think things like Somalia would ever have happened if it hadn't been for this civilianization and for the subsequent disintegration of the unified force that we had had years earlier.

The government had been seized with the duplication, triplication and inefficiency of the Armed Forces, and so they had this very expensive royal commission, the Glassco Commission in 1963, and it came up with a recommendation which I thought was "too horrendous to contemplate." What in effect they were going to do was make a fourth force.

Fifty percent of all the personnel in the Armed Forces do not specifically belong to the fighting arms. They're the communicators, the doctors and dentists, the pay people and all of those service people who are not really specifically related to any one of the three fighting arms. What the Glassco Commission recommended was putting them all under the chairman of the chiefs of staff committee, which in effect was creating a fourth force.

At that time the department was run by committees and there were about 267 committees, I think. They had one member from each of the three armed forces, one from the Defence Research Board and one from the deputy minister's office. So we had five people getting together, spending hundreds of hours in many cases, working through problems that were related to all three of the services, coming up with a recommendation and then having it vetoed by one of the chiefs, so that all of their work was in vain because there was no unified command.

I thought this would be going from bad to worse, so I talked to one of the staff people on the commission. They had thought about unification but decided it wasn't politically feasible, so they hadn't recommended it. The idea of unification started with Brooke Claxton and every minister since World War II had said it was the right thing to do. I also felt that it was the right thing to do. I recommended it.

When I went in as minister in 1963 I wasn't an integrationist and thought that all that was necessary was to eliminate some of these housekeeping items, like getting rid of the duplication and triplication. Then I started working with the chiefs of staff committee and that didn't work. It was really a club of back-scratchers. "If you support my project, I'll support yours." But in fact it didn't always work that way because whoever got there first, when the minister was in a good mood, got the money, and it was usually the air force. They got the bulk of the money and the navy and the army were left without enough.

When it came to important strategic decisions, they had no concept of working with each other. None whatsoever. You had three services planning for three different kinds of wars, one in the air force planning for a two- to six-day war, all-out thermonuclear, over, world destroyed; the army planning for another World War I or World War II — mobilize, get ready, send the troops overseas, turn the broomsticks into rifles and get going, as we'd done twice before; and the navy somewhere in between. I said, "This doesn't make any sense at all." You've got to have a single strategy for the armed services. You have to have them working toward a single set of goals and within parameters that are well understood. They have to set those and come to the minister with a unified voice, not come in one at a time trying to get the minister to approve something without the knowledge or consent of the others, or without having it fit into any unified plan.

I can give you an example. Brigadier Bourgeois, who was the chief of defence public relations, was present at three different briefings at the time of the Suez crisis. They had named a joint commander for the operation, and they called a meeting and it lasted eight hours. The navy was represented by a naval captain and the joint commander said, "Where's the aircraft carrier?" And the captain answered, "Well, I don't know, sir, but I think she's off Bermuda."

"What's she doing there?"

"Well, I don't know, sir, but I think she's engaged in operations."

"Well, we need her as part of this combined operation. Can we get her back?"

"I don't know, sir. I'll inquire of the chief of the naval staff."

The general said that the prime minister is very insistent that the aircraft carrier be made available for this, and the naval captain said, "I will report that too, sir, to the chief of the naval staff." At the end of eight hours no decisions had been taken. As a matter of fact, the aircraft carrier never did get back in time. He was at two subsequent briefings. One lasted 22 minutes and one lasted 27 minutes. The decisions were all made before they left. Decisions made, operation under way.

Unification was a combined thing of saving money and, even more importantly, getting the services to operate as a team and to operate in concert, to have the ability and the training and the equipment to operate and do combined operations without difficulty and without a lot of fuss and bother.

We had just changed our NATO commitments and one of them was to provide troops from Canada in case of emergency, but we didn't have the capability to live up to that commitment, so there was resistance with the military, and there may have been with Cabinet. Unification fit in with the overall strategy of mobility and co-operation between the services, to have the troops trained and the equipment available to put together a combined force and move it anywhere in the world to meet our NATO commitments, United Nations undertakings and whatever else we were asked to do, and to do it efficiently and quickly.

We bought a lot of Hercules transport aircraft and Providers for the navy so that they could move the men and material, provide backup for the fleet at sea and give them a greater range and greater ability to stay on station. This allowed them to have combined exercises, which they hadn't done before, with the navy assisting in assault landings and landings from the sea. They were able to do a variety of tasks and work together as a team, which they hadn't done before. Actually, after unification was the first time that the senior officers of the three services had ever sat down around one table to talk to each other. A lot of people will find that difficult to believe, but it's true. All of a sudden they found that they were in the same boat instead of in three separate boats, often rowing in three separate directions.

I was in fact trying to develop a strategic plan for Canada and to have the means to put it into effect. And we were moving in that direction when the military and civil headquarters were combined, which was in my opinion the wrong way to go. That was the beginning of the unravelling of a strategic objective and of the combined command-and-control structure. Since then it's been downhill all the way. When you combine these things — a command-and-control structure which is not as efficient as it was with the fact that there have not been sufficient funds to provide either the personnel or the equipment to do the job — you have the present sad state of affairs. It's going to take quite awhile to put it all back together again. Because it's Humpty Dumpty and it's going to take a lot of fixing. They're going to have to go back almost to where they left off 30 years ago and put a lot of that back together.

It should start with Parliament, which should say, "This is what we want the Canadian Forces to be able to do. This is the role that we see they should fill." Then after Parliament has said that, the minister should work out the details in conjunction with the military and put together a five- or 10-year plan to make it happen, including getting the personnel and the equipment. That is the way to go, but that has not been done. It's been talked about, but the government doesn't want to face it, apparently, and until we do that we're just going to muddle along.

At the time there was a very strong belief in the military that it was far more important for our navy to operate with the United States's navy, and our army to operate with Britain's army, and our air force to operate with the United States's air force, than it was to have any capability to operate together in one place under a single command. I felt we could have greater ability to operate together, our air force and army in Europe, for example, and still, in other operations like the United Nations, have the capacity to take on a major task that involved elements of the army, navy and air force. These are things that Canada could have done and can still do on its own. Now, of course, with NATO not having a raison d'être anymore, and sort of wallowing around trying to find a reason to continue, I think we could very easily say that we're not necessarily going to be bound by every adventure that the United States gets us into.

And maybe we should not get into some of the things, like the Yugoslav war, for example. I can't understand how it was in our best interests. I think there are other things that we could have done, including saving a lot of money and using it to build up the Forces for other requirements, instead of going along on that sort of rudderless ship.

"Permanent Government" and the "Regency"

The idea of a "permanent government" is not original. It comes from the editor of *Harper's Magazine* in the United States, who said that the permanent government is the *Fortune* 500 list of companies, the biggest law firms in Washington that do their legal business, the biggest PR firms that do their public relations, and the top civil servants, both military and civil. They run the United States. And every once in a while you have this charade called an election. I call it politicians for hire, where the permanent government decides who they want to go onstage and read the scripts. Some read the scripts with less improvisation than others, so they pick people like George W. Bush, for example, who will go on and read the script exactly the way they want it read. So they'll put up the money to try to get him elected and they won't give it to anybody else. No one else need apply.

That is the reality of the situation and we have something not too different in Canada. I'll give you an interesting story. After I left the government, Gordon Robertson, who was the clerk of the Privy Council for part of the time when I was there, and a very powerful individual, was talking to students at Carleton University. My name came into the conversation somehow, and Robertson said, "The problem with Hellyer was that he thought politicians were elected to come to Ottawa to make policy." He had me figured out to a T. That's exactly what I thought politicians were elected to do, instead of just going down there and rubber-stamping policies set by the permanent government, by people like Gordon Robertson.

What you have to have is politicians who are willing to exert, on behalf of the people who elect them, the kind of power and pressure necessary to say, "Look, you may be the clerk of the Privy Council or you may be the chief of the defence staff, or you may be the deputy minister of you know what, but this is what the government has decided on behalf of the Canadian people, and we want you to do it." And as C. D. Howe would have said if they came in giving excuses, "I didn't invite you to come in here and tell me that it can't be done; I invited you to come in here and tell me how to do it." Well, that's what we need.

Now, the "regency" is really the transnational corporations and the international banks. They are the new kings, the absolute kings and queens. The politicians just read the scripts, including the prime minister.

We have to change the system. Because with this permanent government even prime ministers are very much beholden. No party can win an election without the support of the big business operators, and they have limited scope even there. We have to do several things. We have to have an elected Senate which is non-partisan — and in my opinion it should vote with the Commons — and take away the prime minister's dictatorial power so that he is no longer in effect a one-man show, which he is at the present time.

A Liberal MP told one of my friends a few weeks ago that Mr. Trudeau said he was a nobody, not only 50 yards from the House of Commons, but in the House of Commons and in caucus. The same is true of a lot of junior Cabinet ministers. They just don't count. The people who count are those in the big permanent government, like the clerk of the Privy Council. Some of the people around the prime minister have considerable clout because they too have their connections to business councils and spend a lot of time eating and drinking with them. They find out how globalization should continue and how Canada should reduce its sovereignty and boundaries and let the transnational corporations in to save us from ourselves.

So we have to change the system in such a way that the people themselves have some power between elections. I've come to the conclusion very recently that we're going to have to install citizens' initiatives and referenda, more along the Swiss line, so that if somebody like Mr. Mulroney says we're going to have a GST and the people don't like it, they can say that we want that put to a vote. If you had had that, the GST would never have been passed, which it shouldn't have been anyway. If the Bank of Canada is going to bring on another recession with high interest rates, or if we're going to sign a multilateral agreement on investment which is going to lock Canada into a situation where we can be bought, lock, stock and barrel by the transnational corporations and banks of the five major powers, then the people can say, "No, we want to vote on that before the government gives away our sovereignty." There are some fundamental changes that have to be made in the system. Otherwise we will not, ever again, be able to call it democracy. Because it isn't.

Speaking Out
I was the first Canadian defence minister to allow serving officers to testify. Traditionally the minister answers all the important questions in

the committee, and he has an advisor beside him who whispers in his ear if there's something he doesn't know or he needs a little prompting. That has been the British system. Brooke Claxton, who is rated as one of the great defence ministers in Canadian history, wouldn't consider allowing serving officers to open their mouths on anything even remotely related to policy. But the issues were so important that I felt that the Canadian people had a right not just to know my point of view, but also that of the senior officers, whose views in many cases were very different than mine. Some backed what I was doing; some did not. This is the reason that it became so controversial. They were saying things that were in effect detrimental to what the government was proposing.

Our members of Parliament just don't know what's going on. They don't have sufficient information, they don't spend enough time studying what's going on, so how can they criticize effectively? When I was a critic, before the Diefenbaker administration was defeated and the Pearson government was formed, I had to get nearly all of my information from the minutes of the Senate and House committees in Washington. I had a lot of people down there, including Gerald Ford, who later became president, send me these things regularly. It was astonishing, the information that they had about Canada, far more information than our own people were getting about Canada. So I would get up in the House of Commons and ask questions based on the information that Congress obtained from their military people.

How can you have an informed debate without people who are informed, without MPs who are informed? Maybe before they determine the strategic vision they should get experts of all kinds to give testimony to a committee as to what they think would be the proper role for Canada. They could take six months or a year to listen to the different points of view and then come up and say, "This is what would be a good strategic role for Canada and this is approximately what it would cost us. Will the government back it and make it happen?"

I think members of Parliament should be involved in writing a lot of the legislation that the government now writes, and they could use the services of civil servants. There are a lot of difficult areas where a non-partisan approach would come up with better legislation, would be better understood, and would serve the Canadian people better than the present system. The same would be true in examining a lot of the government programs. To have committees that can obtain information, that can subpoena witnesses and get to the bottom of things — that kind of investigation rarely happens in Canadian politics.

Strategic Planning

No one's going to attack us, although we would probably have the Americans to defend us. But against whom? The attack now is commercial and financial, not military. That's the front we're being attacked on and we haven't got our defences up yet. That's where we should be putting our energy and our effort. As far as the military is concerned, we are being asked by the United States to participate in an operation, the antiballistic missile system, which is a repetition of the Maginot Line and just as useless, in my opinion. It's leading people into a false sense of security; it's going to involve the expenditure of hundreds of billions of dollars which could be better spent making the world a better place for its citizens. As far as Canada is concerned, rather than putting billions into that system over a period of years, if we use that to upgrade our mobile facilities, hire the men and women that we need to bring the Forces up to strength, and buy the equipment for them to engage in peacekeeping or peacemaking operations around the world, that is a legitimate function where we can do a service to the world.

But just spending money to go along with something recommended by what General Eisenhower called the U.S. military-industrial complex, which provides a few jobs for a few extra generals and a few extra contracts for a few special contractors, doesn't make any sense for Canada. If we're going to look at strategic ideas, that should be one of the first places that we should look. Does this make any sense for Canada? I don't think it does. There are far more appropriate places for us to spend our money and energy.

NORAD

We've never had decision-making authority in NORAD. That is a myth. We had people engaged in NORAD, but we had a deputy commander who was a deputy commander in name only. Sure, he was in charge until there was something happening, and then he was no longer in charge and the commander, an American, was in charge. The main advantage of NORAD, as far as Canada was concerned, was that we had employment for more people in the air force. That's been true for many, many years now, certainly since the end of the cold war, and to perpetuate it, which apparently we intend to do, may or may not make any sense for Canada.

It would be strongly recommended by the air component of our Armed Forces because it makes more jobs for them, but that is the old way of thinking. What is good for the air force may not be good for Canada, and that's the kind of thing that Parliament and the House of Commons should be addressing. And the Canadian people too — we shouldn't just automatically go along with something because it comes from south of the border. Canada should remain independent so they, the Americans, can have a friend and ally who's willing to tell them once in a while, "This doesn't make any sense, either for you or for us, and we're certainly not going to go along with it."

Civilianization

Unification only became a cropper after the two headquarters, the military and civil, were combined. This then led to the next stage, which was dissatisfaction of the senior military and their determination to scuttle, in effect, what they felt had not been a good move. So they did. They scuttled it and in the process they scuttled everything else that had been achieved and got themselves into the pretty kettle of fish that they find themselves in at the present time.

I get blamed for this unfortunately — still — because people just don't know their history, let alone their military history. Even General Lew MacKenzie, who should have known better, wrote an article in *The Globe and Mail* saying, "When then Prime Minister Pierre Trudeau and then Defence Minister Paul Hellyer combined the civil and military headquarters ..." and he went on to explain why this was not a good thing. I read it with some dismay because a lot of people hold me accountable for 30 years of governmental mismanagement, and although I have broad shoulders, I really don't appreciate being blamed for something that Liberals and Conservatives haven't been able to fix in 30 years.

I called him up and said, "General, I read your article with interest and I'd just like to let you know that I was never defence minister under Pierre Trudeau. I had left that portfolio several years before this took place, and it happened under someone else's watch." And he said, "Well, I must say, you're being very civil about it. If the roles were reversed, I would be" — expletive deleted — "bloody mad." What had been done when I was there, which worked well, and what happened as a result of something else which I would not have ever done were all lumped into one kettle of fish.

The Uniform

The green uniform was a mistake. It was a staff recommendation and because they couldn't agree on any of the traditional colours, it was green. There are really a couple of reasons to have the same uniform, which most people don't understand. One was this whole business of representation with the three separate services. They thought they had to have army, navy and air force at every meeting and cocktail party, and they would start counting the uniforms to see if they were properly represented, whether they had their fair-share representation. I actually insisted after a while that they come to my meetings in civvies so that they would not waste time at the beginning of the meeting counting up the colours to see whether they were properly represented or not.

So that was in my opinion an important consideration, that people stop thinking exclusively in terms of their own service and serving it to the exclusion, and sometimes detriment, of the others. The other reason's logistical. Before unification we had a naval lab technician, female, who was posted to the air force hospital at Cold Lake, and her pantyhose had to be driven up by car from Calgary every week because that was the nearest reserve station for the navy. Now, this doesn't make any sense to the Canadian taxpayers at all.

You could just carry this on around the world with United Nations and other operations where you have a few members of each service there, and if you have to stockpile kit in three different colours in all these places around the world, that is tremendously wasteful.

There were valid reasons, and especially in a small force of our size, which is less than the U.S. Marine Corps, for having a common uniform, although green, unfortunately, was an unhappy choice. I have for years said that what we should have adopted — and what I would adopt if I were doing it all over again — is navy blue for the winter, for everyone, and khaki for the summer, for everyone (which is what the navy used to wear) and then whites for showing the flag in foreign ports and walking out and weddings and that sort of thing. And of course to wear their own distinguishing hats and badges and other things that would indicate which branch of the service they were in.

Even though that was only two to five percent of unification, it was the thing that upset people the most. And I can understand it. I should have overruled staff. As a matter of fact, nearly always when I've gotten in trouble it was because I've taken somebody else's advice when I didn't think it was right or it wasn't going to wash. This was a case where I went along with the staff because they seemed so proud of what they were doing, but in retrospect I should have overruled them.

Rethinking Unification
They are now seriously looking again at what I proposed and did, saying that maybe Hellyer had something and that maybe having the different forces working closely together, training together and having the capability of rapid deployment anywhere in the world was the way to go. I think it's good that they're looking back and wondering if there is something we can learn from what was done at that time, and this of course is good for me to hear. But I'm not sure that a lot of my detractors have yet heard it, and consequently they probably still feel that I'm the villain that they have thought of me as for so many years.

I think the mere development of a new strategy would help engage the Canadian people. If they had a parliamentary committee established and if they spent a few months talking about the various options, and if the newspapers took it seriously and duly reported it, I think this might re-engage the Canadian people. Then if Parliament adopted a new vision, and the government endorsed it and presented it to the Canadian people with a bit of a flourish and said, "Now we are going to provide the personnel and equipment to implement effectively this new vision," I think the Canadian people would be pleased and would feel that we had turned a corner and were going in the right direction.

It has to probably start higher than a minister because ministers can get pulverized in today's system. It really has to be top party policy, which means the highest council in the party in some cases, or the prime minister in others. You have to have a prime minister that says it's time we came to grips with this chronic problem, turned it around and started giving our troops direction and the tools and personnel to carry out our directions. Either that or stop sending them everywhere.

It's easy for the prime minister to go somewhere and on the spur of the moment say we'll send troops. But if you haven't got any troops, he's going to come back and the staff will say, "I'm sorry, sir, can't do it. Our troops just came back from another tour and they're overstressed and overworked. We haven't got any fresh troops to send and we haven't got any fresh equipment to send with them." So it's got to start right at the top and it has to be firmly supported by the prime minister and the party in power. Then you can get a bright minister who will take on the job and see it through and make it happen. I think that the military would welcome some proper direction and a new vision, and certainly they would welcome some funding to allow them to replace airplanes and helicopters that should have been retired 20 years ago.

Decisions and Direction

I think there's always a tendency on the part of people who are there permanently, whether it's in the civil service or in the military, to think that they are really in charge. All too often they are. I have experienced this on several fronts. I had a set-to with the Canada Mortgage and Housing Corporation because I issued them directions. I found out later that I was the first person since C. D. Howe who had sent them any directions. In all those intervening years they had been making the policy and sending it to the minister to rubber-stamp. And something the same is true in the Defence Department. Brooke Claxton was probably the last minister before me who really said this is what we want done and this is what you're going to do. Their natural reaction is, "Well, we're the experts and we're going to tell you what we need and then your role is to plead for it and get us the money to do it."

I can understand this perfectly. I remember Mr. St. Laurent saying it at a Defence Department council meeting one day: "You know, they really are the experts. Can we second-guess them?" Well, I have a very healthy skepticism of experts because I've seen them wrong so many times that I could give you chapter and verse, which would run on for hours, which I won't do. But it's necessary every once in a while for somebody to question them and say, "That's fine, but is this what Canada wants you to do? Is this what is best for Canada? Is this government policy or are you just making this up because you've decided that it would be nice and would help you develop the size of your little empire that fits in with your hopes and dreams?" You need informed politicians who are willing to challenge policy, whether it comes from the Foreign Affairs and International Trade Department, the Finance Department or the Department of National Defence, and say, "We're not sure this is right."

They were really appalled when I cancelled the general-purpose frigate. There were two reasons for it. I didn't know whether it fit into our future plans or whether it didn't, but I did know that if it stayed in, the money wouldn't be available for anything else. I also knew — and this was a terrible habit in the Forces — that they had no plans for the frigates. They let contracts largely, in my opinion, to raise funds for the Conservative Party just before the election in 1963, and certain people went to various shipyards and said, "We'll give you a contract to build a general-purpose frigate, but it would be nice if you would help us get re-elected so that everything will go well afterward." This is often the way things happen, and I just said, "Not sure it fits in. Cancel it. We'll take a look and make sure."

They didn't have any costs. Nobody had the vaguest idea what the total bill was going to be. If you start out on these cost-plus operations, they can run into billions of overrun, and then who gets creamed for it? Why, the minister of course. "How did you let them spend that much money on so few ships, and why weren't you watching and why didn't you insist that they had the plans before they started out?" I said, "Before we reach the 'after the fact,' let's cancel it and make sure that we know what we're doing. Then we'll start out with some ships where we have plans and cost estimates and try to come fairly close to those estimates." That was, I think, a good exercise in ministerial discretion and one I would recommend to a lot of people taking on a portfolio for the first time.

I think the wrong people are making a lot of the decisions. This certainly applies in the Department of Finance, where the policies of the Bank of Canada in the last 25 years have been absolutely ruinous. One minister after another goes out to defend them, even though, in my opinion, they are indefensible, and that is because these people exercise so much power, they intimidate ministers. I have a good case example of intimidation.

Soon after I became minister of defence the air force said they wanted to buy 22 more CF-104s, the "Widowmaker," it was later dubbed. I said, "What do you need them for?"

"For attrition."

"What attrition? Where did you get the figures?"

"They're U.S. test figures."

I said, "Well, don't you get better results after you've flown them for a while?"

"Well, yes."

"How much better?"

They didn't know.

I was doing my own staff work at the time, so I took the file home and worked on it for 10 days and then called them in: "I don't think you need them." And they were absolutely appalled. One of them said, "Well, Minister, it's your prerogative to make the decision." But then he added, "But if the Western world should fall as a result of us not having these planes, you would expect us to tell the truth as to who made the decision, wouldn't you?" And I said, "Yes, as a matter of fact I would."

They were absolutely appalled that a minister would think through some aspect of their request. Then they tried to intimidate him into changing his mind and going along with what they wanted. The end of the story is that my successor, Léo Cadieux, sold 50 CF-104s, surplus, to the West German government. Not only did they not need the 22, but they already had more than they needed. This happens. Not just in the Defence Department, but I would say especially in the Finance Department. And it has resulted in some decisions that I think have been absolutely horrendous in their consequences for the Canadian people.

Changes
Many of the changes that have occurred in the last 30 years have made life more difficult for a lot of people in the military. The introduction of women into the military combat arms, for example, has been very difficult to accept, and I can understand that. I can understand why the women think they should have equal rights, but to be part of the combat forces is very difficult and it has created tensions within the Canadian Forces that are hard to cope with.

The introduction of bilingualism has been very, very difficult for some of the old-timers who have military professionalism and who suspect that the promotion has gone to someone else, not because they had greater military skills, perhaps not even equal military skills, but because they were bilingual. This sometimes creates very difficult tensions. I would hope that some of these things were stages that we were going through, that we will be able to cope with them more easily in the future. At the same time I'm not absolutely sure because it's a different world and there's a lot of interference on the part of organizations like the Human Rights Commission, which is a two-edged sword.

There's another change that's taken place in the last 30 years that I find interesting and difficult too. There's been a general decline in morality and the willingness to accept responsibility. Consequently this has resulted in a leadership that often is willing to pass the buck down to lower ranks for things that go wrong, rather than saying, "Yes, I was in command. It was on my watch and I'm responsible. I'm the guy, the point man, and I should take responsibility for it." Very little of that is happening today and it has affected morale in the lower ranks very considerably. They feel betrayed by some of their senior officers covering their backs for their own careers and not showing the professionalism that they had come to expect from people in command.

Peacemaking/Peacekeeping
Peacemaking is part of the world in which we live and we will never be able to get away from it. There are going to be so many tensions in the world, especially ethnic tensions, where some effort will have to be made to try and prevent people from butchering each other that there will be a legitimate role for the United Nations to intervene, and I underline the United Nations because I hope it will be the United Nations and not NATO.

I think peacekeeping is a lot easier. Obviously when someone has made peace and you're just walking the line and trying to keep people on one side of the line or the other, it's not as risky. It's a lot happier situation by far. Still some risk but not as great a risk.

Where the United Nations with the full backing of its membership has decided that intervention is in the interests of the parties involved and in the interests of the world, then I think Canada should not necessarily back away from that kind of responsibility. The problem is, as of the moment, that we don't have the capability to do it properly. Forces are being put into situations where there is too much risk and not enough backup by way of personnel and equipment. So it comes back to again the strategic vision.

"If, in the future, we're going to ask you to undertake that kind of assignment, you have our pledge that we are going to give you the personnel and the equipment necessary to carry it out effectively. Otherwise we won't ask you to go in." If the Armed Forces had that assurance, it would improve the morale immeasurably, and once again they could take pride in membership in the Canadian Armed Forces and in their country that sends them into action.

Foreign Policy since the 1960s
At the time that I became defence minister I understood pretty well what Canadian foreign policy was, so I started to draft a white paper on defence. I wrote it all myself in longhand. I had some help in doing it, of course, but finally came up with a document that I was willing to show to people and had it reviewed by a number of people internally. The Department of External Affairs took offence: "This is really foreign policy and that's our domain." They wanted to scrap the whole thing, start over again and have a committee write it.

Well, I have never been one who was favourable to committees writing papers, especially when I've seen some of their committees, as large as 22 people, take hours to reach a conclusion on the smallest item. So I thought that was not necessary under the circumstances. Prime Minister Pearson rewrote the section on foreign policy personally, but the changes he made were really insignificant, largely cosmetic, so it came out almost as it went in, which I think is vindication of how close it was to his vision of the Canadian foreign policy at the time.

Normally Paul Martin at External Affairs and I got along splendidly and were members of a team. We always acted in concert, but there was for a while that tension between the two departments. We solved it one day in the Château pool when we were swimming. I said, "Look, Paul, we'll co-operate 100 percent, but we don't want to start all over again and have to go through this interminable ritual." Once we got over this little hurdle there was no problem in the implementation, or in all of the other things that we did. We wanted to get on with the job so that the troops would know what they were doing. We didn't want to take another year to write it.

There was a sea change with Mr. Trudeau. He concentrated power in his office and in the Privy Council Office to an extent that had not previously existed in Canada. Mr. Pearson's government was closer to Mr. St. Laurent's, where Mr. Pearson was the chairman of the board and the ministers had a certain amount of leeway, enough in some cases to hang themselves, and in some cases to have the rug pulled out from under them when they got in trouble. But by and large, as long as we minded our p's and q's, we had a considerable amount of autonomy. And we did have collegiality. Of course the government was smaller in those days, so you could meet around the table. You didn't have just the senior ministers present, as happened later on.

Mr. Trudeau decided that he, and especially Michael Pitfield when he became clerk of the Privy Council, should concentrate a lot of power in his office. There was an interesting story coming out of the Defence Department. I don't know what deputy minister it was, but there was a matter of policy under consideration and somebody said, "I'd love to know what the minister thinks about this." And the deputy minister said, "Well, I would be more interested in what Mr. Pitfield has to say about it." That's an indication of where the real power lay. The Mulroney government, I guess, carried on in the tradition, only more so. It became more presidential and more along the American lines. It's continued with the Chrétien government, where many of the ministers are really not much more than rubber stamps.

C. R. "BUZZ" NIXON
2000

*M*r. *Nixon held many posts in the government before becoming the deputy minister in the Department of National Defence in 1975. He remained in that position until 1982. Prior to joining the civil service in 1964, he held a commission in the Royal Canadian Navy. During the period he spent with the RCN he studied engineering at a number of schools, including the Massachusetts Institute of Technology. He is now retired and lives in Ottawa, but remains an active commentator on defence issues and policy making. He is on the news editorial board of the Defence Associations National Network.*

Since the end of the Korean War probably the best six years the Canadian Forces had with regard to resources, both financial and personnel, were the years when I was deputy minister.

My military experience really wasn't the most profound or the most important aspect of getting to be deputy minister, but I'll give you some of the background.

PLAYING THE OSTRICH

Years in the RCN

I went to Royal Roads in 1944 and left there in 1946 and joined the electrical branch of the RCN. The next three years were at university as part of that training. I spent a year in *Cayuga* out in Korea as the electrical officer, and when I came back I spent four years in naval service headquarters.

I went to MIT and took nuclear engineering, and when I came back I went up and worked for a year in Chalk River on an exchange, so I got some practical experience in the running of nuclear reactors, as well as in designing and thinking about the safety factors and how you make safety equipment for them.

The final important task I had in the navy, in 1963, was integrating all the fighting-equipment aspects of the proposed general-purpose frigates. I had to bring together all of the electrical requirements, not only in power, but how they interconnected with the sonar, the radar, the communications, the displays in the various parts of the ship, the spaces that would be required, the personnel that would be required, and prepare the financial estimates for all of this equipment.

I came up with figures which were quite different than had been presented to the government for those frigates. There were to be eight of them, and if my memory serves me correctly, they were around $30 million at that time, so we're talking about $240 million. But those estimates did not include the price of spare parts, logistic spares, training facilities, the drawings, the handbooks, the federal sales tax or any Canadian production premium.

When I put all those in, the price of the estimate for the fighting equipment practically doubled. When they did it for the whole ship the program came up to around, for the sake of this discussion, let's say about 500-and-some million dollars. At that point I understand Mr. Hellyer, who was then minister of national defence, wrote across the file, "Stop this until we get to the bottom of it." That was the end of the general-purpose frigate program.

My main reason for leaving the navy was that I felt the direction it was trying to go wasn't really related to my assessment of the military and naval outlook for the future. I decided that my best service to the country would be in applying all of the education that I had received to improving the industrial capability of the country. So I resigned and went to the Department of Industry.

Mr. Pearson, who was then prime minister, wanted to have a Privy Council Office that wasn't just scribes, that would provide some interface between Cabinet and the bureaucracy. I was selected as one of the people to act there, providing assessments and integrating what was coming in from departments instead of trying to second-guess them, and advising the prime minister and the secretary of the Cabinet on the type of questions that should be asked. The work I was doing led to my continued time in the PCO, and eventually I became the deputy secretary of planning where I served, I guess, for about two years. Mr. Trudeau was prime minister at the time.

If you asked me the most important piece of background I had for deputy minister, I would say it was the comprehensive systems engineering approach to problems which I developed, particularly at MIT. And I showed, when I was in the Privy Council Office, how you could apply it to government. How's that for a short story?

Education and Leadership
I question all of this recent "it's gotta be education." Many outstanding leaders have had no university degree. My education certainly had an awful lot to do with it, but it was the training and the environment that I worked in when I was a naval officer that was really important. One of the things that's drilled into us is initiative. Don't wait to be told. Look around, see what has to be done. You're the leader, you're the one that's setting the example, and when you're setting an example it better be an example that you can look up to.

Now, at the risk of being trashed, there's a thing in yesterday's paper that the elite diving unit in Halifax has been apprehended for poaching lobsters in Halifax Harbour. They've been doing it for years, so the paper says. Nobody can tell me or convince me that the officers in charge of the diving unit didn't know about it and condoned it. That's not leadership.

In today's paper there's a story about wife abuse in the Canadian Forces. There's no indication that it's more rampant than it is in the civil sector, but where the senior officers are condoning it, turning a blind eye, that's not leadership. The woman said she was being abused in this house, and in the next house all they did was turn up their stereo. Those people aren't just neighbours, they are working colleagues. They may be in the same unit. That's not leadership.

Up at Petawawa we had the case of a car being burnt. I can't believe that there were not senior NCOs and junior officers who knew who burnt the car. But they did nothing about it. That's not leadership. When you have these neo-Nazis and the Confederate flag and this absolutely disgraceful hazing that the Canadian Airborne had, that's not leadership. Officers don't stand by and condone those things, at least not the ones that I know. Something's happened, and it's not education.

I would suggest that leadership is a little bit like democracy. It's terribly fragile, and when you just make the assumption that it will always be there, it can be easily destroyed. You just can't assume that there's leadership unless you, as a senior NCO, or you as an officer, are displaying leadership, and that comes from a very high standard of principles, values and attitudes.

Around Ottawa the bogeyman is the auditor general. It's quite often said, "Oh, you can't do that, the auditor general will observe." The first time I heard that in a management meeting I said, "Look, I don't care about the auditor general. You don't do that because it's wrong!" From then on people knew where I stood and they knew what I expected.

I'm talking about being forthright, honest, having the backbone, when a superior gives you an order which you think is absolutely wrong and is going to be disastrous, to tell him or her so. Then when your leader says, "I've heard what you've said, but do it," you say, "Aye aye, sir" and do it. The main thing is to make sure that your superiors know.

When you're a senior official your main responsibility is not to tell ministers what they want to hear, it's to tell ministers what they've got to hear. Years ago when we were doing the industrial benefits for the aircraft program, I was at a meeting and one of my colleagues in another department made this mouthing about the industrial benefits. We went out of the meeting and I said, "What the deuce were you saying that for? You know you're wrong. Why are you saying that?" He said, "That's what ministers want to hear." Well, it's the same way in the Forces.

I never had a personal ambition, except to do what I'm doing as well as I can and let the chips fall where they may. One of the big failures that we see, and it's not just in the Armed Forces, is when people start to do things for their career or for their future or for their ambition, and they compromise their principles.

The Deputy Minister of Defence
Historically, because of the way that the department and the Armed Forces emerged in Canada, the deputy minister was essentially the bean counter keeping track of the funds. Before the war there really wasn't much defence policy, but during the war the whole focus of the activity changed. Once the government said, "We're at war and this is what we're trying to do," then the deputy minister and the Department of Industry and so on was just supporting the military.

But that relationship carried over into peacetime after the war, and there was some cross-pollination. For example, there was an estimates review committee where the deputy minister was the main figure and the chairman of the general staff was an observer. Then there were the other committees where the roles reversed. When the Honourable Donald Macdonald was minister of national defence, he didn't feel that the organization was giving him what he wanted, and he had an in-depth study done called the Pennefather study. One of the main recommendations was, while the chief of the defence staff would have direct contact with the minister on purely operational military matters, anything to do with the policy and with the financing and support for the military would come under the deputy minister, and the deputy minister would be in charge of the minister's office.

Now, it was felt at the time, by my predecessor and the CDS, that this was a bit extreme. So they came up with this arrangement, that the main role of the deputy minister is to relate Canada's defence activities to the rest of government, whether it's the Department of Finance, the Department of Justice or External Affairs.

At the same time, when you get into the organization and the running of the Armed Forces, that's the chief's problem and the chief's responsibility. But that doesn't mean that the deputy minister should just stand back and watch what goes on. If something doesn't make sense to him, he has a responsibility to tell the chief, "Hey, this stinks," or, equally, to give him the support that he needs.

One time an issue came up with the CDS. I said, "If it comes to that, I'll have to say this to the minister." The CDS was a bit perturbed. "Buzz," he said, "that's my responsibility." I said, "Look, the ministers and Cabinet deserve all of the advice they can get from people who have a responsible position and who understand the situation." And with that he said, "Yeah, you're right." So we got along fine and it worked both ways. But it took constant attention. You can't take it for granted.

In seven years, I forget exactly how much we managed to increase the budget, but we increased the number of personnel from around 69,000 to about 82,000, and it was primarily by my interfacing with the Treasury Board, the Cabinet committees and with the other departments, and having good material provided by the military. But the fact is that the chief has to be responsible for running the Forces and the deputy minister is responsible to relate that to the rest of government.

The 1987 White Paper

I will make no bones about it. When the 1987 white paper came out, financially it just didn't make sense in Canada. And that's what the minister should have been told.

As it so happened, the government of the day was saved a terrible embarrassment because Gorbachev came on the scene with the perestroika and the gradual diminution of tensions, but even by the fall of 1987 there were strong indications that this whole East–West tension was gradually phasing down.

The minister of finance, finally, has the authority and the responsibility for the budget, and when real push comes to shove the only person he has to really answer to and talk to is the prime minister. So while you can win the occasional battle with the Department of Finance, you can't win the war unless the war on everything is going your way, including the minister of finance. In the lead-up to the white paper National Defence may have won a few battles with the Department of Finance, but they didn't win the war.

Civilianization

In the new NDHQ organization of the early 1970s, in certain positions where previously you had military people you now had civilians. But there are an awful lot of places where you have military where previously you had civilians. There was a very interesting item in the *Ottawa Citizen* recently. They compared the ratio of civilians in the Canadian Department of National Defence with those in the U.S. and with other countries. And there's a far greater ratio in Canada than there is in the other places. One of the reasons is that you can have civilians a lot cheaper than military people in uniform, when you take all costs involved. I'm talking about the subsidized housing, the medical, the recreational, the social, the messes and so on. You take all of these costs, and the pensions, and you find out the military is a lot more expensive than the civilian.

The chief of the defence staff is now carrying the main ball and the deputy minister may not be as forceful in these things as perhaps I was. The vice-chief of the defence staff, aside from being the vice in the absence of the chief, is also the general manager of the department and responsible for the allocation of resources within the Forces. Now, the guy's only going to be there three years, but it takes him darn near a year and a half before he really gets his hands firmly around it, and then he's off. If you go to Britain or Australia, that position is like an assistant deputy minister. They call them principal secretaries and second or assistant principal secretaries.

I go so far as to say that if people do not have the high probability of being deployed, they should not wear a uniform.

We have a situation where the chief of the defence staff, with approximately 69,000 people in uniform, says, "I can only deploy, on a contingent basis, 10,000. And I can only deploy on a rotational basis so many." They're very small numbers compared with the 69,000. So I have to say, "Why?" It's because so many people in uniform can't be deployed. So many of your people are logisticians. You have to deploy some of them, but to run these storehouses out in Edmonton and down East, do you need people in uniform? No. Moreover, you have to keep rotating those too. With all of these bases around the country being guarded by military police, we end up with a situation in which, at least in 1994, you had almost as many military police as you had infanteers. What's wrong?

That's a deployment of resources, but who's looking at it? Is the chief looking at that? Is the vice looking at that? Are they doing anything about it?

Integration in the Military

Long before Mr. Hellyer appeared on the scene there were efforts made to standardize and achieve a certain amount of, I would call it, integration — not unification — in trades, but it became very, very difficult. One example, which was given to me when I was a young lieutenant, was that in the navy we only had one type of cook. He's a cook. Whereas the army at that time had a butcher. The naval guy has to do his own butchering. They also had a pastry cook and they had a bread cook, four or five levels of cooks. I'm not saying they were wrong, but I'm saying that it was very difficult to integrate when the navy had only one type of cook. It was the same through many of the other trades.

But the real thing was money. If you could integrate all of these things and have only one set of warehousing, only one group of padres and only one group of medical support, you should be able to reduce costs. I had come to the opinion even before I left the navy that they should pull all of the comptrollers general of the three forces into the office of the deputy minister of finance. That's where you would get the integration of your financing.

But I wasn't by any means advocating either integration or unification. However, having made the step (and it was done when I got there) the only thing to do was to make it work. But there's been a tendency to keep fighting it.

The use of the support services is where the real integration is, and I remain to be convinced why they can't work. When it doesn't make some sense, you don't integrate. I'll use the cook situation again. They're different trades. You see the naval cook in his galley, and then you see the much-to-be-admired poor bloody army cook trying to cook for 2,500 people out of the back of a big truck in the field. At least the naval galley is there. It's in the same place every day and not getting all bounced around. Well, it gets bounced around with the sea. But the army cook! I think it's just a marvel that they ever get fed.

Look at the stores situation. Now, a naval storesman aboard ship knows his range of products, and that range of products doesn't change when he goes from ship to ship. Can you take him and put him on an air base? No. But that doesn't mean to say that the stores depot in Edmonton can't have both naval stores and air stores in it. No problem with that. So there are places where integration works.

Systems

In the army, as I understand it, the regimental system's main raison d'être is the relationship of the officer to the man and the senior officer to the man. In other words it's the family. In the navy they have the divisional system, and it's exactly the same thing. The divisional system is for the officer to be looking after the personnel, men and women. In the air force the old squadron system was there too, but they were always on a base, and the squadron support people never flew, but they were on the base. So you had a quite different relationship.

When they integrated, the Canadian Forces went to a base system. It broke down that relationship, that sense of responsibility of the officers and the senior NCOs for the junior personnel. It meant that when they were out on exercises the regimental people were responsible for the personnel, but when they came back to base it was the base that was responsible. Now, I'm sure you might find people who will say, "Buzz, you've got a twisted understanding or a simplistic approach," but that's the essence of it.

Somalia

When I look through the Somalia report I say, "Why is this? Why did this happen? Why did those people get deployed without enough military police? Why did they get deployed on hard rations? Why wasn't the government told that when you change from a humanitarian mission to an actual invasion the whole ball of wax changes? Why wasn't it told that we can't send 700 people and have a responsible operation?" Somebody in a position of responsibility wasn't saying what he should have been saying.

The CDS one time said to me, "Look, the Airborne Regiment is out there in Edmonton all by itself. They will not work with the rest of the army. They think they're better than the rest. When it was formed up, in 1968, the three regiments, the RCRs, the Van Doos, the PPCLI, all sent their best people because they were supposed to be rotated. But they haven't been rotated as much as they should have been and they're starting to get a cult form in there. They've got disciplinary problems and they've got morale problems. I've got to get them back into the army." That's why they were moved to Petawawa in 1976.

In 1992 they go to Somalia — and I haven't studied the Somalia thing in detail — but a unit commander says, "My unit isn't suitable to be deployed." The response is to change the unit commander without, as far as I can understand, seeing or satisfying themselves that the unit is ready. I can assure you that under the chiefs with whom I worked, while it may not have been their responsibility, the chain of command would have dealt with this before it got to them. At the same time the chain of informal communications is pretty strong, and the CDS would have known and, I don't think, would have let that go by. Why didn't somebody stand up and scream, "Wait a minute!"?

In 1978 Canada got involved with the UNIFIL operation between Israel and Lebanon. It was a Friday evening and I was told about this after I got home. There would be a meeting next morning to arrange for the deployment, so I went to the meeting. The chief was there and as it was an operation thing, it was his ball game. I asked, because the policy people were there, "Where did this come from?" "Evidently the prime minister agreed with the secretary-general." I said, "Any word from External?" and was told that no, they weren't aware of it. "Well how does it relate to the Sharp criteria?"

These were the criteria which the Honourable Mitchell Sharp developed. One of the first criteria in peacekeeping is that there be two legitimate governments. Whether they're legitimate democratically or legitimate by force is neither here nor there, but two recognized governments, and both have asked for intervention and both have said that they would provide access to the places where the peacekeeping was to be done.

Well, in the case of Lebanon there was no legitimate government. Nobody had asked for it from there. We had no idea whether we'd have access, and we were still having our problems with Cyprus. So on Monday morning I was in Mr. Trudeau's study with a member from the PCO and the vice-chief, and I gave the prime minister all the reasons why we shouldn't be there. And finally he said, "OK, we'll stay for 90 days."

Now, that same type of discourse should have happened with Somalia. I don't know whether it did. I would like to hope it did. That's very important because that deputy minister had been in the Privy Council Office when I was doing this in 1978.

Did anything happen between 1976 and 1992 to correct the Airborne? Come on, nothing happened between 1976 and 1992 to correct that situation, and it was known broadly throughout the army. What happened is that the three regiments stopped sending the Airborne their good guys, their good material, because they never got them back. They sent them their deadwood, and we had all that dreadful neo-Nazi hazing and the burning of the car.

Remember, we're not talking about wartime. In peacetime the superior people should always be watching what their juniors are doing. Beno may have made that decision, but what was his superior doing? Did his superior just turn a blind eye? This is where the leadership comes in. You do not constantly micromanage, but when you see something like that, that has that potential, you have to make the assessment as to when you say, "Hey!"

I wrote a letter to the *Citizen* and the gist of it was, "Which is more disgusting, the conduct of the commission or the conduct of the Forces?" When you have a commission do a study of an issue like that, I don't think you are going to be effective by trying to pick up all the minutiae and put them together like a jigsaw puzzle, where you have no picture and no idea whether all these puzzles belong in the same thing. You go to the top.

You get a real good statement right from the top, from the chief of the defence staff, the deputy minister, and then you work down. Do you know what's going to happen? You're going to find discords as you go down, some of them intentional and some of them just because there's a difference of understanding. But as long as you get yourself involved in all the minutiae about who's storing documents and where are the documents and where's this and how many logs are there, you're going to build up a mountain of evidence and come out with nothing. They had a mountain of evidence, but they couldn't put it together. I do not know what the chief of the defence staff may or may not have told ministers, or didn't, or what the deputy minister may or may not have told, but I can surmise from what I've seen. And it leaves a big question.

Problems
In January at the Conference of Defence Associations they had quite a seminar on communication, based on the assumption that the biggest problem with Canada's defence is that there's no communication between the military establishment and the politicians, primarily in Parliament. Well, that's not the problem in my view. Even if you had the greatest of communication there, you still have to get the minister of finance on side and you still have to get a public wanting for there to be something.

I've cited this thing about the lobster poaching. Is that going to make you credible with the public? This wife-abuse thing, does that make you credible? When you get the hazing that went on in the Airborne Regiment, does that make you credible? And particularly, when you say, "I've got 69,000 people, but I can only deploy a very small number on a contingent basis," does that make you credible? If I were a businessman I'd say, "Hey, buster, that's not credible. You better get over and see where your money is going." Another area of credibility, and this relates very much to the Conference of Defence Associations, is the thing about the reserves, the reserves, the reserves.

Today — and it was a fact even in the Second World War — you can train recruits faster than you can get the equipment. So if you really want to have a reserve capability, you'd better have reserve equipment. Forget the people. Barney Danson, former minister of national defence, told us about marching down University Avenue, I believe in 1939, with an onion sack over his shoulder in civilian clothes, with an armband saying he was the Queen's Own Rifles. Reg Roy, professor of military history at Royal Roads, has an article in the *Defence Association Newsletter* where he talks about joining up in 1939 and getting the equipment and the uniforms that they had in 1918 or 1919. Roy also talks about the French tanks from the First World War that they used when they were training down in Camp Borden. The Calgary Regiment, which was one of the more renowned tank regiments in the Second World War, in 1938 trained using Chevrolet cars covered with a framework supporting burlap.

My point is, and I repeat, stop this bloody nonsense about the reserves. It's not credible unless you have the equipment, and if you have the equipment, you can recruit people fast. That's what I'm talking about, credibility. Their story just doesn't line up.

Finding a Balance

Whether we like it or not we're a middle-sized nation, and being a member of the G7 is just one part of our total international operations. Unfortunately, for so many years the military has been the weak link in all of our international capability. If you're going to be part of the international community and you want to work with the other leading nations of the world to create the world you think you should have, you'd better make sure that all facets of your international relationships, your trade relationships, diplomatic relationships, your humanitarian things do that, and the military plays a role in all of these places. I'm absolutely convinced that we came through those terrible years, from the end of the Second World War until 1989, primarily by keeping a credible deterrence in the West. The ability to respond to both national and international disasters has to be there.

Your military is the only body that you have that has the capability to respond to all of these things. I think you need to have a quantity, if you have any sense of moral responsibility, which is commensurate with the rest of your international activities.

Put the shoe on the other foot. Let us just assume that the northern half of North America was the more densely populated and had the real capability, and this thing called the United States didn't have it, that it was very much the subordinate member. How would we feel as Canadians if we saw those people, if you'll pardon me, sucking off the hind tit? We wouldn't like that at all, and they don't like it. I'm not suggesting for a moment that just because the United States says something we jump. But if we agree, that is because it is related to the defence of Canada.

On the National Missile Defense thing, Canada's got to make up its own mind on that. Until someone can show me that this method of delivering a weapon with a ballistic missile is the one most likely to be used — if one is to be used, and it will only be one — I'd say let's just assist in the research and development, but don't bother deploying.

We've been pretty instrumental in getting this world court established and if you're trying to have international intervention, you have to have the court. But you also have to have some method of enforcing it and a good set of international laws. We're talking about an integrated world from this point of view, and that's what we've been shooting for. I think it's been part of the Canadian ethic for a long time and we should be continuing with that. But you can't do it unless you participate across the board.

I don't mean to be callous about the horrors of land mines for the unfortunate people that are maimed by them, but I'm from Missouri and one of the things that I have to ask Mr. Axworthy is, "How do you run a defensive position without land mines?" As far as I understand, they are one of the best defensive things you have if put out responsibly and if you know where they are so you can pick them up. But he got onto this bandwagon and it was internationally approved. Now, if you're ever in a situation where you have to use them, what is Mr. Axworthy going to do? Quadruple the size of the Canadian Forces so that you can do the same as you would if you had a minefield?

By and large this Revolution in Military Affairs is all about going high tech. This is another place where the credibility goes. Take Kosovo as an example. Bomb the hell out of them, but when you really get to the end you've got to put boots on the ground. If we're not prepared to have body bags coming back, then we'd better not be there at all. If you're not prepared to fight and risk lives, then I think it's absolutely immoral to be going and taking them by this mass-bombing technique.

When General MacKenzie was in Sarajevo there was a mortar battery set up next to what he called Beaver Barracks, and he knew that if that mortar station ever fired a retaliation it would also hit Beaver Barracks. So he immediately said, "We've got to dig in and be prepared for that." To me that's wrong. I'm not faulting General MacKenzie, but he shouldn't have been there unless he was capable of saying, "Look, you take that mortar battery and get it out of here or I'll shove it up your nose." If he couldn't do that he shouldn't have been there. At that time there were a few crapped-out T-72 tanks terrorizing the place because nobody had the capability to deal with them. Shouldn't have been there without that capability. That's my view. Incidentally, that's up to the chief of the defence staff to tell the ministers.

Responsibility

To me it's up to the senior official to say, "Mr. Minister (or Madam Minister), there's the responsibility under the treasury bill act that I have and there's the Auditor General Act. Now, under those I have no option but to tell you that you can't do it that way." We've got to have probity and prudence to make sure it goes.

There was a case years ago, before I was in National Defence as deputy minister, when they were building the Tribal-class destroyers. The prices kept going up and up and up and the completion time went on and on, and they got a new project manager. I don't know how many project managers they'd been through, but they got a new one. He put in his estimate, compiled to completion, and put a stop on any more changes and it went to the Treasury Board. He went to the Treasury Board meeting with the then minister of national defence, and the minister of the Treasury Board said, "Well, I can't give you any more money." He apparently said to the ministers, "In that event you better get somebody else to act as project officer because I can't do it."

In my own experience I had a case where there was a large project and the minister was getting a lot of political flak because of the way the project manager was working, but I thought the project manager was doing a very good job. We had a couple of conversations, the minister and I, about removing him. I said, "Why? He's doing a good job. The thing's on time, it's on cost and the review board says it's going well." "Well, I'm getting all of this heavy flak. We've got to stop it." The next time we spoke I was told, "Buzz, get rid of that project manager." My response was, "Mr. Minister, if that's an order, you'd better get somebody else to take responsibility for this project because I won't." I never heard any more about it.

On another occasion some Armed Forces equipment was used to assist a civil authority. This is quite legitimate, but the funds are to be recovered. The bill came in from the command that was responsible and it was sent off to the minister's office and I was told to absorb it. I had a discussion with the minister and said, "You can't absorb it for two reasons. First are my responsibilities under the act. Second, politically it's dynamite for you because if this is absorbed, you can almost be assured somebody's going to raise it publicly and he's going to kill you." "Oh well, I'll suffer that, absorb it." So I went back to my office and wrote him a memo — "In accordance with the directions I received this morning ..." — and sent it off to him. As soon as it was received I got a phone call back. "Forget about it. Tear up that memo."

Defence Policy

There're carts and there're horses and you can get them mixed up pretty easily. The Department of National Defence cannot create on its own a defence policy. The Government of Canada does that. The Government of Canada makes the decision as to how much to put into it. Now, I asked the auditor general and all of his minions, "How in the devil's name are you supposed to put together a long-term plan unless you have some idea of what your long-term budget will be?" That's one of the reasons why I think we made so much progress during the late 1970s, early 1980s.

The first thing I did when I was deputy minister was that I got the minister, the chief, the Cabinet and everybody else to agree that we would have an increasing defence budget, with full inflation plus 3.5 percent. With that we could foresee and plan what we're going to use for personnel and what we're going to use for equipment.

At that time the capital program, the equipment program, was about 8.9 percent of the total budget. We believed, and the more work we did the more we refined this, that it should be something more like about 32 percent. By the time I left we had it up to about 26 percent, and it remained there for two or three years. But now it's not the policy that's missing. It's the fact that we haven't got the funds.

The other thing, to be fair, is to recognize the problem that both the deputy minister and the chief have. How the deuce are you supposed to plan a procurement program which has a five-year time frame when you have no idea what your budget's going to be five years from now? What can you do with your personnel? With all of these cuts, what do you cut quickly? You cut the capital program, the new stuff. You stretch out the old stuff because of the difficulty of getting rid of people. You have to buy them out or else you have to wait till their time is up. That's not the problem. It's the lack of any sense of continuity.

I've yet to hear a prime minister enunciate defence policy and I don't think I'll ever get one. I think the policy you'll get is whatever the prime minister will condone, but it may be made as much by the minister of foreign affairs or the minister of finance, or by the minister of industry. I think that the people in the senior positions have to stand up and say, "I can't give you armed forces of any kind without some idea of where we're going." It's going to be inflation plus 3 percent, or it's going to be a constant 2.5 percent drop or whatever, but there has to be some continuity because this is not a program that you can turn on and turn off.

A minister for whom I have tremendous admiration at a Cabinet committee meeting one time said, "Buzz, defence is terribly expensive." And I said, "Mr. Minister, it's neither as expensive nor as horrible as war." He said, "You're right." The most successful defence forces are those that never have to be deployed because that means you've never had a natural disaster like an ice storm or a Winnipeg flood, you've never had a peacekeeping problem and you've never had conflict. What better? What more do you want? But for goodness sake, don't take the insurance off the house. Who has ever gotten a return on their insurance except the guy whose house burned down?

Accountability and Change

Being tough and telling ministers what they don't want to hear is not easy. It's not something that anyone would want to do every day, no way! It's having these other things like careerism. It's a lack of a good set of basic principles: "Look, I am accountable. I am responsible. The act says this — I must be honest, I must be forthright." Without that it all goes to hell.

Years ago we had a royal commission on accountability. I wrote a 150-page submission to that. I did it myself. It wasn't done by staff. It was based on the principle of feedback. The simplest feedback mechanism you have is the flushometer in your toilet. It turns off when it's full; it opens when it's empty. The same thing with your thermostat to run the furnace. That's a feedback mechanism. You're too hot so turn it off. You're too cold so turn it on.

In any accountability system you say, "What am I trying to do? What have I accomplished?" and you feed that back. "Did I accomplish what I set out to do?" If I didn't, I put a correction back in. That's part of the accountability thing. I described this and showed why it is almost impossible to have that as a strong operation in government: because the inputs are constantly changing.

While I was the deputy minister we introduced the official language commissioner, the comptroller general, the information commissioner and human rights. All of those people were terribly interested in what we were doing in their field. Nobody ever asked me what I was doing about national defence. We've got this plethora of inspectors and regulators, but nobody asks what's happening.

When I first got into the PCO I went to a meeting about the preparation of annual estimates, but the estimates weren't related to programs. It was always for transportation, personnel, property, loans, rentals, pensions, etc. Nothing to do with how much that program cost. I noticed that the ministers sitting around the Cabinet table would just be scratching each other's backs.

So when I was deputy secretary of planning I said, "Every year every department should put in their annual, what I would call, strategic assessment, saying what has happened in this department for the last year in terms of trends, in terms of events. This includes changes — in public perceptions, in technology and in international environment — and how, given the mandate of this department, those changes should be reflected in changes in legislation, changes in regulations, changes in resources, either money or people. Then Cabinet should pull all of these things in from all departments and go through them.

Ever since about 1975 — and I'll take some credit for starting it — there's been an annual conclave of the Cabinet during the summer where they discuss what's happened in the past year, the feed-in from the departments and where we are trying to go. That's where it should happen. Then if the government of the day so wishes, it can refer the strategic overview from National Defence or from Human Resources to parliamentary committee. But it's first within the government.

The contribution of parliamentarians is to check that the government is following through. When government makes a bill it sends it to committee. The committee goes through it and makes some amendments; quite often those amendments come from the government benches. But I'd be surprised if there's any substantial amendment to a government bill sponsored by a government member which the member has not discussed with the minister. I don't mean to say it all happens behind closed doors, I'm just saying that things don't happen unless you have a discussion on these things.

I don't mean to demean the role of parliamentary committees, but as a place of initiation or initiative, or foresight and vision — you're not going to get that. You're going to get that very much from the minister, in the case of defence, from the minister of national defence. That's what the bloody government's been neglected, sorry, been elected for. If they won't do that, then the parliamentarians haven't got anything to work on.

The only standing committees that I ever had were national defence, and it was all about estimates. I've never been on a special committee, except as a witness, like the special joint one in 1994. The only other one was Public Accounts, which was rather interesting. Public Accounts, as you know, looks over the auditor general's report and then goes back to the department saying, "What are you doing about this problem?"

One of the great sins that you had in the past was overspending. That was a no-no. But on the other side of the coin, if you did not spend what you'd been budgeted, it lapsed and fell into a black hole. This meant that if in the Department of National Defence, for example, we had contracted for a bunch of helicopters and the contractor was having a bit of a problem and his invoice did not come in on March 15 — which we'd anticipated — it came in on April 15, the money that we had set aside for March 15 went down the hole. But on April 15 we were still obliged to pay it. It was almost double jeopardy.

I put in a rule when I was in the management. I said, "Look, we are going to budget for zero/zero, but we're not perfect, we're going to fail. The only direction in which I'll accept failure is overspending." So naturally we overspent, but we know that we never overspent more than about two percent. Very small. Well, this got the auditor general of the day all upset, the comptroller general all upset, and I was hauled before the Public Accounts Committee as the condemned. The auditor general and the comptroller general were there as the main witnesses, and the chairman turned to them and asked about this lapsing and overspending.

The explanation got to be quite involved, so I explained it to them, just like I have to you, about the helicopter. You lose the money but you still have the obligation to pay, and the next year money that you allocated for something else has to go here. So it goes short, and from a management point of view it's a bloody nightmare. The members immediately understood it. Guess what happened? They introduced this payee concept, and the payee concept permits that type of thing. The year doesn't cut off buying like that; you have some latitude. A parliamentary committee got into it and when they saw what was going on they said, "OK."

Take a look at the 1987 white paper. The people in National Defence had a responsibility to come up with something for their minister that would be reconcilable with what was going on elsewhere in the government, and they didn't.

Mind you, there are places where this gets out of kilter. When official bilingualism was introduced the CDS of the day said, "This is the policy, I'm going to implement it," and he immediately took steps to increase the francophone input to RMC. He and I went to a meeting on bilingualism because the public service was quite disappointed that they weren't making much progress: "What are you doing?" So he told them. "How can you do that?" they asked. And he said, "Because I'm the chief of the defence staff!"

I'm very much in favour of women in the Forces, but you've got to watch what you're doing because there are other values. The Human Rights Commission came to me and said that at the Canadian Forces Station Alert — way up in the north end of Ellesmere Island where it's dark 10 months of the year — there should be an integrated, mixed workforce. Now, these are isolated posts. They're living indoors all the time, in tunnels, and the service is considered hard labour so they only go six months. I said, "Send all women or all men but don't do both because you're just asking for trouble. Many of them are going to be married, so you're just asking for the destruction of families if you mix the force." And the answer I got from them was, "Well, if the family can't stand that tension, they shouldn't be together."

Oh my God! This is trying to use the Canadian Forces for social-policy things without looking at the broader context. Think of trying to put in a mixed crew in a submarine. Isolation and no privacy whatsoever. It just doesn't make sense to me. We want to have women in the force, primarily because they're very capable people. Actually they are one of our best resources, and they bloody well should be used where you can use them.

The Defence Industry
If the government says that they're trying to increase Canadian industry, the Armed Forces should say, "It's not going to be always Canadian, but we've got to find some way to use the purchases of National Defence so as to enhance Canadian industry."

When the Arrow program was cancelled — and incidentally I think it was the right decision — some people, particularly in the aircraft industry, tried to get into a relationship with the United States to provide the Americans with defence equipment, about the same dollar quantity as we were getting from them. That became the defence production sharing program which was then broadened into the defence development sharing program.

Canadian Marconi got into this in the very early 1960s with a particular radio set. They made those things for years, bloody good equipment, and they did the development as development sharing and then they had the production. Out of that we had the defence industry program for the development of equipment with military capability.

We hear so much about the subsidization in industry and that these industries, like Canadian Marconi, or De Havilland or Bombardier or whatever, don't need anything. Well, wait a minute! In the United States their competitors are receiving an incredibly large indirect subsidy in the form of very large defence research and development budgets, and from that comes all kinds of spinoffs which they then use in the commercial field. That's what our people are up against.

Right now our aircraft industry, if I'm not mistaken, is around about $15 billion a year. About 80 percent of that is exported, and in my assessment, if every industry in Canada, if every dollar the government is spending to assist any program was making returns like that, we would be living in the lap of luxury as Canadians. To criticize those subsidies, you're killing the goose that lays the golden egg.

But to come back to the point. The defence production sharing program went along very well until we got into the long-range patrol aircraft program. I'd just come aboard at that time and the project officer made the assessment, with which I agreed, that it would be unlikely that, even with the defence production sharing, you would get political support to build that aircraft, the Aurora, in the United States, unless there were deliberate offsets attached to that program.

That's where the offset thing started, and it worked very well in the Aurora, at least I think it did, because it hadn't been institutionalized. By the time we got into the new fighter program, not only was it institutionalized, but there had to be a certain percentage for Quebec and a certain percentage for Ontario and a certain percentage for the rest of the country. Well, boom! The contractors, as soon as this became part of the specification, had to allow for it when they were making their estimates. So to get firm X, Y, Z in any part of Canada, they had to put in designators so that they could get them to do something for them. As soon as they did that they had a premium.

Incidentally we're talking about an era when there weren't costs-plus. There were fixed prices for the spares, the handbooks, the training, the whole kit and caboodle. A hell of a lot of the Canadian aerospace industry has grown on this type of defence production sharing, on the offsets, and on the defence modernization program and the defence industrial development program.

Being Realistic
When there's an intent to get into peacemaking, i.e., the international community interfering in what has been heretofore the sacrosanct national grounds of some country, then the UN has to go at this in the same way you would if you were starting up a new country. You have to have some law. We seem to be producing these laws on genocide and on crimes against humanity *post facto*. I would say that's not fair ball.

If you're going to do that, you also have to ask yourself, how are we going to enforce them, both in the form of a system of justice which we now have, the world court, and in the method of policing and physical enforcement? If you're going to do that, then you're going to have to have some form of international force to do it.

From Canada's point of view, or from any nation's point of view, I don't think we should be going into these things unless we're convinced that our people there, plus the other people that are involved, are capable of dealing with the situation.

In this matter of Canada, with alacrity, responding to the UN requests, the chief of the defence staff has to say, "I'm sorry, I can't," or they say, like Somalia, "I'm sorry, I can't put in a responsible unit with 700 for this situation." This is in law. In the National Defence Act, if a province asks for aid to civil power, it is the chief of the defence staff who has the civil responsibility to decide how much it will be. It is not the minister of national defence, nor is it the Cabinet.

This is kind of ironic, but when I was deputy secretary, before I was in the Department of National Defence, the minister of national defence wanted this to be changed so the minister would be responsible. I was asked to study this thing, and I went back and said, "Look, the reason we had this in our Constitution is because we do not have national guards. In the United States the governor can call out his National Guard for his purposes, but here the only thing the attorney general or premier of a province can do, as happened in 1970, is to ask for aid to civil power. It was also asked for at the time of Oka. The chief of the defence staff is the one who had to decide what it would be, and not the minister.

Bowling and Ostriches
The idea of leading by orders and by fear is gone. If you can't lead by example, you're off. The method of team leading is historic, it's by example, it's by all the things that we've been talking about. Unfortunately that has been destroyed.

There's a book called *Bowling Alone* dealing with the breakdown in institutional support. This author, Robert Putnam, has studied what has happened with bowling. Bowling leagues, which used to be a socializing operation as much as anything, have just gone down the drain, and he found that while bowling is still very popular, it's not in bowling leagues, it's in individual bowling.

Then he looks around and finds that all sorts of voluntary organizations have gone down the drain, including participation in political parties and voting. He says that one of the main reasons for this is the absorption of television, which is non-participatory. It's a non-socializing method of human activity. He also goes into other things such as the fact that I no longer know who the hell is running the school board.

John Robson, who is assistant editor of the *Ottawa Citizen*, says that with the increase in the social welfare realm we have lost the reliance on the family and friends. Now, if you run into problems, it's not your neighbour and it's not the family, it's social welfare. Go back to the recent report about wife abuse in the Armed Forces. Two people living next door, probably belonging to the same unit, and yet the man in the one household casts a blind eye on what's going on next door. That wouldn't have happened 20 years ago. It's "me-ism."

See, I didn't come to these things just by accident, these principles and such. A hell of a lot of it I got at home and I got a great deal of it when I was at Royal Roads, as a junior officer watching my superiors, learning from both the good and the bad. Because you can learn an awful lot from the poor ones as well as the good ones. That still applies today. But it starts with the individuals themselves, and we're skirting around the issues. We won't get down to the basics. We're playing the ostrich, sticking our heads in the sand, and we won't recognize that the problem we're running into is very much the individual's values and principles. Without those, any amount of education will only exacerbate the situation. You'll learn how to do it better, even if it's bad!

PAUL MANSON

General (Retired)
2001 (Pre-9/11)

General Manson had a distinguished 38-year career with the Royal Canadian Air Force and the Canadian Forces, culminating in a three-year term as the chief of the defence staff from 1986 to 1989. Trained as a fighter pilot, he commanded at every level of the air force and served extensively with NATO forces in Europe. After he retired, General Manson turned to the business world and worked in several senior positions, including chairman of the board of Lockheed Martin Canada. He is now involved in volunteer fundraising as the chairman of the Canadian War Museum's building and expansion program. He is also a composer.

I joined the Royal Canadian Air Force in 1952 on my 18th birthday for two reasons. I wanted to be a pilot and of course this was very shortly after the end of the Second World War. I'd read all those books about aerial battles in the war and it appealed to me greatly. I'd done a little bit of flying and I also wanted to be an engineer like my father. The air force was offering the ROTP in those days, which was an opportunity for someone like me to get a free education and learn to be a pilot. The obligation was to serve for another four years after graduation, but I served actually for another 34 years.

I retired in 1989. In between I did a lot of operational flying, mostly in Europe, with Canadian fighter squadrons, flying F-86 Sabres, CF-100s, a couple of tours on the CF-104 Starfighter, and the CF-101 Voodoo back here in Canada. As I rose in rank I got into more and more staff jobs, command jobs. I commanded the air division in Europe. I commanded the Air Command in Winnipeg, which at that time was in effect the air force. In 1986 I became the chief of the defence staff. The CDS is at the top of the military pyramid and by definition, and in fact by law, is responsible for the control, administration, the operation of the Canadian Armed Forces, and therefore is the focal point for the exercise of that power. And also by definition the CDS must exercise that power through and with civilians in the Department of National Defence, in the Government of Canada. That doesn't mean to say that the chief of the defence staff is beholden to civil servants, but he certainly must obey the orders of the minister of national defence and the prime minister of the country.

The CDS

The CDS is appointed by the prime minister. In my three years as chief of the defence staff, Brian Mulroney was my immediate boss. But in fact I worked most closely with the minister of national defence of the day, who at that time was Perrin Beatty. But although I did meet him and his associate ministers almost on a daily basis, the real contact with the civilian community came with the civil servants who served in the Department of National Defence, particularly in National Defence Headquarters.

They have their own pyramid structure as well, of course, and the top of that pyramid is the deputy minister of national defence, who according to Canadian law is the alter ego of the minister of national defence and therefore has a very substantial amount of power in his own right. The organizational structure of National Defence Headquarters is such that it brings the military community directly into contact with all levels of these two pyramids on a day-to-day basis, in fact on a minute-by-minute basis. This is a system that was introduced in 1972 and exists basically unchanged today, although there has been a lot of fine-tuning of the structure during that period of time.

The CDS has to make sure that the interests of the Canadian Armed Forces are protected and preserved and brought to bear on all important decisions affecting the national security of Canada. That's done in a number of very complex ways, but because of this unusual structure where military and civilian people serve together in a unified headquarters, this means that the chief of the defence staff and the deputy minister of national defence co-chair a number of the very important committees in National Defence Headquarters.

The most important of these is probably the Defence Management Committee. I can't say how many times during my years as chief of the defence staff I would sit beside Mr. Dewar, who was the deputy minister for most of that time, and the two of us would in effect act as a single entity in listening to briefings and commenting on the situation of the day, and in ultimately making decisions.

Now, that all sounds well and good. But the fact is, because the military and the civilian have their own interests and their own responsibilities, sometimes there are instances where we can't find total harmony in the way in which we look upon any given situation. But during my time as chief of the defence staff, never did the situation break down into a public argument of any substance whatsoever. We worked very hard at presenting ourselves as thinking of like mind.

My interests of course were primarily operational, whereas the deputy minister's interests were primarily financial and administrative. But there were overlaps, and it's in the areas of overlap that difficulties tend to arise. But by and large, if there was some fundamental disagreement, we found ways of sitting down and working it out and presenting a common front to the civilian and military staff. That really is quite important. I am aware that in other instances, with other deputy ministers and chiefs of the defence staff, some difficulties did arise that sometimes would break out into the open. And the harmony that we always tried to find was not always there.

I would say, by and large, over the 30 years that this system's been in operation it's worked pretty well. It was at the beginning so unusual, so unique, that there was a lot of giving and taking. A lot of searching for modalities, ways in which this could be made to work. And by and large, over that 30-year period I think some pretty good solutions were found.

Problems in the System

This system has been subjected to a certain amount of criticism, some of it unfair criticism. I have a feeling that a lot of the ills facing the Armed Forces in recent years have been blamed, rather unfairly, on the system rather than other factors. And there are a lot of other factors at play. But particularly since the Canadian Armed Forces have been reduced so dramatically in size, from 125,000 regular force people in the early 1960s, down to about 57,000 today.

The structure of National Defence Headquarters is probably as good as you'll get in today's circumstances. I don't think, with the Forces being as small as they are, we could afford in Canada to have a separate National Defence Headquarters and go back to a separate Canadian Forces headquarters, or the three separate military headquarters — army, navy and air force — that we had in the years before 1965.

Around 1965, and in the years thereafter, Paul Hellyer did make this dramatic change in the structure of the Armed Forces, in unifying the three services. I think his motives were quite correct to a certain extent. Even with a relatively small Armed Forces at that time, there was a lot of duplication in the three services, particularly in the area of support, in engineering support, in logistics supply, medical, dental and that sort of thing.

I think it was quite right to amalgamate those to cut down on the triplication that existed at the time. Where I think the process went too far was in unifying the forces themselves — in eliminating the Royal Canadian Air Force, the Canadian Army, the Royal Canadian Navy and throwing everyone into a common green uniform. What Mr. Hellyer underestimated at the time was the extent to which this was going to affect the morale and the sense of belonging in the Armed Forces.

It's a well-established fact that military people associate themselves and direct their loyalty primarily to their units rather than to Canada as a whole, or to the Government of Canada or even the Armed Forces as a whole, particularly when it comes to wartime. In wartime, in the dreadful stress of combat, people tend to look at those around them for their support and they give their support to those with whom they're so closely associated, members of their own squadron, their ship, their company. That was severely damaged by forcing the separate forces into a single uniform and into a single service.

What's happened since then is that truth has dominated, and the Canadian Forces have gone back to what in effect is a navy, an army and an air force once again. It's interesting to observe that other nations, such as the United Kingdom, the United States and other close allies, have ended up in essentially the same situation that Canada is in right now but without having gone through the trauma of unifying their armed forces and then disunifying them, as Canada's had to.

And if you look at the organizational structure of the headquarters in the United Kingdom, you'll find that it's not that different from what we have in Canada today. It's a matter of how we got here that's been the problem with Canada, as opposed to the more direct route that other nations have taken.

It was a very interesting time in the 1980s, when the government of the day reintroduced three distinctive uniforms for the three services, because they brought the military back into these three uniforms without really defining what the three services were. We had quite an interesting time unscrambling the egg, deciding which people would go into what uniforms.

This was a relatively straightforward problem and it's worked out quite well, but it did lead up to the period in the middle of the 1980s when, having gone through a traumatic 20 years of unification and reduced budgets, the whole problem of rust-out of the equipment of the Armed Forces came to a point of crisis. This, we have to remember, was at the height of the cold war. Even though the end of the cold war was only five years away, it really was the height of the cold war because the number of nuclear weapons in the hands of both sides had been increasing dramatically. ICBMs were held in huge numbers.

The delivery systems were getting more and more accurate, and more numerous. Thermonuclear weapons were coming into play, and the risk of failure of deterrence at that time, although it wasn't a high risk in terms of the likelihood of failure, the consequences of failure were absolutely enormous. It was very serious business.

Canada, together with her allies, wanted desperately to make sure that we were able to meet any potential threat that was coming from the other side of the Iron Curtain so that we could maintain the deterrent effect. That was really our objective, to prevent this catastrophic situation from ever happening.

But as it happened Canada's military equipment was not in very good shape. Our ships were getting older and older. The army had tanks that were not as well equipped as they should have been. Our fighter aircraft were not in good shape. I was the program manager for the new fighter aircraft program that brought in the CF-18 in the early 1980s. The air force was doing pretty well with that particular airplane, but there were still some very serious problems.

There was what we called a bow wave of unfulfilled capital requirements that amounted to literally billions and billions of dollars. Billions would have to be spent if Canada and the Canadian Armed Forces were to have the capability to fulfill the responsibilities assigned to them by successive governments — and that was a very difficult problem.

This commitment-capability gap had really come to a point of crisis. The approach that was taken in the middle of the 1980s was to produce a white paper. A policy paper on national defence which would've been the first one since 1971. It had been a long time since governments had told the military and the public of Canada what defence policy was. So we undertook to produce the white paper.

It was produced in June of 1987. It was quite a remarkable white paper. It did the sort of things that I, as the chief of the defence staff, felt that a government white paper should do in that it recognized the problem of the commitment-capability gap. It acknowledged the roles and responsibilities that the Armed Forces should be fulfilling at the height of the cold war.

What happened of course — and this was the problem — was it took about two years to produce that white paper. By the time it eventually came out things were starting to change, and change very, very rapidly. Although in 1989 I personally wrote an article in the *Canadian Defence Quarterly* that talked about perestroika and the dramatic things that were taking place in the Soviet Union, I had not an inkling that the Berlin Wall would collapse, that the Soviet Union would collapse within a period of a year or two. It didn't occur to us at that time. Other factors were coming into play, economic as well as strategic, that led to the failure of the 1987 white paper. Of course the whole strategic situation changed dramatically a year or two later with the collapse of the Soviet Union.

After the Cold War
After I retired in 1989 I went into the business world, but I still kept an eye on the Armed Forces and what was happening in the strategic world. It was a very distressing time in many respects. It was a wonderful thing that the threat of the cold war had disappeared and the threat of nuclear annihilation had receded into the distance, which was what we'd been working for in the past 40 years. So that was good news. But other things were happening.

The Canadian public, looking for what was called a peace dividend, really wasn't prepared to fund the still-existing commitment-capability gap. The government of the day and the Armed Forces themselves were having some difficulty defining what the roles and missions of the Armed Forces should be in the post–Berlin Wall era, which was a serious problem because you can't order military equipment without knowing what that equipment is supposed to do, what you want it for, where it's to be deployed and how it's to be used.

A defence white paper was produced in the middle of the 1990s that made a valiant attempt to restructure Canada's defence policy, to identify capabilities that should be held in this new era by the Armed Forces. But as had happened so often in the past, these high-minded policy decisions were not backed up with the money that was needed to allow the Armed Forces to carry out those missions and roles. And that led to the problems that still continue today.

Dealing with the Gap
You can attack a commitment-capability gap in two ways. You can increase the capability, which in effect means more money and a few other things as well, but it basically boils down to money. If the gap is a big gap, it means a lot of money and that's a problem today.

Or you can change the commitment. Now, this is where the real difficulty lies.

The Canadian public, I think, have a feeling that in the post–Soviet Union era the Canadian Armed Forces should be focusing almost entirely on what is being called peacekeeping. But in the 21st century it doesn't look much like peacekeeping. It can be peace restoring or a term that's heard more often, "peace operations." That's a relatively low level of intensity in combat terms, compared to what we would have seen in the days of the cold war, particularly in central Europe, where you required heavy artillery, highly combat-capable aircraft, main battle tanks and so on. But the Canadian public, I think, look upon the Canadian Armed Forces as doing the best thing they can do in the field of restoring peace in troubled areas of the world, like the Balkans, parts of Africa and the Middle East. That's certainly a very noble wish on the part of the Canadian public, but it presents some very serious problems for the Armed Forces.

In effect it would reduce the Armed Forces to little more than a con-stabulary, a police force without this capability that they've taken so long to build up in terms of high-intensity combat. The Canadian Armed Forces have a very strong feeling today that without that high-intensity combat capability, plus flexibility allowing the Armed Forces to take part in some pretty heavy warfare, then the Armed Forces do not have the deterrent capability so important in the 21st century.

To retain that capability there are certain things that have to be done, starting with equipment, with strategy and the organization of the Armed Forces.

A large part of the problem is that it's hard to identify what and where and when a conflict might take place. That's not an easy question to answer, and because the question can't be answered directly, the Canadian public has trouble seeing the need to spend billions and bil-lions of dollars on new ships, new airplanes, tanks and guns.

This is largely the dilemma that the Armed Forces are facing today. In the days of NATO in central Europe, the Canadian brigade group over in Germany were very capable in this high level of combat capability. We were as good as any for most of the past 40 or 50 years.

But now that we've fallen out of that — because we're no longer in Europe on a stationed basis in any significant way — most of our oper-ations these days are peace operations in little bits and pieces in various parts of the world, and on a temporary basis, most of them. That makes it very difficult to structure the Armed Forces in a way that the military feels they should be structured.

The Decline

When I was a young fighter pilot in the early 1960s, about the time of the Berlin crisis, the Canadian Armed Forces had, I think, something like 126,000 regular force members. When I took over as chief of the defence staff it was about 90,000 regular force, and a fairly substantial reserve force as well. Today I believe it's about 58,000 in the regular force.

That is an enormous decline in the numbers of service personnel. In business it would be called a death spiral. When you get to a certain point you get down to a position where, no matter what you do, you can't recover from it.

I think the Canadian Forces may be getting close to that point. We're seeing a situation now where they're having great difficulty retaining highly qualified people who have skills that are quite marketable, by and large, in the civil sector. If they see no brighter future than appears to them right now, a lot of these people are going to find other careers in civilian life. That aggravates the spiral and makes it even more difficult.

Even with the best of intentions and the most massive recruiting campaigns, it's going to be difficult attracting the right sort of young people into the Canadian Armed Forces. They must enter the Armed Forces, as I did when I was 18 years old, with the sense that, "I'm going into something that is good, worthwhile, productive, exciting and a good life." Right now it's pretty hard to convince a young 18- or 20-year-old that the Armed Forces offer all of those things.

When I look at the current situation of the Armed Forces I'm struck that there's one ingredient that seems to be missing, an ingredient that was very important to young people entering military service over the years. And that is a sense that the public is totally behind the Armed Forces. It's not that the public is against the Armed Forces, it's just that they don't seem to care or know or understand what the military's there for and what they're trying to do.

It seems to me that if we want to get the right young people going into the uniform of the Armed Forces, they've got to have a feeling that this is what Canadians at large want them to be doing and that the work they're doing has the full support of the public at large.

Now, that support then translates into political support. But the government of the day, unless they sense that the public at large wants to put more money into new equipment for the Armed Forces, simply won't do it. That's happened a lot over the last 50 years at various times. The public has to be made aware that the military is there for a very good purpose, although that purpose is sometimes very difficult to define. The public must know and understand and support the people who wear the uniform of the country, even at a time when war seems remote.

The Selfish Generation
I don't think it's just the Armed Forces. I think it's a reflection of things that are going on in society at large, with the generation that is being called the selfish generation. Certain things have been happening constitutionally in Canada with the Human Rights Act and the Charter, which puts so much emphasis on the individual and takes away so much emphasis from the organization.

Well, historically military organizations have always been dominant. They have to dominate, and the whole history of warfare is such that, unless you can maintain the cohesion of a unit at the expense, every so often, of the rights of the individual, then armies tend to lose. They lose battles and they lose wars.

Facing the trends that are taking place in society today with this enormous shift toward the individual has presented the Armed Forces with some very serious problems. I faced it as chief of the defence staff when the whole issue of women in combat arose. I spent hours and hours and hours on that particular subject. But this trend manifests itself in so many other ways as well.

The careerism of officers exists more than it did in the old days. But there are some outside influences that are influencing the way in which military officers and military people in general handle themselves. It's a very complex world that a staff officer at the headquarters faces, dealing day in, day out with civilian counterparts, having to understand the machinery of government far, far more than staff officers did back in the 1950s and 1960s. Having to argue cases much, much more strenuously, for example, to acquire a new piece of equipment, than they did in the days when money flowed quite freely from the government to the Armed Forces. Every cent is a struggle now and that means that people have to become in a sense businessmen.

I've been in business for a few years, and it's the way business operates as well. You've got to make your case. You've got to make it right or you don't win your case. That's generated, I think, in the staff officer corps in the Canadian Armed Forces more of a business attitude and less of the old military approach to life. The old ethos that was so much a part of our lives 20 and 30 years ago.

Speaking Out

There's something else that's happening that is forcing military officers to act in ways that are counterproductive and that is that the eyes of the media are always on them. Ever since Somalia, in particular, the media have been watching like a hawk. There are some people making a living out of finding nasty things to write about the Canadian Armed Forces. It hurts the Armed Forces; it hurts them very badly. And they have to be extremely cautious about what they say.

At the same time that the Armed Forces have been moving toward openness in what military personnel can say publicly, there have been changes in this whole concept. In my day we were able to hide behind the edict that said that no military person is allowed to speak to the media without the permission of the minister. That was actually written into the National Defence Act and the Canadian Forces regulations.

But that has all changed, and people are allowed to talk to the media, provided they speak about a subject on which they're an expert. But still, it puts a tremendous pressure on individuals that didn't exist in the past. People make mistakes, they say the wrong things, and the wrong things always make the headlines. So staff officers are working in a very difficult environment these days, and I think sometimes these external influences lead to misinterpretation of what they and others in the Armed Forces are trying to do.

The Military Ethos

I'm still associated with the air force. I wear an air force uniform as an honorary colonel commandant, and I get together with my air force colleagues. I'm impressed with the calibre of leadership in the air force today. I'm particularly impressed with the quality of the senior non-commissioned ranks and the relationship between officers and senior NCOs. I can't speak with the same authority about the army and navy because I just don't know that situation as well.

I think there's a lot of misunderstanding and misinterpretation about the ethos that exists in the Canadian Armed Forces today. They're study-ing leadership far more than we ever did in my day. Maybe that's part of the problem. Maybe in our day it was easy and it came naturally to us. Today, because of this incredibly complex environment in which they work, they have to study and they become self-conscious about their own leadership and about their own relationships with the civilian community in the department, and with the media, and with their own members of their own force. But frankly I don't see a breakdown in the ethos of the Armed Forces to the extent that is being reported today. I think there's a lot of mythology out there. It makes great copy, wonder-ful stuff to write about. And so many people are doing that.

I think the time has come to take a good, honest look at the quality of leadership in the Armed Forces, right to the very top. Also at the junior-officer level and within the non-commissioned ranks. I think a good, unbiased study would find that it's pretty darn good today. That's cer-tainly my impression.

The CAST Brigade
To understand the Canadian Air-Sea Transportable Brigade Group, the CAST commitment to Europe, you have to go back to 1968. It was at that time that the Trudeau government cut the armed troops in Europe in half. They reduced us from about 10,000 down to 5,000, almost overnight. It was a terrible blow to our esteem among our NATO allies.

And our NATO allies really hit us very hard when Canada did this because they were really counting on Canada — even though our force was relatively small — to stay in Europe in the larger formations. Because that showed Canada's intent of being a good, solid member of the NATO alliance. However, we were cut in half. And partly to over-come the reaction of our NATO allies, the government of the day agreed to commit this brigade group to the north flank of NATO.

It would be flown over and sent over by roll-on/roll-off ships at a time of crisis, and position itself on the vulnerable north flank. It was an extra commitment that would help to fill the void that had been left by the cuts in 1968. Well, it was a good idea and it certainly did help to restore, at least in part, Canada's image with our allies on the European continent. But the fact is that in strategic terms and in tactical terms it didn't work.

We relied on foreign ships to send that brigade group over there. It would take weeks to get them into position. Exercise Brave Lion, which took place, I think, in about 1984, demonstrated that very clearly. That was really the death knell of the CAST commitment. And so the decision was made in the 1987 white paper to eliminate that commitment and instead to use that brigade to reinforce the Canadian 4 Brigade in central Europe.

In other words, rather than spread our resources very thinly from the north flank of NATO down to central Europe, we were going to really focus our commitments on central Europe. And that was the end of the CAST commitment. It wouldn't have worked in war. It did serve a political purpose during the time that it existed, but it wasn't based on strategic reality. Our allies, being very smart people strategically, understood that it was just a chimera. It really wasn't something that was going to be useful if a conflict ever did break out.

The decision to cancel the CAST commitment to the north flank generated a lot of acrimony within the NATO chiefs of staff committee, of which I was a member, together with my colleagues from the other 15 NATO nations at the time. They were really very upset that Canada had decided to change this commitment and to reduce it.

But we stood our ground. They couldn't argue against the absolutely solid logic that the CAST commitment wouldn't really have worked in wartime anyway and that it was better, in the final analysis, to take those units and move them to support the existing brigade in central Europe, which was a very important reserve unit in the Central Army Group. That made a lot of military sense, and in the final analysis our NATO critics quieted down.

The Gulf War
In two ways Canada's contribution to the Gulf War was superb. One was the navy and its conduct of the blockade. Even with some very old ships

and some antiquated equipment, Canada did extremely well. The people in the navy were so good and they did their job exceptionally well. The second area in which Canada did well was with the CF-18s. The CF-18 aircraft, the Hornets, and their crews performed very well indeed during the Gulf War. And our allies have acknowledged this in very clear terms.

Where Canada was not able to contribute effectively was with land forces, and the reason is pretty obvious. We really didn't have much that we could offer to augment the land forces in the field. We did provide a field hospital, and we were really just getting that up and running when the war ended. That was a pretty meagre contribution on the land side, but in the other two areas we did very well.

I personally saw no evidence of a loss to Canada's prestige whatsoever. But it's very difficult to measure things of that kind. It's a kind of a gradual loss of prestige as Canada becomes a smaller and smaller player in the total strategic picture. That is reflected in a number of ways: in the ordering of Canadian military equipment by our allies, for example. Whereas in the past they might have been inclined to come to Canada to buy high-tech electronic equipment, perhaps after the reduction of Canada's commitments they would be more inclined to go to their European allies for that equipment. But again, it's extremely difficult to measure consequences of that kind.

NATO
Canada has really lost a lot of its place within the halls of power in NATO. Not so much in NORAD, we've kept up a pretty good commitment there, but certainly among our European allies, with the reductions that took place in 1968, and then throughout the 1970s and then again in the middle of the 1980s, and now in the 1990s as well. Canada's voice in strategic bodies in NATO and in other political forums has declined for very good and obvious reasons. But that's part of the game. If you can't play as a full-time member of the club, then you don't have full privileges of membership. And that's clearly understood.

I'm sure the government of the day in 1968 understood, when they were reducing Canada's military contribution to the continent in half, that we were going to pay a price for it in economic and diplomatic terms. But that's a price that was obviously accepted at the time. On the other hand, Canada constantly points out, and we pointed this out to our allies after the white paper in 1987, that we look after our own continent pretty well.

The Canada–U.S. region is a region of NATO, and Canada, together with our American allies, serves very well in NORAD, in protecting the periphery of the North American continent and keeping track of what's going on out in space. Also, with our naval allies in the United States we look after a very large chunk of the Atlantic and of the Pacific oceans. This is something that our European allies tended to forget, conveniently. We constantly reminded them about it, that we're not a European nation. We have made enormous contributions to the security of Europe, in World War I, World War II and throughout the whole of the NATO era as well. And our NATO allies, I think, understand that.

After the 1987 White Paper
The period following the February 1989 budget was a very, very difficult time for us because the 1987 white paper had built up some very high expectations. At last it appeared the government had recognized that there was a commitment-capability gap, looked at the strategic situation and declared its intent of resolving that dilemma for the Canadian Armed Forces. So things looked pretty good.

But in early 1989 the fiscal situation in the country did not look very good. I spent many hours talking with people like Michael Wilson, the finance minister, and his staff, making our case for substantial budget increases to actually do the things that were called for if we were to resolve all of these problems. And we were looking for a substantial up-front investment in capital equipment, with real growth in the defence budget over a 15-year period.

But it was just too rich for the Canadian government and for Canada at a time when the debt-to-GDP ratio was totally out of control. Our deficit and debt were racing away and the government, with a sense of fiscal responsibility, decided that they could not afford to pay for all of the good things that the white paper called for. At the same time perestroika was rampant in the Soviet Union, and it started to look pretty clear that the strategic threat as we'd known it for the past 30 years was dissolving.

That reduced the interest of the Canadian public in paying high taxes for Canada to re-equip its Armed Forces and get rid of this bow wave of unfulfilled capital equipment requirements. In the budget of April 1989 all of these high hopes basically disappeared and we had to explain to the public, and more particularly to the members of the Armed Forces, that we weren't going along the path that had been outlined in the white paper. That really was a very difficult time.

Public and Parliamentary Apathy

One of the common themes in my entire period of service, including my time as chief of the defence staff, has been the absence of interest on the part of the public in general toward the Armed Forces. That translates to not much interest through their representatives in Parliament.

We look wistfully south of the border and see the powerful committee structures surrounding the Department of Defense in the United States and the way in which congressmen and senators get involved in very important decision-making and budget questions involving the United States armed forces. Whereas in Canada members of Parliament don't have any such power or authority whatsoever. They do sit on a committee called the Standing Committee on National Defence and Veterans Affairs and individual members of Parliament get a chance to interview senior members of the Armed Forces and ask them questions.

All too often, in my experience, the questions degenerate into local matters about the constituents and local problems with their bases, rather than high-level strategic matters.

It certainly could be better. Perhaps not to the extent that the Americans have, with their very complex, very powerful committee system where the committees have enormous resources for research and some very bright people advising congressmen and senators so the right questions tend to come out. The net result is that by and large they come to some pretty good conclusions that have a very real impact on the evolution of strategic direction within the American armed forces. We don't see that in Canada, unfortunately, and I'm not sure there's an easy fix for it. But I have a feeling that if we were to engage parliamentarians more in strategic matters of the Armed Forces, that would rub off on Canadians.

One of the factors that comes into play in the link between the Armed Forces and the public is that military strategy, military tactics, military technology are infinitely more complex today, compared to what they were 50 years ago. It was easy for the public to understand what was going on in World War II and in the years afterward, compared to the intricacies of military strategy today.

Particularly with the Revolution in Military Affairs, as it's called — the impact of high technology on armies and air forces and navies, and the way in which they conduct their business. So that's broadened the gap, the void, between the public and the Forces.

Over the years the polls ask Canadians, "Do you feel the Canadian Armed Forces should be well equipped, well trained?" Answer: "Oh, absolutely. Yes, indeed."

"Do you feel the defence budget should be increased to do this?"

"Oh, no. No."

So there's a great inconsistency in the minds of the public. But governments read that mind to the extent that they can, and they respond directly. And that response almost always is in terms of the dollars and cents allocated to defence.

All too often they've read negative ideas from the public, and therefore the defence budget has gone down. It went down in the 1990s to an extent that it started to hurt the Armed Forces in very visible ways. The reaction is taking place now, and the government is responding to that reaction by upping the budget, at least to a small extent.

When I first took over as executive assistant to General Dextraze in 1972, when he had just been appointed chief of the defence staff, one of his first orders that he asked me to promulgate was that instead of headquarters staff wearing civilian clothes four days a week and uniform one day a week, he was reversing that. We would wear our uniforms four days a week and on Fridays, to allow us to go shopping and so on, we were allowed to wear civilian clothes if we wanted. He understood a problem that has become even more intense today, in that the Canadian public really doesn't know the Armed Forces.

Back in the 1950s, 1960s and 1970s every major city in Canada had a large military base or two. The tendency with the reduction of the

Armed Forces has been to close bases in the city, bases like Downsview in Toronto, Rockcliffe in Ottawa and so on, right across Canada. They've moved these bases by and large out into the hinterland, up to places like Cold Lake, Alberta, and Bagotville in Quebec. So the Canadian public isn't aware of the physical existence of their military. I've heard it said many times that there are a lot of Canadians in this country who have never seen a military person in uniform. I believe it's true.

One of the things that I tried to do as chief of the defence staff was to institute something called Veterans' Day, where each of our bases across the country would host veterans and their families — bring them onto the base and show them what we do now and give them demonstrations. Show them our vehicles, our equipment, and talk to them and try at least to close the gap between the veterans community and the military, which surprisingly, I found, was widening back in the 1980s. It's even wider today because many of the most severe critics of the current Forces, if you read letters to the editors, are veterans. I can understand that the veterans are very upset and concerned about what they see to be a deterioration in the ethos and the standards. But it's just part of a larger problem.

It's a great military tradition that retired senior officers will stand up and criticize the forces of the day. I think it started with Genghis Khan and Julius Caesar. It's a tradition that will go on into the future. It's part of being a retired military officer to insist that those young people in uniform today aren't "nearly as good as we were in my day."

I don't believe it for a minute. From what I can see, the young people in Canada's military today are better trained than I was in my day. They know an awful lot more about the high-tech world that they live in than we ever knew. They work very hard at their jobs because the shrinkage of the Forces has meant that they're working longer hours than we ever did in our day.

So it's very painful for them, I'm sure, to be criticized by the public at large or by ex-members of the Armed Forces. But by definition those who have served before know a little bit more than the average public, and their input, I think, can be valuable, provided it's rational, it's temperate and it's understanding. Which it not always is.

Social Change

Before I was chief of the defence staff I was the assistant deputy minister of personnel for both military and civilian people in the Department of National Defence. And during that period and in the years immediately afterward when I became chief of the defence staff, I must say that the most persistent, nagging problem that I had was trying to accommodate the Armed Forces to the changes in society that were taking place all around us.

The problem was in accommodating to changes in the Canadian Human Rights Act and in particular the Canadian Charter of Rights and Freedoms. The legislation changed the structure of our military and the way in which we treat the members of our Armed Forces.

I think that five days out of six on the job I had conversations with the judge advocate general (JAG) about human rights questions, and I spent an inordinate amount of time on these very difficult questions. For example, women in combat, which sounds old hat today because there are so many women in the Canadian Armed Forces. But in those days there weren't, and they were limited in the roles that they could perform in. During my watch as chief of the defence staff we increased the occupations that women could serve in enormously, to the point where by the end of that time there were very few that women couldn't join.

But at the same time I had some very grave concerns about the rapidity at which these changes were taking place, and the pressures that were coming to bear upon me and the Armed Forces for adapting to fit the mould that society in general was going through.

The point is that we could make all of these things work, and we did, in peacetime. But the big question was, what would happen if the Canadian Forces found themselves in a real shooting war, in combat? Would it work? And many people even today, members of the Forces who have been through combat, swear that women in combat occupations will not work, or certainly won't work very well. The experience of the Canadian Forces during my time — and since — in bringing women into the combat arms has been a pretty dismal story.

With the best of intentions and the best of will it's been a difficult process, even in making modest gains in bringing women into occupations that were forbidden to them in the past.

The problems with the inclusion of people with physical handicaps in the Armed Forces, which the average person might not understand, were profound. You can't just fire somebody who is grossly overweight, or fire somebody because they don't meet what have been designed as physical standards. If you have to keep them in, there's a gradual deterioration in the average physical fitness of the Armed Forces, which means a deterioration in the ability to do the real job of the military — which would be to fight a war, if we ever had to do that.

Every time you retain somebody who can't go out to Kosovo because of some physical infirmity, then you have to find a special job for that person. And the person who is fit has to go to Kosovo that much more often to fill in for the people who can't go there. These problems are still with us. They present severe difficulty to the leadership in trying to keep in step with major social change in our society without degrading the Forces' ability to do their job.

Before he retired the last chief of the defence staff made a statement that raised ire among the veterans community by saying that today's Forces are more combat ready than they were 10 years ago. Basically he's saying that the individual members perhaps may be more combat ready, in that they are better trained, they've had more combat experience, operational experience than I had in my time.

But what he's not saying, and what I think is misunderstood, is that the Armed Forces as a whole certainly cannot be as combat ready because we're only half the size of what we were not that many years ago. Our Forces are very good, but they're spread very thinly. So it's difficult. When you ask, say, a foreign military officer, "How good are the Canadian Armed Forces?" they almost invariably will say, "You've got very good people."

Then they very politely will say, "But your Forces are very small relative to your gross domestic product, relative to the contribution of your allies, and your contribution has been declining year after year after year, to the point where Canada's military today is almost inconsequential in the total international equation." That's a sad thing to have to acknowledge, but I think it's quite true.

LOUIS DELVOIE

2000

*L*ouis Delvoie is a senior fellow at the Centre for International
Relations and an adjunct professor of international relations at Queen's University. He joined the Canadian foreign
service in 1965 and has served abroad as the ambassador to
Algeria, deputy high commissioner to the United Kingdom and
high commissioner to Pakistan. In Ottawa he was director general of the bureau of international security and arms control in
the Department of External Affairs and assistant deputy minister for policy in the Department of National Defence during the
Gulf War.

I'm a career foreign service officer. I started in the Department of
External Affairs in 1965 and served as a foreign service officer for the
following 30 years. I was frequently engaged in politico-military affairs
in the department, and toward the end of my career I did a two-year
stint as assistant deputy minister for policy in the Department of
National Defence, on secondment from the Department of Foreign
Affairs. My final posting in Foreign Affairs was as high commissioner to

Pakistan from 1991 to 1994, followed by a one-year stint at Queen's University as a foreign service visitor.

The assistant deputy minister for policy has a bit of a grab bag of responsibilities. One is obviously the development of defence policy, that is, the preparation of strategic assessments and of policy documents which the public comes to see in the form of defence white papers. Another side of it is following day-to-day developments in the world and deciding on how to react to them, usually in consultation with the Department of Foreign Affairs. Another function is to make defence policy known to an interested Canadian public through public affairs events, through programs such as the Security and Defence Forum, which provides support to centres for the study of security affairs at 12 universities across Canada. The job also has the responsibility for the relationship between the department and some of the central agencies, for instance, the Cabinet office and the PCO. So in one sense it's a policy think tank and the developer of policy, but it's also to some extent a secretariat which serves the department and the central agencies.

Defence Policy/Foreign Policy

Any theoretical discussion of the subject of foreign policy and defence policy will automatically assume that defence policy should flow from foreign policy, that defence policy is in many ways the handmaiden of foreign policy, and essentially that has been my experience. This does not mean that there are not occasionally some differences of views between the two departments. There frequently are, for instance on matters relating to arms control. The perspective of the diplomats in Foreign Affairs is not always the same as that of the soldiers in National Defence, but these get reconciled in the process of discussion, and sometimes adjudication by the political level. The relationship between the two departments is one that is based on a constant series of contacts, on a day-to-day basis, between the defence and security bureaus in Foreign Affairs and the policy and operations side of the Department of National Defence. By and large it is a system that works very well.

The perspectives of the Department of National Defence are of course more focused than those of Foreign Affairs. Foreign Affairs must deal with defence issues, environmental matters, trade policy and economic policy, the protection of Canadians abroad and a whole host of other things. Defence, on the other hand, is more focused on Canada's alliances, on defence and deterrence, on peacekeeping, and associated with that, operations to provide rescue to people in emergency situations such as earthquakes and famines around the world. It is far more definable than the mandate of the Department of Foreign Affairs.

There are old stereotypes that die hard in both departments. In the Department of Foreign Affairs it is still possible to hear people refer to "those mindless Rambos over in DND," and in DND to hear references to "those pantywaist, diplomat cookie-pushers over in Fort Pearson." However, by and large the relationship is one of mutual respect and one based on a recognition of each department's own particular responsibilities. I have found over the years that probably the closest relationship that the Department of Foreign Affairs has with any other government department is with National Defence, and it is perhaps the most problem free. The relationship that Foreign Affairs has with Finance or with Industry presents more problems and more policy conflicts.

Gaps and Bluff

The famous commitment-capability gap, a term which was coined in the early 1980s by Professor Rod Byers to describe the situation of the Canadian Armed Forces at that time, has continued to be a feature of the Canadian Forces. Although a lot of commitments have been shelved in the last decade, particularly the presence of Canadian troops in Europe, both army and air force, certainly the reductions in the budgets and personnel of the Department of National Defence have meant a different set of commitment-capability gaps. The same thing has occurred in the Department of Foreign Affairs. The last 10 years have also seen serious cutbacks to that department's financial resources and to the department's personnel, but an ever-increasing agenda in international affairs in the form of new countries coming into existence where representation is required and new issues coming onto the agenda. Twenty years ago nobody would ever have thought of, for instance, the environment being the sort of issue it is today in the Department of Foreign Affairs. And yet there it is. It has to be staffed. Yet the resources are still well below what they were a few years ago.

You can carry on bluff for a very short period of time, but the rest of the international community is not totally deprived of intellect and they see through the bluff pretty rapidly. Machiavelli said that money is the sinews of war. Well, money is also the sinews of peace and money is also the sinews of diplomacy and international relations. You certainly need the trained personnel to be out in the field and on the ground carrying on your diplomacy. You also need to back up that diplomacy with financial and sometimes military resources. All of these depend on the Department of Finance, whether it's the aid budget, the amount of money you have for the Export Development Corporation to support Canadian exporters abroad, or whether it's the amount of money you have for the Canadian Forces to support not only their maintenance, but their deployments abroad. In the absence of money, sooner or later you are left largely with words. And I suggest words get seen through pretty rapidly.

The Gulf

There is a frequent miscalculation that says that in order to be counted as being serious you have to put in massive amounts of money or troops. The idea of presence and involvement is frequently enough. Let me take an example: the Gulf War. We sent to the Gulf three Canadian naval ships and a squadron of CF-18 aircraft. Some people claimed at the time that that was insufficient, that we should have done far more, that we should have sent ground forces and all of the rest of it. The simple fact is that there was no need to send any more. The Americans had decided very early on that they were going to have in place American forces sufficient to complete the job rapidly, as surgically as possible, without depending on anybody else.

The military contributions of others were largely politically symbolic. To be able to counter the Iraqi propaganda that this was purely an American attack on Iraq, the Americans produced a remarkably broad-based coalition of 35 countries and could demonstrate to the world that it was not just an American effort, that it involved countries from Africa, the Middle East, Asia, as well as North America and Western Europe. There the interest was primarily in having a presence. And it did not matter that we did not send more troops. Other situations are somewhat different. When you have a case like Bosnia or Kosovo where after the end of the fighting it is decided to send in a semi-enforcement mission from NATO, then the number of troops do begin to count. If you are just putting in a skeleton force, it comes across as a skeleton force. There they really do need the troops on the ground. And so the situations differ.

Casualties are of course a consideration which is taken into account in any rational decision making about the deployment of forces, but it was not the primary reason, not the secondary and not the tertiary reason. It was reasonably far down in the list of factors examined. The first reason why we did not send more to the Gulf, or ground forces, was that the contribution we did make roughly corresponded, relative to others, to our level of interest in that particular conflict. We did not have a level of interest comparable to the Americans, comparable to the British or comparable to the French, which have been heavily engaged in that region for decades, which have alliances in the region, major interests in the oil production of that region, and which have major markets for, among other things, defence equipment in the billions of dollars. We have never been in that league. So relative to others, the contribution we made was perfectly reasonable, and it compares favourably with the contributions of countries with similar, or perhaps even higher, levels of interest, such as Italy, Spain and Australia.

The third thing, nobody asked us to send more. We were asked for a few additional things, all of which we provided. The British asked us to provide the elements of the field hospital. We provided that. The Americans asked us to provide some backup support in our bases in Germany. We provided that. But nobody asked us to do any more.

Those are the three main reasons why we did not send land forces to the Gulf. Certainly the difficulties of getting them there were a consideration, the length of time it would have taken us to get them there was a consideration and the prospect of casualties was of course a consideration. But it was those three main ones which led to our decision not to do it.

There were various contingency plans that were done which envisaged, more or less, reinforced brigades for the Gulf. They seemed to range roughly between 9,000 and 12,000 men, which on the surface seemed a bit broad, in that the French had what they regarded as a full division there that had 10,000 men. There were debates back and forth and there was a whole spectrum of possibilities examined, but nothing ever got fixed on any one thing.

Big Power or Middle Power?
One of the central faults in much thinking about Canadian foreign policy is an attempt in some cases to play the role of the least of the big

powers, and in other cases to play the role of the greatest of the middle powers. It's the old trick of riding the Roman circus horses when trying to do both. Usually the result is a very strained groin. This has appeared repeatedly in Canadian policy.

For instance, in pursuit of things like the land mines initiative or the international court of justice, or other initiatives in the so-called human-security agenda, Canada portrays itself as a leading member of the right-thinking middle powers.

But when you get into the economic agenda, Canada wants to be in there voicing its views with the major powers and having its say in international economic co-ordination and management. Sometimes the two clash because the role of leader of the middle powers frequently leads one to criticize the great powers. The role as a member of the great powers, G7, G8, leads you frequently to take actions which disregard the interest of the middle powers. It's a very difficult role to play.

For instance, in the government's statement on foreign policy, *Canada and the World*, which was published in 1995, if you flip from one page to another, you have Canada on one page portrayed as a member of the G8 and on the next page as a struggling small member of the international community that has to preserve its economic interests through multilateralism, through alliances with like powers. There's a real contradiction there.

Let's put it this way. A major military role is not a requirement for membership in the G7. The Germans have reasonably large armed forces and the Japanese have reasonably large self-defence forces, but they do not play military roles in the world. They are in there on the basis of their economic clout. Canada largely is in there on the basis of its economic clout, not the same as Germany or Japan, but still in that league. But what membership in the G7/G8 does require is that you have a reasonably global foreign policy, that you be involved in the things which other members of the G7 and G8 are involved in. This makes it far more difficult to pursue what some political scientists suggest should be Canada's role, that is one of niche diplomacy, of finding certain areas where we are good or where our interests lie and abandoning the rest of the world. You can do that if you are going to be just the leader of the middle-power pack. You can't very readily do that if you want to have a voice in the G7 or G8.

Peacekeeping

This commitment to peacekeeping as part of, shall we say, the national ethos, takes you part of the way in understanding our involvement in peacekeeping, but only part of the way. Our initial involvement in peacekeeping had everything to do with our security interests. Our primary security interest throughout the years of the cold war, from the late 1940s to the late 1980s, was the avoidance of a global nuclear conflict, which would have had devastating impacts on Canada. In the pursuit of that we became engaged in collective defence and deterrence through NATO and NORAD. We also, because of our capabilities, became involved in peacekeeping as a way of dampening conflicts which, if they had not been dampened, might have escalated to the point where they would have engaged the superpowers in a global conflict. The containment of these regional conflicts was a central policy purpose of Canada's involvement in peacekeeping throughout the period from the late 1940s through to the late 1980s.

With the end of the cold war that particular policy rationale largely disappeared. The central rationale of avoiding a global nuclear conflict ceased to have any relevance. The superpowers disengaged, one collapsed and there was only one left. So the conflict of a global conflagration opposing two superpowers ended. Part of the peacekeeping operations that were put in place in the early 1990s were in fact operations to bring about the winding down of the cold war, in places like Nicaragua, Namibia, Cambodia. Those all had a purpose relating to the traditional purposes. Similarly, the kinds of operations that were mounted following the Gulf War between Iraq and Kuwait were traditional things that had a clear-cut security rationale to them.

It's when you started getting into responses, not to policy imperatives or well-thought-out policies and criteria, but responses to the CNN factor of horrible sights being conveyed into living rooms by the television news services, that the thing began slowly but surely to lose focus, and the phenomenon which had been noted many years earlier by *The Globe and Mail* as Canada's "Pavlovian" peacekeeping response to any international crisis began to take hold.

We continued to be involved in a variety of peacekeeping operations, some traditional, some humanitarian, some nation building, but the rationales have changed from one to the other as we've gone along, whether we're doing it in pursuit of a human-security agenda, whether it's purely humanitarian or whether it is related to international peace and security. We have abandoned the traditional policies and criteria for the peacekeeping of the first 40 years, but we have not yet put in place a new set of policies and criteria which take into account those things we want to do instead.

The questions of why, where, when and with whom we should be involved in peacekeeping have not genuinely been asked. It was simply a response to situations and to the corresponding cry, "Isn't it awful? Something must be done!" This gets you then into a phenomenon that can probably best be described in terms of a CBC comedy program, *Madly Off in All Directions.*

Peacekeeping was an extremely useful instrument throughout the cold war period in containing regional conflicts, regional conflicts being by and large conflicts between regional states where you interposed observers or forces between the armies regularly constituted of sovereign governments. The whole process had to it a certain orderliness and a certain discipline. You could, if something went wrong, deal with the government of one or another country.

The expansion of the concept to the humanitarian, civil wars and so on, has diluted the whole thing, and in fact much of what is described as peacekeeping nowadays is nothing of the sort. It is in fact peace enforcement, which is a perfectly legitimate thing under the Charter of the United Nations, but it is a totally different thing than peacekeeping. One of the greatest problems encountered by peacekeepers in the field in the last 10 years in various operations, whether it's Somalia, Rwanda or Bosnia, has been that what starts off as a peacekeeping mission gets transformed into a peace enforcement mission without the necessary change in the mandate and without the necessary change in the rules of engagement.

This has resulted in humiliating situations that have discredited the UN most unfortunately, and have discredited many of the countries participating in these operations. Canada seeing some of its peacekeepers in Bosnia attached to posts, being used as hostages, hardly did Canada's credibility any good and certainly did not do the UN's credibility, or our support for peacekeeping, any good.

One of the concomitant obligations upon a government once it has decided to deploy forces is to deploy them in such a way that you run the minimum risks for your forces. That may require changes in where you deploy them, in the kind of equipment you give them, in the kind of training you give them and in the kind of logistical support you provide them. If those do not follow, then this is an irresponsible use of the forces, which leads to a broader question. If you are, in the name of a human-security agenda or humanitarianism, engaging in military interventions to protect people in situations where there is no truce or armistice or peace to keep, what is the obligation of the Canadian Forces to lay down their lives in support of people in places where Canada doesn't have any particular interests?

Canadian troops are sworn to lay down their lives if necessary, to make the ultimate sacrifice in defence of Canada, Canadians and Canadian interests. They do not have any such obligation, in terms of their contract, to do it in defence of Bosnians, Serbs, Haitians or whomever else you wish to choose. This is a very broad question when you no longer have a policy rationale in terms of Canadian interests to justify your involvement.

Certainly a review of peacekeeping in the past 10 years would indicate that countries like India, Pakistan and Bangladesh have leapt forward as primary contributors of peacekeepers. Sometimes they have had literally thousands of troops in peacekeeping, whereas the rest of us were contributing 1,000 or 2,000. The question arises whether this is the best way of going about peacekeeping. Some of these countries certainly do not view peacekeeping in the same way as the traditional peacekeepers did — the Scandinavians, the Australians, the New Zealanders and the Canadians — as being a responsibility of the United Nations to simply provide for peace through a neutral role. Many of these countries see peacekeeping as a way of protecting interests of friends on the ground.

For instance, some of the Muslim countries saw peacekeeping in Bosnia not as a neutral activity between Serbs and Bosnians, but as a way of being there to protect the Bosnian Muslims. Another feature of this new kind of peacekeeping has been the fact that some countries have seen peacekeeping as a way of acquiring new equipment for their forces from the international community and of securing high rates of pay for their military personnel, much higher than these military personnel would ever achieve in their own armed forces.

There are some valid questions to be asked about the future of UN peacekeeping. Are we returning to some of the bad old habits of an earlier era in European affairs, where when conscription arose the sons of the nobility could buy their way out of military service by hiring some peasant to go and do their military service for them and thus avoid the unpleasantness and risks of military service? Have we reached a stage now where people, for money, Bangladeshis or Indians or what have you, will be taking on the risks and the unpleasantness at our behest and we will become simply the bankrollers?

One of the simple facts of the Somalia operation is that some of the incidents relate precisely to very messy new rules of engagement as to what the troops could do and could not do, should do or should not do.

Of course the torture death of Shidane Arone is unforgivable, unacceptable under any circumstances, and the personnel involved in that are criminally responsible. The question of looters being shot may have far more to do with something systemic than any question of individual responsibility, in that the rules of engagement became extremely murky in Somalia as the mandate crept forward, and virtually every single contingent had to develop its own rules. That lack of clarity can lead to unfortunate accidents.

In acquiring basic political intelligence about a country the Department of National Defence, if it does not have a defence attaché in the area, depends on the Canadian mission to provide that, but the fact is that we do not have a diplomatic mission in Somalia. The mission accredited to Somalia is located approximately 1,000 miles away in Nairobi. On the basis of two or three visits of one week's duration every year to Somalia, one hardly is in a position to mount a serious intelligence collection-and-provision operation.

The Canadian peacekeepers are handicapped by getting involved in countries where we have no diplomatic representation. Somalia was one. Rwanda was another.

Once Canada commits forces to the UN, it ceases, except for basic personnel management, to exercise any direction role. That rests with the UN commander of the force. The Canadian contingent must respond to the mission commander, who is a general usually, appointed from one country or another by the United Nations. It would be extremely improper for the Department of Foreign Affairs to be giving direction to a Canadian contingent commander on the ground.

Over the years I've frequently been involved in briefings for outgoing peacekeeping observers or commanders. It's a regular part of the job in the deputy's bureau of political military affairs, or what is formally called international security and arms control, to provide briefings on the basis of diplomatic information and intelligence assessments to out-going participants in Canadian missions. It is not, however, the respon-sibility, as I say, to provide direction.

Frequently you have a question of public expectations, and sometimes the expectations of politicians, that once a decision has been reached it is immediately implemented. You announce that you are going to par-ticipate and send a force to country X, and within 24 hours that force is in country X because the pictures on the television screens are horrible.

Canada has never developed the resources necessary to be able to respond in those kinds of time frames. We do not have the command-and-control systems to mount operations instantaneously. We do not have the strategic airlift necessary to get troops on the ground some-where within 24 hours. So the process of planning and development does sometimes get shortened, unnecessarily so, in the face of political or pub-lic pressure. I think that certainly a lot of the normal planning steps were skipped over in the course of some of these operations.

Africa, 1996

In 1996 several hundred thousand human beings, refugees from Rwanda and from parts of Zaire, seemed to be at risk of starvation and disease. The idea was to intervene in such a way as to permit them to return to their homelands and thus escape the threat. But beyond that, what exactly motivated Canada, rather than some other country, to take the lead? It's not a region of the world in which we have engaged a lot of resources. It is not a region of the world where we have any major inter-ests. It is not a region of the world where we have any major influence.

After 40 years of independence in two of the countries involved, Burundi and Rwanda, we have never opened up a diplomatic mission in either one of them. In the case of Zaire we had closed down our mission a couple of years earlier and did not reopen it until a couple of years after the proposed operation. So these were not countries that were of great importance or had a great Canadian presence. Therefore our knowledge of the local political situation was far less complete than that of many other countries which did have diplomatic representation and major aid programs in that region. When you come right down to the crux of it, it was a spontaneous reaction on the part of certain political leaders in Ottawa to the simple horror of the television pictures.

I think it was *The New York Times* which many years ago published an article in which it said that the most boring headline in any American newspaper was, "Another Worthwhile Canadian Initiative." We are initiative-prone as a country, and sometimes those initiatives are indeed thoroughly worthwhile. At other times it is simply "a desire to be seen to be acting."

And in the case of the Zaire Great Lakes initiative, even if you take the CNN factor fully into account, that would justify our offering to do something and advocating that something be done. It would not necessarily explain our saying, "We will lead this whole thing," especially with the lack of intelligence about what was going on, on the ground. That is something which rests somewhere in Ottawa, in the bowels of the Prime Minister's Office or the office of the minister of foreign affairs, but it was extraordinary and in the end, thank God, it didn't have to be tested.

The Canadian Armed Forces, at roughly 60,000, to go in and take the lead in an operation in a region where Canada has absolutely no experience of military operations, did not have the logistical capacities to sustain fighting forces that distance from home — and these would have been fighting forces, not just peacekeeping. To actually put in place the command and control necessary to operate a multinational force, including Americans and Brits, was simply beyond the capacities of Canada.

Soft Power

The human-security agenda has a companion piece to it, and that is the notion of soft power, as put forward by Mr. Axworthy in his various statements and speeches. Well, on at least two occasions the human-security agenda as envisaged in terms of the preservation of life and human rights and so on has demonstrated quite clearly that soft power ain't enough. That was certainly the case in the Zaire Great Lakes operation, and it became subsequently the case with Kosovo, where to bring that to a resolution which was deemed acceptable by the Western international community, it required far more than soft power. It required hard military assets. I think that the advocates of the human-security agenda are slowly but surely coming round to the notion that a mix of both hard power and soft power is necessary if that human-security agenda is going to be carried forward.

One of the problems with soft power is that nobody has any very clear definition of what it means. People talk about it endlessly. If you are talking about soft power as the projection of culture, ideas, the arts, the academic and the scientific, as assets in your foreign policy, then that is a perfectly valid concept. It is one that has been practised by most Western countries and other countries for decades. It's called public diplomacy, cultural diplomacy, academic diplomacy or what have you. It has on many occasions proved its worth to Canada. In dealing with problems like leg-hold traps in the European Community or with acid rain in the United States, our soft power diplomacy has been a great asset to us.

On the other hand, we do not have the same soft power capabilities as the Americans do, simply because they are the one superpower whose every action, mode of thought, mode of dress is observed and very frequently imitated worldwide. The McDonald's phenomenon, the blue-jeans phenomenon or the hard, medium and soft rock phenomenon. All of these are elements of American soft power in the world. We cannot hope to rival that.

Some politicians do understand it and some don't. I think it has ever been thus and it will ever be thus. What you hope for as an official or as an academic observer of the situation is that those who do understand will have a preponderant voice in Cabinet, but they don't always have one.

The original article on which this whole soft power thing is put forward was by a very distinguished American author, Joseph Nye, who was looking at this simply as a complement to traditional foreign policy and to traditional defence and security policy, not as a substitute for it. Some have chosen to make it a substitute for everything else and it doesn't work because when you come up against guys armed to the teeth, it's not much use telling them that the joys of reading Lucy Maud Montgomery will bring them to the true fulfillment of their aspirations.

Defence Scenarios

The current international situation is an extremely complex one that is constantly throwing up new challenges, so the difficulty of developing solid, longer-term policies is considerable. But there is certainly a division of opinion, clearly evident within the government, as to what this policy should look like if it were indeed ever developed.

There are certain quarters in the government reflecting certain strands in, shall we say, the chattering classes, which say that what we should be doing henceforth with the Armed Forces is making them into a constabulary force capable only of classical peacekeeping. There's another school of thought that says you should be capable of doing largely mid-intensity peace enforcement actions. Finally, there's another school that says you should have a full spectrum of military capabilities and the ability to fight with the best against the best.

All of those scenarios have implications for what our future policy options are going to be and for what our commitments are going to be. I think the divisions of opinion within the government, as well as among the academic communities that feed into the government, are very divided. That is one reason why there has been reluctance to really focus in on some of these basic questions.

I think it was Jack Granatstein who said that sending in the Canadian peacekeepers had become a sort of automatic reaction, comparable to "Ready, aye ready, sir," and that it had become a substitute for thought. In the last 10 years Granatstein's point has indeed some validity to it. There is not sufficient analysis of realities, there is not sufficient analysis of interests, not sufficient analysis of capabilities before decisions are made to actually act and intervene and "take initiatives."

One of the greatest difficulties in the foreign policy process is drawing up priorities. Officials, who by and large are charged with taking a rational approach in terms of national interest and capabilities, do try to draw up priorities. Those priorities frequently get dissipated once they reach the political level because the politicians owe so many obligations to so many different constituencies. Supposing a foreign policy list of priorities were to be drawn up on a basis of regions of the world for Canadian involvement. In terms of Canadian interests certainly sub-Saharan Africa would probably be the last priority on the list, whether we're looking at it in terms of political-security interests, economic interests, immigration, investment, whatever you might have in terms of Canada's foreign policy.

To suggest, however, that we are going to let sub-Saharan Africa drop off our foreign policy agenda and concentrate our interests where we have more direct interest will automatically bring you, as a politician, a host of protests from churches, non-governmental organizations, Canadian communities drawn from sub-Saharan Africa, as well as, perhaps, from some international organizations. All too often the politician chooses to avoid prioritizing because it puts him in difficult situations with one constituency or another. So theoretically everything becomes of equal importance and you disperse your resources rather than concentrating them. This is a very real problem and it's not in Canada alone. In many, many countries the same thing is true.

RMA
In terms of broad purposes I think that the Revolution in Military Affairs reflects two things. One, an ongoing desire on the part of the United States administration to be able to field forces with the maximum amount of destructive capability and the minimum amount of risk to personnel — with precise destructive capability, the so-called smart weapons and so on. Diminishing the risk of casualties is certainly driven by a political agenda in the United States, where the public has repeatedly shown that it is not prepared to accept body bags as a result of American military interventions abroad.

The other driving force behind it, it seems to me, is the defence industrial base, which has lost an awful lot with the end of the arms race with the Soviet Union, and which sees in the Revolution in Military Affairs a way of sustaining the demand for new procurement, new equipment, new technology and so on. The two come together and constitute a force for carrying forward these ever more complex forms of military equipment and military forces.

There is a major question that arises out of this, however. With whom is this race to improve things being conducted? In fact with ourselves.

Certainly it is not being conducted in a race with Russia or China, which technologically are falling further and further behind. You don't need to vastly change your forces to keep up with them. On the contrary, you could stay absolutely still and you'd still be several light-years ahead, technologically, of the Chinese, and by now some time ahead of the Russians.

It becomes something driven by an internal, largely American agenda. The question for allies of the United States then becomes, how much should we emulate the United States in this, and how much are we prepared to expend by way of resources to do so? The primary thrust from a military point of view is that we must do it because otherwise we will cease to be able to operate with the Americans in any military theatre. We will become irrelevant, and therefore we must go ahead with this piece of gear or that piece of gear. The obvious question is, if there is no adversary, with whom we are racing? Is the solution that the Americans slow down as opposed to the rest of America's allies speeding up? I think it remains a valid question.

Another thing about the Revolution in Military Affairs, of course, is that you are producing an ever more complex form of military organization and an ever more complex soldier on the ground, who with all sorts of gear is wired into computer systems, intelligence-gathering systems and so on, and supposedly can do all sorts of things which soldiers have traditionally not been able to do. But if you have your soldier weighed down with all of his fighting gear, his protective armour, his computers, his suits to combat biological and chemical weapons and so on, he's likely to come onto the field looking like the Michelin Man, and if he has to in fact chase a guy through a jungle with nothing but a rifle and a few bullets, he's going to be in real trouble.

I think it's always wise to remember the lessons of some of the wars in which the United States and others have fought in the last few decades. Vietnam was a case where the United States had clear, undeniable technological superiority over the North Vietnamese and the Vietcong, but in the end the war was lost. The same thing was true of the French in Algeria.

This is a rather impressionistic view of some of the problems associated with the Revolution in Military Affairs, but I do think that it demands that some questions be asked. They should be asked by the American military, by the American civilian authorities, as well as by the United States's allies.

Foreign Policy in the Future

In the last foreign policy pronouncement, *Canada and the World,* in 1995, there was a firm statement of purpose to democratize Canadian foreign policy. What does democratization of foreign policy mean? At one end of the spectrum you can say it means more parliamentary involvement in foreign policy making, parliamentary debates, more and better-equipped parliamentary committees examining various policies, making recommendations and so on. At the other end of the spectrum it means carrying out a referendum every time a major policy issue arises. In between you have the whole business of consulting with interested groups, such as non-governmental organizations, academic think tanks, the general public and so on. There's this whole gamut of possibilities. But where are you going to get the best policy from? Which end of the spectrum?

There's a much broader spectrum of government involvement in foreign policy. Certainly the idea of foreign policy being made exclusively by foreign ministries in co-operation with prime ministers' offices is a thing of the past, and it has long been a thing of the past. All sorts of other government organizations get involved, the departments of Fisheries, Environment, Industry, Finance and so on. Parliamentary committees have, with ups and downs, been more active. Parliamentary debates on foreign policy have become somewhat more frequent in the last decade than they ever were before. Non-governmental organizations are demanding to be heard and are being heard, and certainly are making more and more of an input. And this is all to the good.

But after listening to all of this, who makes the final decision? The advice you get from non-governmental organizations is frequently interest-based. A non-governmental organization interested in the protection of the environment may give you one kind of advice. Another non-governmental organization interested in poverty alleviation may give you a quite different piece of advice. In the final analysis it still comes down to somebody making the decision, and I think that is not amenable to all that much change. The consultation process can and should continue to be expanded. But in the end there is only one organization in the world that has as a mandate to promote and defend the interests of Canada and Canadians. That is the Government of Canada, the one that was elected by the Canadian people to do this.

This cannot be delegated to the Business Council on National Issues any more than to Amnesty International or to Oxfam. It has to remain a government responsibility. If the public does not like it, then the government can be thrown out at the next election, but foreign policy decision making must remain based on those who have the authority, the responsibility and frequently the knowledge to make the decisions.

The last review produced the rather extraordinary situation where the defence policy white paper came out three months before the foreign policy white paper equivalent. There is frequently a disjoint between those two documents. The defence white paper makes, for instance, no reference at all, virtually, to the whole human-security agenda, which is featured very prominently in the foreign policy white paper. How does defence fit into the human-security agenda? Certainly looking at those two you don't see it. Similarly, rather intriguingly, I find, the commitment to NATO is far more strongly expressed in the foreign policy white paper than it is in the defence policy white paper. There are conceptual gaps there. At least that's the most charitable way of putting it.

Intervention

I think that the old saw about consistency being the hobgoblin of small minds has a certain merit to it, but it can be taken too far. Let's take a recent example from 1999.

A situation develops in Kosovo where thousands of people are being displaced and hundreds are being killed, and in the name of some set of universal principles you say it is necessary to intervene to stop this. And on the basis of those principles of human rights, avoidance of ethnic cleansing and so on, you intervene militarily. Fine. Six months later a situation which is qualitatively not all that different occurs in Chechnya and you do not intervene militarily.

Well, there's good reason for not intervening militarily. It's one thing to bomb to smithereens a rump state in the Balkans. It's quite another to do that to a nuclear-armed Russia. Realism dictates that you don't do it. But obviously if you have justified the first on the basis of universal principles and you justify your second action on the basis of realism, then your universal principles are open to question and you are open to being accused of double standards, hypocrisy and all of the rest of it. That is where problems of consistency do indeed arise.

The same thing is happening now in relation to Sierra Leone, where a most appalling civil war is taking place with all sorts of brutality being committed. And questions are being asked. Why aren't the United States, Britain, France, Canada in there with troops to stop this, as they were in the case of Kosovo? The answer coming from certain people is that it's just a case of racism. Whites were in danger in Kosovo, but it's blacks in danger in Sierra Leone. That is the dividing line. Of course that is not really the dividing line, but you certainly leave yourself open to those kinds of accusations if you constantly state your foreign policy in terms of universalist principles, as opposed to more pragmatic calculations of interests and achievable results.

Financing the Future
One could think of many ways in which the Armed Forces could take onboard a whole series of lessons from various operations, including Somalia. But one of the things necessary to make change is money, the sinews of war. To say, for instance, that you are going to shift the Armed Forces to a new set of roles requires very frequently a whole new set of equipment, and if the money is not there to buy that equipment, you simply cannot take on that role.

If we were, for instance, to say we want a Canadian navy suited to our requirements today, it would mean in fact scrapping those 12 spanking new frigates of the Canadian navy because they were largely constructed on the basis of a capability for combating Soviet submarines in the North Atlantic. The design of those ships and the decision to build them was made back in 1978. The first one of them came on stream in 1990, just as the cold war was winding down. But the idea of scrapping those ships, which have cost us billions of dollars, and starting anew is totally out of the question. So frequently your intentions to bring about change are limited by your equipment dollars, as well as by the extremely long lead times in defence procurement.

You see, the Americans have throughout the last 50 years been far more willing to devote resources to defence than has Canada. In all of the normal calculations the ratios between Canada and the United States are roughly 10 to 1: population, economy, industrial production and so on. When you get into the defence sector, whether it's in terms of size of forces, budgets or equipment, the ratios are 25 to 1, 30 to 1. That is one of the real reasons why the flexibility in Canada to make these changes frequently doesn't exist.

The media does have to my mind an important role and a constructive role to play. If the media were to put its nose only where it was invited, there would be an awful lot of unemployed journalists. The media has a responsibility to put its nose where it's not invited, and I have always been somebody who considers that the media can have a very positive effect in terms of foreign policy. When talking to my students I some-times ask them to imagine what would have happened if there had been a CNN crew on the first ship that transported slaves from the west coast of Africa to North America, or if a CNN or a BBC World Service team had accompanied Napoleon on the march to and from Moscow. Would the world not have been a better place for it? And my clear answer is yes.

COLIN KENNY

2000

A former executive director of the Liberal Party, Colin Kenny worked in the PMO as a special assistant, director of operations, policy advisor and assistant principal secretary from 1970 to 1979. He was appointed by Prime Minister Pierre Trudeau to the Senate in 1984. Senator Kenny was a key sponsor of the Senate Standing Committee on National Security and Defence and currently serves as its chairman. The committee was reinstated in 2001 after several years' hiatus. He also serves as deputy chair of the Special Committee on Illegal Drugs and is a member of the Senate Subcommittee on Veterans Affairs and the Canadian NATO Parliamentary Association.

As a young boy I was involved in cadets and I went to a military college in the United States, but my real interest in the military started about five years ago when I was asked by the government to sit on the special committee examining the future role of the Canadian Armed Forces. We spent six months looking at the Forces from every angle we could think of and came up with a report that ultimately constituted a significant part of the government's white paper which governs military policy in Canada today.

As a NATO parliamentarian, I chair a committee on the future of the Armed Forces. I'm the only Canadian on the committee and the vice-chair is an American congressman. The other vice-chair is a French senator and the rapporteur is an Italian senator. We've just come back from a meeting of the committee in the U.K. and we'll be off to Budapest at the end of the month for another meeting. That keeps one focused, but I maintain my interest mainly because I'm concerned about what's going on in Canada.

Government Oversight

The (Douglas) Bland study of Parliament generally indicated a fairly low level of knowledge about the Armed Forces. We have very few veterans left. I can't think of any in the Senate. There may be some in the House of Commons but they don't jump to mind. The level of interest in the military in Canada right now is, I think, at an all-time low, and it's to some extent as a result of the success of the military. We won the last war; we've had structures in place like NATO and NORAD that have kept the peace. We're a country that is surrounded by three large oceans, which means we really haven't had any serious threat facing us, and as a consequence Canadians don't focus on the military very much and their parliamentarians reflect that.

The parliamentary role of oversight is not being properly executed. Part of the problem is structural. We have a Westminster-style Parliament. So when the estimates for military spending in the coming year come forward, Parliament's members have to accept them all or reject them all. They can't pick and choose which ones they like and which ones they don't like. If they decide to reject them, that means the government falls. So government members tend to vote for all of the estimates as they come forward each time, whether they like them or not. Secondly, legislation comes forward once in a blue moon, so parliamentarians don't have much opportunity to take a look at the military from that perspective. Thirdly, the governments generally haven't been very quick at coming forward with white papers. That process generates debate that's useful and causes people to think more carefully about how the military is functioning.

The Senate is sadly lacking in not having a defence committee. The problem is, I'm an optimist and optimists often don't do well in the Senate. We're going to have a defence committee, I just don't know when. Whether or not the other place can clean up its act and have an effective defence committee, I don't know. But right now I don't think any reasoned observer believes that it's doing as much as it could to scrutinize the Armed Forces.

You need to have chairs who stay on a committee for a period of time, who become knowledgeable and who are prepared to revisit issues regularly. Part of the concern is that parliamentarians haven't been aggressive enough about it, and we could certainly improve our surveillance of the military significantly if there was a political will to do so.

When we went out and travelled across the country with the special joint committee, we attracted people in every city we went to. We held hearings in every province and attracted people who were in favour of having no military at all and also people who were in favour of having a vastly larger military. We structured the hearings in such a way that we created a debate that the media were interested in. Frankly, having a defence committee sitting in Ottawa holding hearings simply doesn't catch the attention of the media. You have to go out to the people and then you get the media coverage and the debate develops.

One of the recommendations from the special joint committee was that there be a joint House and Senate defence committee. At the time it seemed like a good idea and I supported that recommendation, but I cease to support it anymore. The Reform Party, the Conservatives, the Liberals and the Bloc worked well together on it. I don't recall there being an NDP member at that time. The Bloc crapped out in the last two weeks and disassociated themselves from the report. Up until then they had agreed with absolutely everything that we had. We'd gone a step at a time and they were onboard. I thought that was a useful process.

But since then I've had a chance to look at how the defence committee functions in the House and frankly I don't like the amount of control the government exerts over it. It usually has a parliamentary secretary on it who serves as the minister's watchdog, while the chair of the committee tends to get shuffled every year or two. This is not how you have an effective committee.

The Senate banking committee is arguably one of the most powerful and influential that we have on the Hill. We had the same chair in place there for about a decade. After you've been around for a decade looking at issues, bureaucrats don't fool you so easily, politicians don't scare you anymore and you have an opportunity to go back and to revisit issues and to be quite effective.

Another good example would be the Special Committee on Terrorism and Public Safety. Senator Kelly, a Conservative, chaired that. I sat on two of his three committees. They were terrific because the first time round we got the same old answers from the same old bureaucrats and they thought the committee was going to wrap up. Well, we did wrap up, but then a year later when we saw no action, we struck the committee again, went back at the same questions. Lo and behold, we started seeing some action and some improvement. Having the capacity to revisit issues is very important for a legislature, and that's one way that the executive is brought to account.

I found that when I sat on the Special Joint Committee on Canada's Defence Policy that it took awhile to work our way up the learning curve. Defence provided two colonels and a naval captain to do research for us. I suppose they were combination researchers and spies for the deputy, but they tended to be helpful. I think that it's only when a committee is in place for a period of time that you attract good researchers and there are an awful lot of folks around who are prepared to provide free advice. There are a lot of retired military folk who know what they're talking about and who are prepared to translate it into language that politicians can understand. It wouldn't take me 10 minutes to find half a dozen who would come forward on different subjects and provide good professional advice.

Once a committee's been functioning for five or six years I don't think you'll hear the deputy minister of finance saying, "Gee, it's too bad that those dummies on the Senate banking committee don't know what they're doing." They know what they're doing. That could be said for defence if you had people with an interest who were consistently on the committee and putting the same effort into it. I don't think the people on banking are smarter than the people on defence. They've just been around longer, they have an institutional memory, they focus on the issues and they don't let go. If they get fooled once, they make sure they're not fooled the second time when the same witness comes back.

The special committee wrote its report with the firm understanding that we were going to be dealing with $11.5 billion and we're dealing with more than $2 billion less than that now. If we'd known that, we would have written a totally different paper. Had we known it was going to be funded at this level, we would never have approved our report and we would have objected to the white paper.

Targeting the Military

It's ironic, but there are folks on the right who talk about cutting the size of government and a very easy target to cut is the Department of Defence. And there are folks on the left who don't like the military and don't want us to have a strong defence posture, and so they aim at the Department of Defence. The end result is that we have a department that is ill equipped to do very much.

Our credibility abroad is directly tied to our ability to project force. There are some people in this government that don't understand that. There are others in the government that don't believe it, but the reality is that other countries look at us and measure very precisely our ability to project and to sustain. We don't have the ability to project a force and we don't have the ability to sustain it. As a consequence we are not listened to very seriously in a lot of councils because we're not players. Bluffing only works once.

Foreign policy should drive defence policy, but having said that, if you don't have an adequate defence, then it will drive foreign policy because it will put absolute limits on where your foreign policy can go. And it will determine that there are whole areas that you simply cannot deal in from a foreign policy point of view because you have nothing to offer. Our allies understand this very clearly.

It's offensive to be overseas and have people in other countries point out very clearly the deficiencies in our Armed Forces. I lost two cousins overseas in the last war. My father and my uncle were prisoners of war. My family went over and liberated Europe, and to have Europeans come back and talk to me about us not pulling our weight is offensive.

But if I take a look at the level of their defence spending against their GDP and the level of our spending, we don't measure up. I look at what's been happening to our troops and how they're equipped, and I find it offensive. I've arrived at the point where I'm not prepared to see any more of our boys and girls sent overseas if they're not properly equipped.

Now, I was over in Bosnia and I saw our kids over there, the 18- to 25-year-olds in lousy equipment, not only driving lousy equipment but wearing lousy equipment. That doesn't make any sense. My position is, until we equip them as well as we can, until they're the best equipped in the world, let's keep them at home and not have a foreign policy that calls for sending them off on peacekeeping missions or any damn missions.

Our allies know we're cheating on our commitments. They not only know it, but they say it. They'll sit down in front of you and they'll have the list of the spending — the figures aren't a secret — and they'll say, "How come you're not measuring up?" They don't come over here and make speeches to Canadians saying that, but if you're visiting their country, they'll tell you, clearly, exactly what they think.

We're left out of a whole range of consultations and councils. People wonder why we weren't part of the inner group being consulted during the Kosovo exercise. It's real simple: the people being consulted were the people who were bringing something to the party. What we brought to the party was good, but very small.

I'm going to a briefing tomorrow for the next NATO meeting. I guarantee you one of the things that we're going to be briefed on is just how good we are and how well we're pulling our weight. "Here are some arguments you can give back to the folks when they start crapping on you." We all know the arguments won't stand up. Then the message comes back, "Well, tell them we're contributing in other ways." So we say to the bureaucrats, "What are the other ways we're contributing?" "Oh, well, we don't have a briefing note on that!"

The Canadian public is pretty bright and understands issues pretty well, but no one has made a case to the Canadian public about why we need a military. The case isn't being put by anyone that I can see. But if you sit down with a farmer in Saskatchewan and say, "Look, you're in the wheat-selling business and you have to ship it overseas. Now, is it important to you to have stability in the countries you're shipping it to?" that wheat farmer will say, "Yes." Then, if you say to that wheat farmer, "Is it worthwhile for us to have a foreign policy and a defence policy that brings stability to where you're shipping your wheat?" that farmer will say, "Yes." "Well, since your wheat is going in ships, would it be useful to have a navy to keep the sea lanes clear in case there were some problems?" Again that farmer would say, "Yes." But nobody is sitting down with the farmers in Saskatchewan and talking defence policy, and that's what you've got to do with any policy if you want Canadians to get behind it and to support it.

Post–Cold War
As we matured as a country we liked the Pearson legacy. It meant something to Canadians and they identified with it. Over the past 50 years Canadians have been proud of the fact that we've participated in a significant number of United Nations peacekeeping missions. Having said that, the case has not been made about how you have to go about it. As peacekeeping changes to peacemaking and the level of violence rises, Canadians haven't adjusted and aren't focusing on that.

Canadians are still adjusting, as the rest of the world is, to a situation where we had a cold war with relatively static lines and a relatively clear understanding of who the friends were and who the enemies were to a situation where we have what are called rogue states and where we have developing problems that are potentially very dangerous and very destabilizing. The cold war at least stabilized a lot of states that now seem to be throwing their weight around, but Canadians haven't adapted to that and haven't come to an understanding of the role that they can play in providing that stability.

Now, if we're going to be part of the G7 or the G8, the major economic players in the world, we have to ask ourselves the question, "If we're in this league economically, should we not also be prepared to provide the stability so that the world continues to flourish economically?"

Inter-operability is a problem that all NATO countries have to one degree or another. The Americans are moving leaps ahead of the rest of NATO in terms of how much they're spending, how sophisticated their equipment is. There are real problems with other NATO countries communicating with the Americans and functioning in theatre in an effective way.

I have great difficulty with our sourcing policies. I don't understand why Canada goes out of its way to build military equipment the way we do it right now. I'd have no objection at all to us building military equipment if we also were building equipment that we were exporting and the industry stood on its own, but we're building equipment that's heavily subsidized and takes a huge amount to design and create. Sometimes I think we're using it more for regional development purposes than we are for military purposes.

I've heard estimates that we're paying a 30 percent premium on the equipment we're purchasing. A good example would be the frigates. We have 12 terrific frigates in Canada right now. I haven't met anyone who doesn't think we've got terrific frigates, until they start talking about the helicopters and say, "What's the point in having a frigate if you don't have a helicopter? It's a vulnerable piece of tin and you'd better keep it in port." But everyone makes the point that you've got terrific frigates. Now, we made them in New Brunswick and Quebec. It doesn't make any sense if you've only got a run of 12 to make them in two separate shipyards. No sense at all.

The question you have to ask yourself is, would we be better off having regional development policies that subsidize those areas or subsidize those areas in a line of work that would be ongoing? Why do we have five shipyards in Canada? Why do we have a shipyard on the West Coast, a shipyard in Quebec, a shipyard in New Brunswick, a shipyard in Nova Scotia, a shipyard in Newfoundland, when this country doesn't have enough shipbuilding to sustain one shipyard? It doesn't make any sense at all.

It would make a lot more sense for us to tag on and buy the last 12 frigates from an American run. We'd drop our price by 30 percent, the taxpayers would save the money — and they could spend it supporting those regions if they wanted to — and we would also be solving our inter-operability problem at the same time. But let's not subsidize at huge cost pieces of equipment that we can't economically build. The test is if you can sell more than your own needs. We've got a helicopter plant that's exporting helicopters all over the place. We've got a GM plant in London that's making terrific government vehicles and there's a market for them all over the place.

We have to convince the taxpayers that there's value in having a robust Armed Forces. We have to demonstrate to them that there is a return for that. Until politicians are able to do that, you're going to see the military budget being whittled away until we have a military that's of no consequence.

The Credibility Gap — Canada's Obligations
The best thing that I've seen happen in the last year is that the chief of the defence staff said publicly that he did not have any more people to send overseas if the government called on them. Once you start seeing that sort of pushback coming from the military, the message comes to the politicians that they have to put up or shut up. Either they've got to fund the military properly or else they've got to stop making these promises that we're going to go waltzing around the world keeping peace hither and yon. And while we're at it, we've also got to remember that we're not going to be around to help with the floods in Manitoba or Mel Lastman's snow problems. The reality is that if politicians aren't prepared to fund the military, then they should stop sending them overseas.

The politicians have a credibility problem, but I don't think the Armed Forces have a credibility problem. It's true that we are not threatened anywhere. I think it's fair to say that it's very unlikely that somebody is going to set up an armada and sail across the Atlantic or Pacific, or that somebody's going to march across the Arctic to invade us. We all understand that clearly, and we're blessed that way.

But the blessed have certain obligations. We didn't have to go over in 1939 to deal with Hitler. We went over because there was a moral imperative to do that. Now, if we want to talk about self-interest, we're a trading country and a great part of our prosperity depends on our ability to trade. If we want to continue to be a trading country and expand our markets, then it is in our interests to make sure that we do have a stable world.

If we want to have influence with other countries, we have to have the Armed Forces to demonstrate that we can participate in keeping a stable world. If Canada sees its role simply as an honest broker shuffling back and forth between warring parties, that's fine, you don't need an army. We can produce all the pinstripe suits we want and see if they have any

effect. I can tell you that you have to be asked to be a credible interme-
diary. We don't get asked that often.

It's very hard when you look around the country to try and develop a
group of knowledgeable people who are prepared to come forward and
talk about these issues. There's certainly a deficit in terms of the attention
Parliament gives to the issue. There's a deficit in terms of the obligation
politicians have in explaining the role of the military to the public, and
there's a deficit in what the military does in terms of speaking up.

Now, it's partly my job as a parliamentarian to encourage debates of this
sort. I try to do it by writing and speaking periodically on the subject. I
try and stay knowledgeable through the work I do with NATO. But the
case has to be made to the Canadian public. The Canadian public has a
very open mind on it. I think our natural bias is not to be warriors.
Canadians don't see themselves like the British, who are forever sending
off expeditionary forces. Canadians are quite comfortable with the concept of being peacekeepers. That's a role Canadians value and would like
to nourish. Having said that, they have to respect the fact that there's a
cost associated with it, and so far no one has explained the nature of that
cost in very simple issues like sustainability.

If you want to keep a battalion someplace overseas, you need to have
three other battalions back in Canada to keep the fourth overseas. That
means you have to have a lot of people involved. If we're not going to
equip our troops properly, the only moral thing we can do is to withdraw and stop pretending that we're players. We're a middle power. If
we're not prepared to equip our troops accordingly, let's stop pretending we're a middle power and say we're something less than that. Let's
stop trying to have a role that's bigger than what we are.

We can't pretend that we're big shots at the UN and then not pony up
when the time comes to send troops to a troubled place. We can't pretend to be world leaders in the G7 and then not be able to send off
troops that are well equipped, to East Timor or wherever else troops are
needed that day. Canadians have to decide what level of responsibility
they want to assume in the world, and if they decide that they want to
be isolated in an American cocoon and want to say to the Americans,
"Look, we're going to rely on you to defend us," the Americans, being
practical people, are going to say, "OK, but there's a price associated with

this. There's no free ride here, Canada, no free lunch. If you expect us to protect you, what are you going to pay? Where are you going to give it up?" There's going to be a price somewhere.

The obligation lies first and foremost on the political leadership in the country. That's why we're here and it's our obligation to provide leadership, not just wait to see where the parade's going and then rush around to get to the front of it. But having said that, water doesn't run uphill. There has to be a willingness among the Canadian population to understand this.

Canada has a proud history of citizen soldiers who, when the call went out, joined up at great sacrifice, and the world is significantly better for the contribution that our parents and grandparents made. The issue that faces my generation and my son's generation is, are we going to continue? Are we going to be able to ensure that the world is a safe place? It doesn't stay that way just by accident. People have to earn it, a generation at a time.

EDWARD "TED" MCWHINNEY
2001 (Post-9/11)

*T*ed McWhinney has a worldwide reputation as scholar of international and constitutional law. Elected to two terms in the
House of Commons (1993–2000) representing Vancouver Quadra,
he served as parliamentary secretary to the minister of foreign
affairs and international trade and to the minister of fisheries and
oceans. At the time he was one of the few members of Parliament to
have had military experience. In his professional life he has been a
Crown prosecutor, royal commissioner of inquiry, consultant to the
secretary-general of the United Nations and an advisor on constitutional and international law to several Quebec premiers, the premier of Ontario and the federal government. He was also a member
of the Permanent Court of Arbitration, The Hague, and special
advisor to the Canadian delegation to the United Nations General
Assembly. He recently completed a two-year term as president of the
Institut de droit international in Geneva.

The cold war was on when I was a student. I read and wrote about the
Soviet Union, Soviet foreign policy, Soviet law, the Soviet approach to

international relations and law. I've written four books on terrorism, which grew out of this East–West confrontation. The obvious solution for international terrorism in the 1960s and 1970s was East–West co-operation, and in the end that's how it worked. The Russians were actually more gung-ho on pursuing terrorists than even the Americans were. The notion of compulsory extradition of every terrorist was something even the Americans found difficult to accept.

Many of the ideas I developed on federalism carried over to East–West relations. If you're going to get into nuclear disarmament, you have to negotiate on the same principles as in federalism — pragmatism and balancing of interests. You don't offer the other side anything that you're not prepared to do yourself, and vice versa. The process of problem solving is not a difficult carryover from federalism to international relations, even cold war style.

Advisor to Candidate

I remember a Quebec premier saying, after I'd given him a report on language policy, "This is a brilliant report. It's got everything there. But you didn't tell me what to do." And I said, "No, I'm a specialist advisor. My function is not to tell you what to do. That's for your political advisors. What I do is analyze the problem. I quantify the alternative costs of the various solutions put forward, I lead you right up to solution but not the final choice." He said, "The problem with my political advisors is, they're so emotionally engaged that I can't trust their views; they get coloured by their emotional preferences." So I said, "On that basis, if I were in your position, I think I would do this." And he said, "Fine." He accepted 50 percent of the advice and went ahead and it was quite successful. So if you advise somebody, you sit next to them and you are competent, meaning you don't try and exceed your function, you soon find people saying, "Would you like to be a candidate?"

So for the last 30 or 40 years people of different political parties and different provinces have asked me if I'd be a candidate, but I've always been too busy. I'm writing that next book on nuclear disarmament or a new study on international terrorism. It just happened, finally. In 1990–1992 the country was in a mess federally because Meech had failed, Charlottetown had failed and the divisions were very clear, very bitter. So two national leaders came to me and said, "Would you be a candidate for our party?" And they actually said, in each case, "You've given a lot of free advice, now you should put up or shut up. Come into the arena." There was a window of opportunity and I took it, but I made the condition that I would serve one term and re-examine, but at the most two terms and then I'm going back. I'll postpone a few things but I'm going back. And that's how it worked out.

When I was asked to be a candidate nobody offered to appoint me. In fact John Turner, my predecessor in the seat I ran in, said it's the kiss of death in British Columbia to be appointed, you've got to win it. So I had to go out and learn how to win a nomination for a party — a contested nomination with four, five other candidates who had been working for a year or two — how then to win an election, and then of course how to be re-elected. It's a science and if you apply intelligence, you can do it. And we did it. But it took me about six or eight months to win the nomination and then win the election. Intensive work. I haven't worked as hard since I was an 18-year-old flying cadet.

A majority government in its first few years tends to ride with its electoral mandate. It's very confident; it usually doesn't do very much. You sit back. Look at Trudeau, for example. His first term wasn't his best term. Some say his best term was his second term, the minority government. So there really wasn't much to do. One of the conclusions from the 1993 campaign was that people, even though they'd experienced Meech and Charlottetown, were just bored with the Constitution. They wanted to bury it. And so that large area was out. There was no discussion. There's been very little happening on it in Parliament since 1993.

Similarly with foreign policy. The Berlin Wall had fallen in 1989. A lot of the ideas I had put forward scientifically and nationally were already in operation. Nothing much happened in foreign policy, so we were left with a budget on which I had strong views — $42.8 billion, the deficit budget we'd inherited. It was absurd. It couldn't be tolerated.

The other thing was how to make economies that keep things going: medicare, education, higher education, advanced research. The provinces were strapped for funds, the money had been cut off. The federal government didn't have the constitutional responsibility, so I made my main objectives getting pure research supported federally, getting a massive inflow of federal funds in spite of the need to balance the budget.

I set myself goals — tangible, realizable goals. I discussed them with my constituents fully and we agreed on this and we won. We got federal money for higher research, for purer research, we got money for higher education. We got the universities back on a track of competition with leading institutions elsewhere.

So I don't regard my time as wasted but it was essentially bilateral, dealing within the government. I would go to a minister if I had a minister that I had good relations with and confidence in. Paul Martin, the finance minister, knew he had to make his austerity budgets, but he believed in higher education. The science minister, who was John Manley, impressed me enormously with his capacity to read briefs and understand problems in those areas in which he had no background.

I discussed with the transport minister, Doug Young, ways of keeping Canadian airlines alive, very important to my constituency, and we basically succeeded. So there were very few targets that I set that we didn't achieve. By the end of each year I felt I'd done enough. Within the caucus, if you know how to raise an issue properly, you can win. The thing you don't do in caucus is make 20-minute speeches. Three minutes is about the maximum tolerance level.

You've got to explain complex issues in very clear language and you've got to keep coming back again and again and go directly to the minister. And when you meet a minister in your field, you've got to be better informed than the minister. So you've got to study, read the files. It's a science. It can be done.

Parliament and the Executive

We mix up the two things, the executive and the Parliament, or the legislature. I'm not sure it's very healthy to mix them these days. The qualities required to be elected as a member of Parliament are not necessarily the qualities to be a good executive. And certainly the reverse is true. I've seen many excellent people in industry, business and labour who would be very good members of a cabinet in the United States, but couldn't possibly be elected in Canada. They don't have the personality or the patience or the discipline to go about being elected. The executive talent available in Parliament is very much weaker than in the United States.

Correspondingly, since our members of Parliament are already into this double function — the potential of being an executive member and having to be elected and re-elected — I don't think they're able to give the time to the legislative process. The committee system, because it's tied into the parliamentary executive, is weak and ineffectual, and the membership of committees is controlled by the party whips.

The committees, I think, pale in comparison to American committees. The work they get done in the United States on legislation just isn't done in any comparable way here. I have friends in the United States, U.S. senators, and they'd much rather be a senator than a cabinet minister.

There's no job more pleasant than being a United States senator, and frankly, if you organize yourself in your six-year term, you are very fully informed. I dealt directly with state senators and congressmen and they were very well informed, very well disciplined, and if they didn't have the background themselves in an area, they had the staff.

It was always said, of course, that under a strong prime minister the parliamentary system produced an executive stronger than in the United States. Great Britain under Lloyd George, for example, as prime minister, or Winston Churchill, or in recent times Margaret Thatcher, had a stronger executive power without the constitutional restraints you get in the United States. It's the periods in between where you have the problems of course, where you get a weak prime minister and little support from the Parliament.

Consensus building in the United States is through the elected Congress. The executive is selected for totally different reasons. You select them for their specialist confidence or their overall capacities. I couldn't have seen Colin Powell being elected, for example, as a senator or a congressman, or having the patience to put up with it, but he's a great secretary of state. The only way we can bring people into our system is to create a by-election, get somebody to retire, put them in our appointed Senate, which is a joke by comparison with the American Senate. But with Powell you're speaking of the chairman of the joint chiefs of staff.

The case of General McNaughton is the best example. Poor General McNaughton was commander of the Canadian Forces in World War II and Mackenzie King wanted him in the Cabinet. He tried twice to find him a safe seat, but he got beaten each time. He was totally hopeless as a communicator, but in terms of the direct conversational exchanges with the prime minister or others as commander-in-chief, he was excellent.

The American Congress is the permanent consensus-building institution. The cabinet comes and goes according to the changing political attitudes of the country, but the president has an enormous freedom of choice. And even where the president is in a minority in the Senate, so that the opposition party controls his choices and the veto over cabinet selections, the rules of the game are at par, except in the extreme case of confirmation.

Every president leaves his mark. In Ronald Reagan's first term he inherited people and it wasn't much of a term. But in the second term his staff was there. The people he selected were excellent and they carried him into history.

Committee Membership

As a junior member of the government I was both a member of the foreign affairs committee and then parliamentary secretary. But as a parliamentary secretary I was a representative of the government. I was a member of the committee and I would communicate to the chair (who was always, of course, a government member) government positions. It was my obligation to do that. I'm not sure that constitutionally it is a good plan.

The minister doesn't have much choice about who the members of the committee are. This is good in one sense — that the minister shouldn't put yes-men or yes-women on the committee. But it does mean that you get a committee that doesn't necessarily have any expertise in foreign affairs. It always puzzled me in Ottawa why the whips didn't use their talent better. If you get a fisheries committee, you have expertise there. It may be specialized expertise, but you say, "This man knows fisheries; I'll put him there."

Committee membership, I think, is a way of keeping backbenchers happy. Foreign affairs is prized because it has a lot of money for travel and you will end up in interesting and not unpleasant places in the spring, before the snow has melted in Ottawa. So there's intense lobbying to get there.

Our committees don't have a great deal of expertise. The majority, the government, controls the calling of witnesses. The opposition, because they don't, I think, use their expertise to the full, aren't really very helpful in putting forward useful, interesting witnesses who will say things different from the government line. It's not the parliamentary secretary's role, by the way, to produce balance among the witnesses. All I can suggest and what I did suggest — and by the way I met no resistance when I did this — was say, "Look, we need more information. Here are some interesting people."

For example, on the Balkans we do have some Canadian experts. You don't have to get the people that you've funded as NGO representatives to go to various international conferences. There's an awful feeling that some may be singing for their supper when they come back as witnesses.

The other thing that as an ex-lawyer always puzzled me was why the opposition didn't ever ask, "What's their expertise?" If you go into a court and you say, "This is an expert on heart diseases," and you examine them and you find their medical practice has all been in maternity cases, they're dismissed as an expert. I never found any great sophistication in government. And in the opposition I found very little sophistication in bringing forward witnesses who might have a different viewpoint.

Svend Robinson was not always popular in his own party but sometimes did ask the unexpected questions. I also found the Bloc good because this is an area of foreign affairs that doesn't have too much impact on traditional Quebec sovereignty issues. The issue of the Balkans, Kosovo — is there a Bloc Québécois position or not? I found that they were well-educated, thoughtful people and they were very helpful in committees. But the committee's strength is pale by comparison.

The strength of committees in the United States lies in the ability to summon witnesses. I've been a witness and my testimony's been sought by American committees. And their range is very wide and they at least read what's being written. They know enough to say, "We need something to balance our viewpoint; let's have it."

The Canadian Role
I think it is true that the Canadian role has diminished significantly in the last 25 — even perhaps the last 50 — years, but that was almost

inevitable. When the United Nations was formed it had 40 members and the British Empire was not decolonized, the French Empire was not decolonized. It's now 185 members. So there we were among the 40, the 21 Latin American states and the 19 others.

In those early years we just happen to have had the congruence of two quite interesting but complementary personalities. We had Pearson and we had Paul Martin, Sr. They're both interesting people: different qualities, but they had an element of wisdom. Wisdom is knowledge and experience, putting them together.

And you know, India, when it came into independence, 1947, Nehru was the prime minister, Krishna Menon the foreign minister. They could talk to Pearson and Martin and there was a sort of common dialogue and common sympathy before decolonization was achieved. Then the United Nations jumped in 1955 from 60 to 78 members, and so we were swamped. As newly decolonized countries developed their own political elite, usually educated with the confidence that goes with it, they didn't seek our advice. Moreover, we probably had taken our role for granted and we didn't do the work.

Pearson, Martin, Sr., were people you don't see much of in Parliament today. They were not narrow specialists. They had a large view of the world, a Weltanschauung, a conception of international society and Canada's place in it. And that sort of overview helps take positions that are not necessarily politically opportune at the moment.

Under Dean Acheson, under the Truman foreign policy, and I think the Eisenhower foreign policy, there was a close American relationship and lots of these things have disappeared since. Although we have foreign ministers from time to time who have, you might say, objectively good qualifications for foreign affairs, you don't get this larger philosophical outlook or the ability to articulate it all that very often.

The early post-war period soon became dominated by the cold war. This bipolar conception of a world public order meant it wasn't such a big jump to adjust to a situation where a policy was made in terms of its impact on either Moscow or Washington. So your part as a member of the alliance was talking candidly but quietly to your ally and perhaps getting them to share their analysis of the problem and changing their positions. We were, I think, in the 1960s and 1970s an important element in the détente process. We were able to back the Americans up where they wanted to take unilateral initiatives. And even on American bilateral initiatives like nuclear disarmament we were able to say, "This isn't selling out to Communism."

For example, the Moscow test-ban treaty, President Kennedy's treaty, was a novel, in some ways a revolutionary, act. Even before that, President Eisenhower's action, the 1959 Antarctic Treaty, in which he basically brokered with the Russians a deal to demilitarize Antarctica. There was a suggestion then that nuclear waste materials be dumped in Antarctica. They thought of the ice as being solid. Then the Outer Space Treaty in 1967, keeping people out of orbiting nuclear weapons in space. That would have been a crazy idea but it was circulated.

Until the end of the 1960s we were part of this relatively simple bipolar world system. It's a very conservative system; there's very little territorial change. The ethnic extremists that you now see in the 1990s were kept under order. They were in the Soviet bloc. They'd keep them in order. They behaved at Moscow's behest. It was a simpler world order and the main emphasis was on problem solving, pragmatic, empirical problem solving. And we did very well then.

The 1990s
There were two problems in the 1990s. One is obviously the limitations of expertise and the failure to build our new cultural communities into community decision making and ultimately foreign policy making. For example, when the Balkan conflict arose, people had been predicting that once Tito died, in 1980, Yugoslavia would collapse. But there was clearly no game plan and operation for that eventuality. There was certainly no expertise in our foreign ministry. We had to start from scratch in the beginning of the 1990s. I don't think there was anybody there who spoke Serbo-Croat.

The other problem is the remoteness from World War II. It's rather strange, and it ages me a little bit to say it, but I was the only member in the last House of Commons with direct military experience. And you deal with a succession of ministers of defence who have no military experience at all.

You feel confident when you get somebody like Colin Powell in control. He had been a fighting general. He's known how to use power and how not to. He was part of two crucial decisions. One, to conduct the Gulf War under the aegis and under the control of the United Nations, even if the United States was the spearhead. The second decision was, having gained the objectives stipulated by the United Nations — pushing back Iraq from Kuwait — he stopped at the front when people in the United States said he should have bombed the hell out of Baghdad and killed Saddam Hussein. Colin Powell certainly made that decision.

So you feel very confident in this renewed crisis, in the new international terrorism movement, of somebody with a certain knowledge of the economy in the use of power. It's one of the first lessons you learn in a military school, economy in the use of power. You have the enormous power, but you don't have to send a battleship to do what a motor torpedo boat would do. So that expertise, that sort of feeling that "I've been there" has been missing. It affects Great Britain, Germany too, the successor group, the first baby-boomers group.

From the beginning the Gulf War command operated under the United Nations, the authority of a bundle of resolutions. Security Council, General Assembly, there was lock step all the way. Although effectively the military command was American, it was a UN operation. I think in that sense there was a sufficiency of Canadian support, parliamentary and other. This was of course the Conservative government in operation, Mr. Mulroney as prime minister and George Bush, Sr., as the American president.

Kosovo

In the Kosovo operation there had been some innovations which I had helped contribute to. I had argued that we should have a debate in Parliament before we engaged the Canadian Forces. It's in the American constitution, as you know, if you declare war, you've got to have Congress's authority. It has been said, since President Roosevelt, American presidents have made a point of not declaring war so they didn't have to go to Congress.

Our government had non-binding, non-voting debates in Parliament at various stages of the Balkans operations. They were always in the evening, usually after regular business was finished, so you would have a House in which perhaps three members would be present and the opposition would politely not challenge for the lack of a quorum. While at least there was a debate, there wasn't, I would say, a good deal of impact on government policy. There were alternative routes.

It might have been a different operation within the United Nations. In my own contribution there over Kosovo, I suggested going through the General Assembly. If the Security Council becomes immobilized because of the veto of a permanent member, you can go to the General Assembly. That was the basis of the United Nations action of the Korean War in 1950. It's a well-known precedent. I don't suppose I should have been surprised but nobody seemed to have heard of it, although it has been used several times since by the United Nations. But I think we went too quickly into a NATO-based operation and it does present problems. In theory, if you act without an international law base, you may be subject to prosecution and national tribunals. So I think the legal ends with regard to Kosovo could have been tidied up and should have been tidied up, but they weren't.

This was essentially the debate between experts. I read the evidence before the British House of Commons committee and it's very, very critical of the lack of an affirmative legal base for the Kosovo action. I think a more effective parliamentary system, with perhaps votes on some of these issues, might have corrected that aspect. But as far as the Canadian public was concerned, the witnesses we heard were essentially the conventional witnesses, NGOs and others. I don't think we had General MacKenzie testify to us.

There were other people who might have appeared, but the committees operate in the context of the Canadian system. There are dozens of committees. There's limited time available and perhaps the foreign affairs committee was able to give eight hours, maybe more, on this. If you get a witness who insists on reading a text, as many of the academic witnesses insisted on doing, if the chair doesn't correct them, the time is gone. I wouldn't say the committees were very effective.

Speaking Up
When I spoke in the House I usually spoke only in areas where I had something to say. I'd indicate that I wanted to speak and in general the whip usually pushed me in very quickly. But the whips' offices and the

government supply members with speeches. I made the point that, "I will read the speeches, just to make sure I know what government policy is so I won't get out of line unconsciously, but I'm not going to use them. I give my own speeches." And the whip accepted that. But so much of the speechmaking on both sides of the House are texts that are prepared by the research bureaus attached to the parliamentary parties, operating through the whips' offices.

When I was in the Fisheries Department — I was parliamentary secretary there — they used to write these speeches and they'd start out with platitudes: "Canada stands on so many oceans and frontiers, extends from one ocean to another." I said, "This is junk. Why do you do this? Who does it?" "Well, we're retired civil servants, we're paid to do it." They seem to think members expect this. So we did make some pleasant changes in Fisheries. They accommodated quite readily to the notion they should start saying something substantial, but I think the speech writers had low opinions of MPs, and possibly of ministers, because ministers' speeches are written too, for the most part. They rarely refuse to read them, even if it's not good stuff.

I once sat as the commissioner examining the legality of televising parliamentary debates. It was commissioned by the B.C. legislature, Dave Barrett was the premier. Our stuff actually became the basic stuff for people who later decided to televise, but some of the things that could have been anticipated, and should have been anticipated, weren't. There weren't really any legal problems. Parliament has enough discipline and decency, I think, to control abusive use of time. But what should have been anticipated was that it would concentrate those areas that were televised into a soap opera in a certain sense, and the Question Period now has come to dominate everything.

So for 45 minutes each day — if you leave out the statement of the government members, it's 45 minutes — everybody's there. You get probably two-thirds of the members of the House present, you get the galleries packed, usually by school children and others, who sometimes come out in horror.

You get this bear pit where questions are asked, but the answers are non-responsive and everybody knows that. You get this soap opera which has very little relationship to reality. The questions are framed rhetorically, the answers are framed rhetorically. Some ministers are not very good on their feet, others are excellent. One of the best is Herb Gray because Herb developed this capacity for giving a boring non-response, deliberately low key. He's one of the brightest members of the House. But you know it's theatre.

It isn't reality. When I was a parliamentary secretary I would often have to substitute for the minister in Question Period. We'd begin discussing potential questions, potential answers at 11:00. It would go on until 1:30, and you'd go in the Cabinet room and you'd rehearse the sort of answers to give to questions and make sure your answers co-ordinated with government policy. I would see the Bloc Québécois people begin work at 8:00 in the morning on the Question Period. So between 8:00 and 3:00 their time is taken up with particular problems isolated out of context.

Is it an efficient use of time? Can we turn it back? I don't think so. I think the fundamental reforms of Parliament probably have to go to the issue of a complete change in the Constitution, separation of powers, American-style and European-style. The country's certainly not yet ready for that.

The failure to obtain the prior authority of the United Nations regarding Kosovo meant that we were faced with some very embarrassing questions. For example, aerial bombardment. The law has been codified since Suez, since World War II, since the Korean War. You have actually quite draconian controls on aerial bombardment, including aerial bombardment of collateral objects. In other words objects that are not necessary to the immediate purpose of the mission.

If these issues had been tabled before the UN, that would have cancelled the desirability of going back to the Security Council and saying, "Can we get a dispensing interpretation of the Geneva protocols of 1977, 1978? Can we at least get that authority, on behalf of ourselves, as somebody with an air force commission?" Many years ago it would have been a nice thing to know — if you were carrying out an aerial mission with authority on your side.

We cite this as the perfect example of an operation in compatibility with international law. The Cuban missile crisis was Kennedy's finest hour.

He had people saying to him at his National Security Council, "Go and bomb the hell out of the Cubans." His advisor told him that in international, as in military law, you escalate carefully through various degrees of power and if you don't have to bomb cities, if you don't have to bomb even military targets on the mainland, that's the way to go. And they did.

They applied what was called the quarantine. They took great care to allow Khruschev, the Russian leader, an ability to retreat without political loss of face. And there's the solution. It's a textbook case of how you handle power in a dangerous situation. I wish we could get into that sort of process ourselves and I think we will.

It has been said that the NATO Rambouillet positions on Kosovo were designed deliberately to spark Serb rejection. This comes out, actually, much more clearly in the counter-opinions, interpretations in the British House of Commons. The report of their House committee is excellent.

The Senate Report and the UN

I'm very much opposed to a non-elected Senate. It's a constitutional no-no. It's a constitutional oxymoron. But some of the Senate committee work is excellent, and their report raises all these issues and the problems they present. It seems to be suggesting that any future operation we're involved in, I suppose including any continuing military action, should be done in lock step with the United Nations. Would you get a veto in the United Nations? Would the Russians or Chinese veto?

But even if they do, on the basis of the Korean War the General Assembly is quite competent, by two-thirds majority, to confer legal authority. But in conferring legal authority it usually will offer suggestions and modifications. That's where the consensus comes in, the international consensus.

I think the government is aware of second thoughts on whether the Kosovo operation was handled as it should have been — in terms of the bypassing of the United Nations and in terms of the cardinal point of the Pearson–Paul Martin, Sr., foreign policy, that we act through the United Nations simply because you have got a reasonably representative world community there. You may not get unanimity, but if you can get two-thirds of the 185 on side, as I think you could, for example, in the present response to the September 11 terrorism, you're pretty sure that you're acting sensibly and the law is probably going to be on your side. If any dispensation, though, is to be given from existing norms, the very severe norms restricting aerial bombardment, for example, it should come from the Security Council. A military alliance like NATO can't give it. It can't hoist itself by its own bootstraps to a jurisdiction it doesn't have.

Choosing Politics

A peace-time army — unless you're in Austria or Hungary in the 19th century with those beautiful uniforms — it's not exactly an attractive profession, a sexy profession, is it, the military? That's part of the problem. It applies to Parliament too. You're certainly not getting the sort of interesting, bright people that you used to get, say, 30, 40 years ago.

I think it's really a career only suited to very young people, of whom the Bloc has a very considerable contingent, and the Conservatives. Bright kids who are into one or two terms. Or people who are basically retired, sufficiently independent to be able to say, "I'm not going to bother running again, I've done my bit." You're not getting interesting, dynamic people anymore because there's more competition in going into a multinational company. Probably if young people leave by the time they're 30, they'll never go back to politics, they've had enough. People these days, I think, are more interested in doing things, in making decisions, contributing to them, rather than going after particular offices. If you're worried about getting a pension, you're in the wrong profession. You should be out in business.

It's a wonderful experience. The whole point of going into politics, I think, is, "I've got some ideas, I'd like to put them into operation." Power is participation and decision making. It's not an office you hold. I spent a lot of my eight years in Parliament persuading American congressman and senators, and the State Department, to apply a benign rule to their customs and immigration laws that won't hold up people crossing from Windsor to Detroit each day to work, or from Vancouver to Bellingham. Be sensible and practical and they'll come aboard.

It's possible the new security measures after September 11 will change all that. I hope not, but the trend, once we signed the free trade agreement, is that sovereignty becomes ever more abstract. So you do what comes naturally. You make decisions across borders. You go directly to American senators. If you want a treaty on Pacific salmon, you don't go through the Foreign Affairs Department and the State Department and Mrs. Albright. You talk to the senator from Alaska who is the power in this issue, and you get your treaty.

And that's what happened.

MICHEL DRAPEAU

Colonel (Retired)
1994

After first serving as an infantryman in the militia, Michel Drapeau was commissioned in the Royal Canadian Army Service Corps. He was promoted to colonel in 1984 and served as director of the NDHQ Secretariat and as secretary of the Armed Forces Council. After 34 years in the military Drapeau took up a civilian appointment at NDHQ. A graduate in both civil and common law, he completed his articles of clerkship at the Federal Court of Appeal and was recently called to the bar in Ontario. He currently runs his own law practice.

I joined the Canadian army in 1961, and I served pretty well through every province in Canada, and abroad, including the United States, until I retired in 1992. My career was principally in the logistics branch, culminating in 1982 as a director of the National Defence Headquarters Secretariat, where I was working at the corporate centre for both the chief of the defence staff and the deputy minister. I was promoted to the rank of colonel in 1984 and retired in 1992.

When I left in 1992 I took up an appointment as an executive with the Public Service Commission and I became the director of corporate administration of National Defence Headquarters. A short 24 hours after my appointment I was appointed by the deputy minister as the Defence Department's acting director general of corporate management services — again working directly for the minister in a civilian capacity. So I had my feet in both waters, right in the middle of it, because I headed the bureaucracy, the senior management, at National Defence Headquarters.

The Need for Change
Changes have to be made. Either we run the system we now have with substantially less money, or we do away with a lot of stuff that we do now and get full value for the money.

We have a defence establishment, a large proportion of which runs National Defence Headquarters, which is staffed with 10,000 individuals, civilian and military. We have the navy, air force and army and they have headquarters. And they in turn create their own levels of headquarters. There is a proliferation of such organizations and the headquarters have become bloated over the years. These don't give you much bang for the buck.

We need to look at the number of executives that we have because these tend to perpetuate themselves. They tend to create more jobs and the ultimate value to the troops that we deploy in foreign postings is questionable.

There are many ways to start to cut, but not from the bottom. There, fundamentally, we have a good structure in place. Our combat units and their record are as good today as they were in 1945. I think you start from the top down, but before you start you've got to make sure that you have individuals in place who are willing to listen, willing to examine, willing to consider changes.

And today — and with the new technology and the amount of money the defence establishment has spent in the acquisition of such technologies — we'd better bring in some savings in return. Often we bring in new methods but we keep the old, not only in DND but within the bureaucracy itself.

So you pare down your headquarters and you pare down your system. You make sure that you constantly ask, "Do we need this? Are there smarter ways to do it."

Contracting Out

The buzzword that is being used within the Canadian bureaucracy now, and certainly within DND, is "contracting out." That's one way to do it. There are more services available to the Canadian military at a cheaper cost doing it outside than doing it inside. It's a way to look at the acquisitions programs. There is equipment that can be purchased off the shelf without having to go through an expensive and extensive renovation program or modifications before it can be adapted to military use — the purchase of trucks, for example.

Why don't we look around and purchase a truck that can meet the minimum requirements of the military and buy it off the shelf, as opposed to trying to manufacture one designed specifically for the Canadian military? Often we spend millions. The value that we get in return is, in my books at least, questionable.

There is value in creating a Canadian industrial base. Unquestionably this maintains our own sovereignty. It ensures that Canada can raise and can feed its Armed Forces. But there's a limit to it. There's a limit to how many dollars the Canadian public is prepared to invest in defence. If we don't spend wisely and we spend instead to create industry, something has got to give. And that's probably a defence capability because we're not going to have the bucks required for it. So I think you do this and you do it very cautiously. I for one do not believe that we should spend scarce defence dollars to keep defence industries afloat. There may be some exceptions there, but that should not be the aim or the objective of the defence dollar. Defence dollars should buy the maximum bang for the dollar that we can have.

The finance minister has a different agenda. He has to have a different agenda and it is wrong to expect a finance minister to be writing defence policy. It is wrong, also, to have to wait until February of every year before you find out how many dollars defence will be given and then decide what the defence priorities or policies are going be. Right now the finance minister is driving defence policy and defence priorities.

Look, I think the first thing DND has to do is make sure its own house is in order. It has a significant amount of our tax dollars and it has to optimize on this amount first and foremost. Now, admittedly the finance minister may take a little bit away from it or may not increase it to keep up with the economic increases, inflationary pressure and so on, but that's something else. Within the current budgetary envelope there's a lot that the Department of Defence can do to make sure that we get more bang for our dollar. And that creates a demand upon the leadership. It requires vision and leadership is vision. It requires hard choices. Again this needs leadership, and I don't think we have leadership at the level we want.

Leadership

Why is there a military leadership gap? A whole host of reasons: because we have leaders of a past era in place; because we don't have new blood coming in; because we have the clubbish type of attitude within the defence establishment, both the civilian and the military; because we don't encourage dissent, we don't encourage a broad spectrum of views on defence.

The number of people serving in uniform who actually contribute to the defence debate and actually contribute to the development of the defence policy is very, very small. In an organization the size of National Defence Headquarters these people ought to be far more involved in what we do. Year after year, defence policy is dictated by a very small band of individuals. And they tend to be the same, year in and year out. I think it's time for new blood. Right now it's the people who have left the uniform who speak out on defence.

Criticism is the kiss of death at DND. Criticism is not something that you want to encourage. I normally say that at National Defence Headquarters we don't like surprises. Even a good surprise is not welcome. Criticism is certainly not encouraged and is certainly less evident today in the written form or verbal form. I mean positive criticism, criticism that is not sought after. It's a missing link in the development of a sound defence policy.

Most of the reductions implemented since 1989 — when we had a number of bases close and the submarine program cancelled — tended to be at the lower echelons of the Forces. We haven't had a corresponding shaving up the pyramid, at the top level. Quite the reverse. The most recent defence estimates indicate that the defence establishment is going from nine lieutenant-generals to 10 lieutenant-generals. It says the number of senior executives on the civilian side of the department is going from 151 down to 150. Somehow this organization was left intact. This is difficult to explain while the rest of the Forces are being slimmed down considerably.

I recognize it's just human nature not to create any more difficulty for yourself than you need. The current climate of defence reduction is creating a lot of work for the Defence Department executives. But at the same time they have to bleed in the same way and proportionate to the rest of the Forces themselves. And that has not taken place, either in absolute numbers or in rank levels. We certainly don't need 10 or 11 three stars to run this establishment. If you were to cut this down in size, it'll have a ripple effect all the way down through the chain, and a salutary effect both on morale and efficiency.

It's exactly the same on the bureaucratic side. I suggest to you it's even worse because in the intervening three or four years we have had a significant increase at the assistant deputy minister level, one level down from deputy minister. We have recently created four more positions. Absurd. As we are reducing the size of the Armed Forces, we're increasing by four the number of assistants to the deputy minister. That's difficult to explain. Difficult to accept and difficult to stomach if you're one of these lower-ranking individuals who's received his pink slip and is out looking for a job.

NDHQ
National Defence Headquarters is just like a Siamese twin. At the very top you've got the chief of the defence staff and the deputy minister. They effectively form an entity. Together they run the department and the Canadian Forces. They each have their own distinct duties and so on and so forth, but they have to come together in order to run the department.

At the same time you have the assistant deputy minister. Assistant deputy ministers of personnel are military. A three-star lieutenant-general is responsible for both the Canadian Forces personnel and the defence establishment civilian employees. The position of the assistant deputy minister of finance, a civilian individual, is equivalent to the rank of a three-star lieutenant-general. He also provides financial support to both the civilian and the military side of the department. It's a fully integrated National Defence Headquarters.

When you get down into the field, at command level, the two entities are more distinct. It's easier to see them as separate. But at National Defence Headquarters they're one and the same.

I think overall the Canadian Forces lost in the exchange. They've lost because our senior military officers retire at 55. They tend to spend most of their career in the field or abroad. They don't have the contact, the day-to-day working knowledge of the bureaucracy of National Defence Headquarters. They tend to arrive in Ottawa late in their career, at high rank. All of a sudden they're dealing with a civilian executive with decades of experience, and in some cases decades in the same job. While the military comes and goes every second year with the posting cycle or as retirement approaches, the civilian executive stays there. So the power over the years has shifted to the civilian side, manifested by the deputy minister and also the assistant deputy ministers in their civilian capacities.

During the Gulf War I attended meetings on a daily basis, chaired by the minister with the then associate defence minister. Also at the table were an equal number of high civilian executives of the department and the military. It was difficult to discern who was totally responsible for one aspect or another, civilian or military. The advice given to the minister on the conduct of operation was given by the chief or through the chief of the defence staff. But the chief had to rely upon a civilian for logistic advice because the then associate deputy minister was a civilian. But the civilian himself had to rely on the military for advice about logistics.

The military advice given to the minister came from the chief of the defence staff. But on questions of policy and finance, that advice came from the civilian side of the department, the DM. It's not all black and white. There's a bit of this and bit of that. And the advice has to come together. The chief of the defence staff and the deputy minister were sitting alongside one another, nodding in agreement over the same point. And the minister was getting it in stereo from both the civilian and the military. That said, I think that at moments of real crisis the overwhelming influence is the deputy minister's.

I read recently about the difficulty that we had to deploy and sustain a force that we sent to Somalia, a force of 1,000 people. Compare this against what our fathers had to do from 1939 to 1945 or in the Korean conflict. Somalia may be a far, distant location, but we sent 1,000 personnel and we had problems in preparing them, in equipping them, because of the way National Defence Headquarters and the Canadian Forces headquarters are organized. Something has to be done. I believe we are going through a leadership crisis. It may be that we have been at peace for so long and we have suffered so many setbacks, financial and otherwise, that it's quite natural to have such a leadership crisis.

Taking a Stand

The thing that made me most uncomfortable in my career was what I saw as a certain politicization of the senior cadre of the military. In my last four years in government, DND would say to the government what the government wanted to hear, not what the military options were, what the military choices were, not what the nation ought to receive from the Canadian defence establishment in response to its investment of tax dollars.

When was the last time a senior Canadian bureaucrat resigned on principle about the way the defence establishment is being run? I haven't seen a single resignation. And I question why not.

We always seem to agree. We agree to deliver to the government precisely what the government wants. We let our elected officials make the decision. Within a democratic system the military man must speak, and speak in a more forceful way, because only he can present the range of options and provide military advice.

But there's a vacuum here. We are not presenting these options. You must tell the politician that if he or she wants to send troops on peacekeeping and peacemaking missions, then they need the right sort of armoured vehicle; they need the right sort of training; they need to have the numbers to deploy effectively to enforce the peace in a distant land. I don't see that. I see a very timid approach, with timid advice given to the government.

At my retirement mess dinner, in my final address I emphasized the point that ambition, which is not necessarily bad, must be tempered with the responsibilities of leadership. Indeed, when you look back on your career it's not really important what rank you have achieved. It's far more important to see what you've done.

And far more important also not to look back and say, "I regret not having taken a stand here. I regret not doing so when I should have." It's too late in your retirement year to say, "I'm sorry." From my perspective I left contented. It's my feeling that there are many, many senior officers who are leaving the Forces and who've missed an opportunity to speak out. Individuals don't like to speak out. They see their duty as keeping the peace within their organization, as opposed to a duty to better the organization by speaking out. You often hear U.S. military senior officers speak out and take a stand on issues to add their knowledge and their expertise to the public debate. Not here.

JOHN FRASER
2001 (Post-9/11)

John Fraser is the chairman of the Minister's Monitoring Committee on Change in the Department of National Defence and the Canadian Forces. This committee was established in the fall of 1997 to oversee the implementation of the large number of changes that various reports and commissions, including the Somalia inquiry, had advised the government that the Canadian Forces needed. Following the completion of their reports in 1998 and 1999, the Monitoring Committee's mandate was prolonged to provide the minister with specific advice on the process of restructuring the Land Force Reserve. Fraser has been elected to the House of Commons six times. He has served as minister of the environment, postmaster general and minister of fisheries. In 1986 he became Speaker of the House of Commons, a position he held until 1994. He is currently the honorary colonel of the Seaforth Highlanders of Canada.

I volunteered in Vancouver as a private soldier in the West Coast Signal Regiment a week after the Korean War started. I was just finishing my first year of university. Later on I transferred to the Canadian Officer

Training Corps and I was commissioned as a second lieutenant and was posted with the 27th Brigade, First Canadian Highland Battalion as an infantry platoon commander in Germany. The fighting in Korea stopped that summer. I came back to Canada, finished law school and stayed with the reserves until 1962.

I was elected to the House of Commons in 1972 and re-elected through to the election of 1993, in which I did not run. At that point I retired from political life. I was then appointed by Prime Minister Chrétien as Canadian ambassador for the environment. I did that for nearly five years and I was then asked to establish a fisheries conservation council on the Pacific Coast. In 1997 I was asked to join a committee to monitor the implementation of over 300 recommendations for change and reform in the Armed Forces.

In the spring of 1998 I became the chair of that committee, and more recently we were also asked to establish a smaller committee, headed by myself, to recommend a series of specific things to revitalize the Canadian Army Reserve. That has been done and we are monitoring the implementation of that. We also continue in a role of monitoring leadership, training and education in the Armed Forces. To the accusation or the lament that the government doesn't care, remember our committee was set up by the minister with the support of the Cabinet, so you have to be careful where you aim your fire.

The Monitoring Committee

Our mandate was specific. It covered a great deal of ground; there's no question about that. We were asked to weigh what units, what troops and which personnel, and what people in the chain of command would be in charge, and we were asked to recommend a way that the logistics, the transportation, the military-police side, the medical side, the liaison with other forces and civilians should all be determined.

We went to the former Yugoslavia and we went to different areas in Canada. We spent a lot of time saying, "Are you doing what you were told to do?" The short answer is, yes, they are. And there have been remarkable changes.

We gave very high marks to the Department of National Defence and the Armed Forces in implementing many of the substantive recommendations that make up the 330-plus recommendations approved by the government. Now, that was no mean feat because it was done at a time when the Armed Forces were trying to cope with reduced money, reduced numbers, old equipment and things that were wearing out. At the same time the Forces faced increased obligations, especially in foreign deployments.

But they weren't perfect and I don't think anyone would have expected that. We had continuing concerns in the area of education, training and leadership, and they had one failure, which was in the restructuring of the Army Reserve. A lot is being done in that regard now, but it's not finished.

We found that within the command structure and in the department there were certainly some who were open to change, but there were others who were not nearly as benevolently attuned to either the need for change or for bringing it about. That didn't surprise us. What I think is important is that a great deal was done, and I don't think as much would have been done if the minister had not had the good sense to set up an independent committee to monitor it.

This committee does not remove the policy direction from the minister to a civilian committee, but what it does do is establish, in a very acute way, a kind of oversight which frankly the Armed Forces is not used to, and neither is the department. In effect we became an oversight committee. It's true our function was to monitor the implementation of these recommendations. That's different from telling the minister how to run the army or the air force or the navy.

But it was clearly oversight because the committee had to inquire of a lot of people, "This is the recommendation. Exactly what are you doing?" We had to at times deal with people who came back and said, "Well, we've decided to do it a different way," or to not do that but do its equivalent, and we would have to say, "Wait a minute, we have to report to the public and there's the recommendation. That's what you have to do." Some people were quick to say we weren't blind to what was happening. We did do a lot of this and we didn't need to be nudged.

I think the fact that we were there made a difference, but I take nothing away from a lot of people who worked hard within the department and the Armed Forces to implement a great deal of what was given to them. And under difficult circumstances.

The Armed Forces and Parliament

It's fashionable, and has been now for some years, among the people who write columns and who set themselves up as experts from either a sociological point of view or a military point of view to say that the Armed Forces have to reflect the Canadian community. Of course they do. And there should be a relationship between the Armed Forces and the public. We could all say, yes, there should be. But where there absolutely has to be, in my view, an effective relationship is between the Armed Forces and the Parliament of Canada. And if you asked me point blank if I think this relationship has been effective in all the years since I was a young soldier, I would say no.

When popular magazines started to write stories about abuse in the Armed Forces, sexual abuse and physical abuse, started to write articles about the standard of living, the quality of life of our Armed Forces personnel, all of a sudden parliamentarians were alerted to this. The situation changed, money was spent on it and that is to be commended. One has to ask, though, why didn't it happen a long time before? Were the committees of the House of Commons and the Senate not hearing any of this? Were the Armed Forces not telling members of Parliament that this was a problem, that it was real, that it would affect the morale and fighting quality and fighting capability of our Armed Forces?

But you have to go farther than that. Surely to goodness one has to ask if the relationship between the Armed Forces and the Department of National Defence and Parliament has been working effectively. Where was Parliament in all this? Where were the members of Parliament in knowing enough about the military to even be critical in a patriotic way?

Provided the Armed Forces made the mandated changes, especially the army, because this was very much an army problem, we do not think we'll have another Somalia. Now, it's very important to point out when we go back and talk about that unhappy and inexcusable thing that it didn't happen because the Armed Forces didn't have a code of honour, of duty, of sacrifice, of discipline and self-discipline. That's not why it happened.

It happened because some people within the system abandoned that very code. That this all happened because somehow or other the Armed Forces didn't reflect the wonderful values of Canadian society is a lot of academic claptrap. The Armed Forces know exactly the difference between right and wrong and so do the officers and soldiers, and to pretend that they don't is nonsense. What happened is that through a breakdown in discipline and self-discipline and failures in the chain of command, those fundamental tenets that make the Armed Forces something honourable, something patriotic, something effective and something of which we could be proud were forgotten, or got put aside.

Post–Cold War

When I was elected in 1972 there were quite a number of members of Parliament in different parties who had actually had some military experience. By the time I left politics in 1993 there were very few members of Parliament with any background in the military. For a lot of the years in which the present members of Parliament grew up and took their place as adults, we were engaged in an awesome impasse with the Soviet Union. The consequences of any carelessness would have been devastating to humanity.

But this created a kind of stability and a kind of certainty and it enabled Canadians to luxuriate in the notion that we were peacekeepers. It was very convenient to forget that our troops in Europe weren't there just to keep the peace. They were there to fight an awful battle if the Soviets ever lost control of their senses and rolled westward.

After the so-called end of hostilities between the West and the Soviet Union, when the Berlin Wall came down, a lot of people thought we were going to get a great peace dividend. We could quit worrying, and that suited a lot of people who I think are terribly well intentioned, but they'd serve the community better in prayer than they would in proposing great defence policies.

But we suddenly came upon a very ugly reality. The world was not more peaceable. We faced a different kind of threat and it was breaking out all over and it was very ugly. It took awhile for the Canadian public to realize that what we were trying to do, for instance in the former Yugoslavia, wasn't just peacekeeping in the old sense, where both sides had politely agreed to let us in there.

We were in the middle of a savage business and we didn't have the authority from the United Nations to do what we should have been doing. We weren't backed up either because there was this lovely notion floating around that we were just there for peacekeeping. And wasn't everything going to be lovely and isn't that our great tradition? We had plenty of Canadians going around saying that it's not our job to have to fight or to fire our weapons orto ever have to go to war because we're a peacekeeping country.

What we've been asked to do since going into Yugoslavia in the early 1990s, almost consistently, is to participate in situations in which our troops had to be ready to fight if the occasion came upon them. They could not do what they were being asked to do unless they were trained in combat. Now, that does not mean that they shouldn't be trained in how to control crowds and how to defuse tension. You have to do all that. But you can't do any of that if you're not trained to be combat capable. This is what we have started to learn.

Now, the consequence of the so-called peace dividend and national finances is that we've run the Armed Forces down in terms of numbers and in terms of equipment. We can get more equipment, but right now, if we had to do something, we've got a real problem getting enough people.

Supporting the Armed Forces
There have been people in our country for as long as I can remember who are noted for two things. One is their anti-Americanism and the other is the determination not to support our Armed Forces, although they've said that the Americans will have to look after us anyway. It's a dichotomy that you can't resolve — either in logic, in common sense or in practical terms. But we have been collectively deluded by this foolish notion.

The fact of the matter is that to the degree that we abandon our share of the military obligations of the free alliance to which we belong, people are going to pay less and less attention to what our views are. There's a moral problem to this because ultimately most great issues are moral, and it's a very dangerous notion to espouse that somehow or other we don't have to do our share because somebody else is going to look after us anyway. Now, that's not the way I was raised and that, by the way, was not the view of most of our soldiers in the past. I don't think it's the view of most of our Armed Forces personnel today. But it's certainly the view of some people in this country.

Now, some of them are trapped by very idealistic notions about the beneficial effects of constantly talking about peace and other ways of persuasion. I think these people are misguided because they lead us into a position of neutrality, which leads us next into a position of helplessness and next leads us into a position of no influence at all.

But there's another side to this: the bean counters of the system. It has suited their purposes to take that propaganda and use it to persuade others that we don't need to spend any money on the Armed Forces and defence. This is a delusion that people can indulge in if, and only if, they don't have to face reality. They do a lot of counting, and you need bean counters. But you should never let them set policy. Many of them have used that sort of pacifist, do-gooder approach for a far more dangerous real purpose, and that is to cut down the resources that we need to have an effective military.

Parliamentary and Public Responsibility

The Armed Forces have a problem in a parliamentary system. How free are they to say what's really on their mind? This issue is going to become, at least in my view, much more the subject of debate. There is a notion that in a parliamentary system where you have a minister who's responsible for defence, those who are involved, both in the Department of National Defence and in the Armed Forces, are severely restricted by what they can say about the state of the Armed Forces.

And certainly, if saying something means that the chief of the defence staff is going to hold a press conference and blast the government and his or her minister, I would say, yes, you've gone beyond the pale. But when you're in front of a parliamentary committee, whether it's the House of Commons or the Senate, and you're asked direct questions, then there is an obligation not to fudge. That's a very important obligation to keep in mind because if members of Parliament are told, not lies, but only half the truth, they are not going to be in a position to do their duty as elected members from this country.

When the military and the Department of National Defence go in front of a parliamentary committee, it's very important that they give enough facts to the members of Parliament so that they can decide for themselves what ought to be done. Now, the Defence Department officials and the Armed Forces services personnel do not have to say what the policy ought to be, but they ought to tell people what the situation is. In my view, both as a lawyer and as a former member of the House of Commons, doing that isn't crossing any forbidden boundary at all. If the presentations to a parliamentary committee are written by spin-doctors to make sure that nobody asks a specific question, or if the submissions are, "Don't worry, everything is just perfect," then you're not telling the members of Parliament what they need to know.

Some MPs think that because it's defence, because it's the Armed Forces, they don't have to ask the same kinds of questions that they would cheerfully ask of almost any other department. But that's what the whole tradition of Parliament has been about. It's what the Estimates were all about. Because you didn't get supply if the departments could not persuade the House of Commons that that money was needed and it was going to be well spent. It's fundamental. I don't accept the argument that our parliamentary system makes it impossible for members of Parliament, members of the Senate and the committees to elicit the information they need. They may not be getting all the information they need, but that's not because they can't get it.

We live in a parliamentary system where the majority rules. Governments have been known sometimes not to give resources to committees that are going to ask embarrassing questions. That's a political difference of view, a difference that members of Parliament have got to argue with, and they've got to involve the public. If it were shown by enough members speaking up that they didn't have the resources to do the job, things would change.

But fundamental to all of this is that there has got to be enough exact and clear information about the status and the shape of the Armed Forces so that members of Parliament can understand what it is they're dealing with. It doesn't stop with the members of Parliament. It's also got to go to the public.

I would like to think our Canadian military is a repository of our best values. But I am convinced that momentary fashions are not the enduring values. If they don't have real values, our soldiers will be of very little use to us when we're in real trouble, and the rest of the citizenry has to depend on these particular people to defend us, to keep us safe, to put their lives at risk. Ultimately that's what it's all about and it's very important that everybody understands. You can't have a military that can do its duty if it doesn't have values.

The other side of this is that people must understand that the military's got to be supported because if we have no military, we are defenceless. Somebody else can perhaps look after us up to a point, but what we should be doing for ourselves is not being done. Without a military we can't meet our obligations to our allies. If we can't do that, we can't meet the obligations that many people who don't support the military believe we have to humanity. You can't do that when the chips are down without a military that knows how to fight and has got the kind of values that you know we can depend on.

There has been a sense that the Canadian public was not backing up our Armed Forces personnel. In some of the cases where people were sick or injured there was the suggestion, and sometimes the allegation, that they weren't properly looked after. That people coming back from overseas duty where they faced danger were not being cared for, were being dismissed back into public life without support. All of these things have happened and they're wrong. But one of the reasons they happened is because nobody knew about it. Now, one can ask, "Why didn't the senior leadership in the Armed Forces go public?"

They probably didn't want to hold a press conference. But as it seeped out that we had a problem, not only did the members of Parliament pay attention and make sweeping recommendations, but the public said, "What have we been doing? How could we be neglecting these brave people? They're prepared to put their lives on the line, that's the unlimited liability that goes with their enrollment in the Armed Forces. How could we have let this happen?" Then of course the bean counters realized the jig was up. And quite extraordinarily, the bean counters found money to start to do something about it.

It's not much comfort to anybody that our committee has not been hesitant about insisting that the Armed Forces be given the resources to do what needs to be done. They need to have a mobilization plan so we know what has to be done in a crisis. Sitting idly back in a kind of glib comfort because some people think that we would have years of warning before anything might happen to us has really got to stop.

We didn't have years of warning before the Gulf War. We didn't have years of warning before the worst aspects of the former Yugoslavia. We didn't have years of warning in East Timor. We didn't have years of warning in Africa. And while some people warned that sooner or later some terrible terrorist act was going to take place in North America, that wouldn't have fit into the so-called warning schedules that occupied the time of those who predicted we'd have years and years of warning before anything happened.

What happened in New York and in Washington is not beyond the norm of military intelligence to expect. It isn't beyond the imagination of the ordinary Canadian either. And the greatest mistake would be for some of these people, well intentioned though they may be, to delude themselves again by saying, "That's an American problem, not ours." Well, it most definitely is ours.

JOEL SOKOLSKY

1994

Joel Sokolsky teaches in the War Studies Programme at the Royal Military College in Kingston. Professor Sokolsky is a graduate of Harvard University and is an expert on Canadian and American foreign and defence policy, as well as international security trends. He has appeared as a witness before various parliamentary committees and participated in a number of ministerial defence reviews. He is the author of numerous articles and several books dealing with the Canada–United States defence relationship.

In 1985 Joseph Jockel and I wrote *Canada and Collective Security: Odd Man Out*. We looked at Canada's military posture, highlighting areas where we felt we had made commitments we couldn't fulfill. We also criticized the approach to defence policy, which seemed to view military commitments as a means of buying political influence abroad.

We suggested a military posture which was radical at the time; it called for withdrawal of troops from Germany, a concentration on the northern flank in order that the Canadian Forces would be militarily more useful to the NATO alliance. We also commented on the high moral tone that Canada sometimes took on security issues. As one U.S. diplomat put it, Canada seemed to be the stern daughter of the voice of God on disarmament questions. We tend not to view our activities abroad in terms of our national self-interest. We tend not to explain it that way. Particularly on military security matters.

This is in contrast to trade issues, where we know clearly what we want. We know we want to get our pork bellies and shakes and shingles into the United States. We want to sell them to make money. On national security issues we tend to adopt a broad tone which equates our well-being with global stability. That's very altruistic because we're doing this for the good of the world not for Canada, and in many cases what we do benefits the world.

The legacy of the cold war, however, is that we continue to identify our national security issues with regional conflicts around the world which really are of no direct relation to our physical security or our economic well-being. In the cold war, because any conflict anywhere in the world might touch off a superpower confrontation leading to annihilation, we were generally concerned. What I've been arguing now is that the link has been broken. You can have conflict in central Europe or in Southeast Asia that doesn't necessarily threaten Canadian economic or physical well-being.

Canadian Commitments
In the context of the cold war, what the NATO alliance was looking for were commitments of forces as political symbols for allied unity. And the United States accepted this and our allies knew full well what our capabilities were. I think we also made the commitments on the understanding that should war come, none of this would make a difference: we would immediately go to a nuclear confrontation. So we never expected to actually be called on and in the interim we were paying for our seat at the table. In that context it made eminent political sense. In the case of war it would not have made strategic sense.

But our political leaders knew full well what they were doing: you make a commitment when you don't always have the forces to back it up. However, that's not what you're interested in. You're interested in meeting the NATO quota for that year. You're interested in showing the alliance you're doing something. For our principal ally, the United States, compared to the problems it had with other allies, the fact that Canada didn't fulfill its commitments was of very little significance. The fact that Canada made a commitment was politically important and I think that's all the Americans were looking for. In my view it bought us maximum international participation at a time when a declining percentage of national wealth was being directed toward defence. It may have cost us some credibility, but from the standpoint of Canada's political leaders that wasn't as important as making the commitment.

As far as the capabilities go, you have to be very careful. We were buying world-class equipment. We just weren't buying enough of it. The CF-18, the Leopard tank, the Aurora aircraft and these new frigates, which were bought for NATO, are world-class weapons. Our training and the capability of our Forces are definitely of international standing, but we did not have enough if the balloon had gone up. By the end of the cold war we had too many commitments, not enough troops. We continued to make commitments abroad for which we lacked adequate resources. The irony is that Canada is more engaged globally today than it was during the cold war.

The principal problem is that peacekeeping is starting to look a lot like war. It falls heaviest on the army, the branch of the service least able to sustain itself because it has not been given the type of equipment it needs for these roles. There's a more fundamental problem, which is that we continue to identify our national self-interest with broad global stability. That makes every conflict everywhere of interest to Canada and we feel we have to send troops there if the UN calls. These regional conflicts do not affect us directly. We have a range of options. When we do intervene, as we have in Bosnia or Rwanda, the reality is this is primarily for humanitarian reasons. We're there to save lives.

We are not now in a position to support an overseas expeditionary force which would allow us to participate on the ground in something like the Gulf War. My solution is that we don't participate. If we can offer ships, let's offer ships. If we can offer planes or logistics, let's offer that. But let's not go out and buy ourselves an expeditionary army simply because we want to participate in these conflicts. Let's make a decision now that we're not going to maintain that capability because the reality is, we can't afford it.

In the case of the Gulf War we did not have a direct interest. We sent forces commensurate with our interest and with our capabilities. I think it's erroneous to believe that if we were to double our ground forces or send greater forces, our allies would give us a greater role in the diplomacy. Look at Haiti. The Americans have gone in, we are supplying. We will supply forces from the RCMP and some military police to train the Haitian police forces. That's a useful function. We shouldn't be ashamed of it. If they don't like it at the Pentagon, then we don't have to go. It's really not in our interest to go in the first place.

Confronting a Crisis

Let's say Saddam Hussein starts moving this week: we could deploy a ship, we could send aircraft. We will not be able, given fiscal realities, to deploy the kind of forces that will make our allies stand up and cheer. At the same time we have deployed useful forces. I think you'd have to take a look at the performance of the Canadian navy in the Persian Gulf to see where a small group, highly professional, performed a valuable role. That may be all we can do. We're not the only country in this position. We're not the only country that doesn't send large ground forces into these foreign excursions.

If we were to restrict Canadian defence interests to North America and to a modest traditional peacekeeping role where there's no risk of high-intensity combat, we would have more than enough Canadian Forces personnel today. The impetus to get Canadians on the ground because if we don't we might look bad in front of our allies is Dieppe-type thinking. Our troops should only go in where they can be militarily useful and where there is a good chance of success. But simply to have Canadian soldiers on the ground because we don't want to be laughed at by our allies is a wrong way to approach it. We make the contributions we can, given the fiscal and other constraints on the country. Had we deployed the tank unit in Germany to the Persian Gulf in the fall of 1990, I have no doubt it would have performed well. But I also have no doubt that it wouldn't have given Canada one more iota of influence over the political direction of that war. That's an illusion we have to avoid.

In the present international environment there's a whole range of things Canada can do and prepare for. Given fiscal realities, defence policy choices are going to have to be made. In particular what I'd like to see the parliamentary committee do is not talk in broad terms but talk in terms of actual capabilities. I would rather have the debate, not about broad issues, but about hard equipment needs. What are you going to buy the army to do its peacekeeping? What does it say it needs? Can you afford to buy that and keep flying CF-18s and sending ships abroad? Those are the questions. It's more important perhaps to have the minister of finance before the committee and the president of the Treasury Board than the minister of national defence or the chief of the defence staff.

It reflects the reality that defence, whether the military and academic strategists like it or not, is a low item on the national agenda. It's below health care. It's below welfare reform. It's below federal-provincial relations. Canada is not directly threatened by anybody. Its military contributions are meant to support its diplomacy, so you can't go out and say, "The sky is falling. Unless we buy this helicopter our entire nation is going to be at risk." The Americans can go to their Congress and say, "We are the world leaders and our security depends on our armed force. We need this."

It becomes very difficult for a Canadian politician to stand up and say, "You can have this helicopter, but you can't have this daycare centre. You can buy this tank but, I'm sorry, we're going to close hospitals in Alberta." Now, I support defence policy but reality in foreign policy begins at home, and it's really a futile debate to rail against this notion that non-defence issues have primacy.

The Reluctant Ally
During the cold war we very often sugar-coated what we were doing on defence policy. When Pierre Trudeau launched his peace initiative, Canada in allied councils was saying yes, yes, yes to the very weapons, the cruise and the Pershing, which were causing the problem for the Soviets.

We tended to sell ourselves as a reluctant ally, when we were a very staunch ally in terms of support for broad allied policies. The end of the cold war has left us in a position where we have to define our national security interest very much on our own, and that's been difficult because as it turns out we haven't had any national security threats. There's a role for the Armed Forces in supporting our diplomacy, in supporting our UN activities, in providing a hedge against uncertainty. The problem is you can't oversell it.

I'd like to see the government simply say, "We're trying to support the UN in humanitarian efforts on their own merits. We're not trying to save the world from the Saddam Husseins. We're not trying to spread democracy around the world. We're not going to tell you that the Soviet Bear's never going to rise again. But all we can do, given the fiscal constraints, is maintain a capability."

We need to maintain a capability because the world may turn against us at some point. And if you're going to maintain the Armed Forces, the Armed Forces must prepare and train for war. A war-trained, combat-trained soldier is the best peacekeeper you can send. It's the duty of the Armed Forces to train for war. When push came to shove in the 20th century, we went to war and we did well.

The danger comes — and we keep coming back to this — when for political reasons our government dispatches troops abroad that are ill prepared. That's something we have to watch out for.

DAVID BERCUSON

2001 (Post-9/11)

*D*r. *Bercuson has published widely in academic and popular publications specializing in modern Canadian politics, Canadian defence and foreign policy and military history. Since January 1997 he has been the director of the Centre for Military and Strategic Studies at the University of Calgary. From January to April 1997 he was special advisor to the minister of national defence on the future of the Canadian Forces, and in October 1997 was appointed to the Minister's Monitoring Committee on Change in the Department of National Defence and the Canadian Forces. He has written, co-authored or edited over 25 books, including* Significant Incident: Canada's Army, the Airborne and the Murder in Somalia. *His latest book is* Bismarck!, *co-authored with Dr. Holger Herwig*

There are really two different kinds of people in the Canadian military. I found that there were those who had grown into military bureaucrats, who were mostly found at the high command — they were very political. And then there were the people out in the field who actually did the work. I'm not sure where I divide the one from the other. Maybe it would be a division on the basis of rank; maybe it would be a division on the basis of attitude. It seemed to me that there was a disconnect between them and what I heard when I interviewed real soldiers at the bases — both those serving and those who had been in the Airborne Regiment prior to my starting on the book — and those at the top. I really found very, very big divisions between them.

I think that in armies in peacetime there is always a tendency to downplay warrior spirit and to reward those who are good at playing the bureaucratic and the political game. It's natural and it's understandable. It's frustrating as hell to a military historian, but the facts are that the most important thing that the high command can do in peacetime is to fight for a larger share of the budget. The more political you are and the better you are at playing the bureaucratic game, the better the chance that you are going to succeed. When the peacetime militaries go to war you find an almost complete replacement of the middle, if not the high, command with people who are not necessarily good at balancing the books and fighting for training dollars, but who know how to lead men in combat.

The most significant problem with peace-time armies is when they are faced with challenges that come unannounced, unplanned, usually as total surprises. Who would have ever known at the beginning of June 1950 that four months later there would be a shooting war in Korea of significant proportions? Who would have thought on September 10, 2001, that we would be facing the tragedy that we faced the day after? The only war that I know of where people really had some kind of a warning was the Second World War. But it usually doesn't work that way. Usually these things just sneak up and grab you. The problem with peace-time militaries, especially today, is that they're slow to adapt and they're slow to change.

On the one hand you want militaries that are adaptable, that are capable of reacting quickly to what we call "come as you are" wars. On the other hand, when you do get those kinds of militaries, they seem to be a threat to the civil authority during peacetime because they're too active, they're too bellicose, they're too belligerent. The more military the military is, the less they get along with the civil authority and vice versa. But the other way around leads to ineffectiveness.

Reality Now

I think now we are developing a more flexible, more adaptable officer corps. But I don't see that flexibility and that adaptability when I look back to 1990. The major problem throughout the 1990s was that everything kept changing and it seemed every year there was a new challenge, there was a new mission that was different than the last mission. Peacekeeping changed dramatically and rapidly and the officer corps could not keep up. To me the essence of the Canadian military in the 1990s was not being able to stay ahead of the curve, not even knowing where the curve was half the time.

In my mind the question was always, where does the political authority assume responsibility for military operations? They certainly do at the highest policy levels in a country where the military does, or is supposed to do, what the politicians tell them to do. Is it the job of politicians to prepare for changes in the international military environment, or is that the job of the professional military? Or is it the job of both of them? In this country, historically, in peacetime we've had militaries that have usually not kept up, that have not been able to keep up, have not trained or prepared to keep up with changes in the international military environment. We've had political leaders who were not interested in the international military environment, who've had their own take on the way things were going and basically were going to tell the military what to do, whether the military were capable of carrying out the missions or not. As far as I am concerned, the problems that we had in the 1990s were generated both in the Cabinet and at National Defence Headquarters.

It's really interesting how the government seemed to ignore most of what came out of the Somalia inquiry when they decided to go into Zaire. What the evidence was saying loudly and clearly during the Somalia inquiry was, "You didn't have a formation that was prepared for the mission; you didn't properly prepare the formation for the mission. The mission wasn't clear; the people you were sending to do the mission were not clear themselves as to exactly what it was they were supposed to be doing." Very shortly afterward they were about to inject a force into a similar sort of a situation in a different part of Africa. Would that happen today? It's hard to say.

When you learn the lesson, and in effect the Somalia commission of inquiry was a lessons-learned exercise, the lessons learned always apply to the last campaign. The real lesson that needs to be learned is flexibility and adaptability. Did the military learn flexibility and adaptability? Did the government learn flexibility and adaptability? I think there is often cause to doubt whether they did.

There's always a disconnect between the chief of the defence staff and the people that advise the CDS, and to a certain extent the force commanders are the guys that do the lessons learned. It's like somewhere out in the Gulf of St. Lawrence there's a line where the saltwater ends and the clear water begins, but you can never really show where that line is on any particular day. Where does the line between military advice and political action, or political reaction, end or begin?

There was the perfect example of the chief of the defence staff acting as a government cheerleader. I'm not getting personal about that particular CDS. I think it's true of every CDS. I think it's inherent in the position of the CDS that the CDS is going to say, "Everything's OK, nothing's wrong, we're doing it all correctly and we're always going to be able to do more with less. We're going to be more force-effective, even if we're going to be smaller, because we're going to have better this and better that." That's his job. That's what he's there to do. He's really there as the transmission belt between the political decision making and the military. If the CDS does not particularly care to keep his job, of course he can always come back from a place like Zaire and say, "I'm sorry, Minister," or "I'm sorry, CBC," or "I'm sorry Canadian public, there's just no way we're going to do this," despite the fact that he knows the minister wants it done. Well then, OK, take your pension and go. Some chiefs have done that in the past. But it's not instinctive for anybody to do a self-sacrifice routine in the middle of a burgeoning military career. So I don't think we should expect those kinds of things from chiefs of the defence staff.

There's a certain way of thinking that develops among high-ranking soldiers of the Canadian military. I think it goes like this: "This is not a perfect world. I can resign. I know that much of what I'm saying, or some of what I'm saying, is absolutely incorrect — or I'm hiding the facts or I'm not being forthcoming. I know this government is not doing everything that it says it's doing. I know it's a bad thing that we're waiting so long for helicopters. But if I leave, maybe somebody who takes my place will do a worse job than I will. At least I think of myself as someone who is a protector of the nation's military interests; I believe in myself and I believe in the military and therefore I'm going to stay and I'm going to fight for the best deal I can in this imperfect world." That's something that I can understand. I think very often that's what's going on in the minds of these people, vice-chiefs and deputy chiefs and even chiefs of the defence staff. They have no friends out there. They are responsible directly to the government.

Parliament plays no role whatsoever of any consequence in the making of defence policy. The people's elected representatives take no proprietary interest, no real proprietary interest, in the Armed Forces. So these guys at the top are alone with the ministers and it's "my way or the highway," and they know that. And I guess sometimes they think, well, I'm better to stay onboard and try to guide this ship through this fight than I am to leave.

I think the parliamentarians don't know the right questions to ask half the time. I think they don't have correct information on the basis of which they can ask questions. It's a very big difference between the system of government we have here and the one we're always comparing ourselves to south of the border, where Congress votes the money for the armed forces; where Congress, since the beginning of the Republic, always took a proprietary interest in the welfare of the individual men and women of the armed forces; where in a sense there are two authorities to which the armed forces are responsible, the executive branch and the congressional branch.

That is not the case here. SCONDVA (the Standing Committee on National Defence and Veterans Affairs) cannot summon anybody who doesn't want to go, and when SCONDVA does summon them, they're not appearing in the same way that they would be appearing before, let's say, the Committee on Armed Services of the American Senate. There's a very, very big difference. So I don't think the CDS lies to Parliament. I just think that the CDS answers only that which the CDS chooses to answer, which reflects the best light on the Armed Forces. Because if the CDS doesn't do that, the minister may say, "Hey, Joe, what the hell are you doing out there, putting this government in a bad light. Who do you work for anyway?" That's just the way it is.

The only way that we will ever achieve some degree of continuing military effectiveness is if the Standing Committee on National Defence and

Veterans Affairs or some similar committee of the House of Commons, or of the House and the Senate, were to somehow gain more authority.

Now, you can gain authority by getting more authority through the law. You can actually change the law. I see that as problematic. I don't think any government is really going to give a committee of Parliament independent control, but I do think that SCONDVA has a great deal of moral authority. But they need to ask the right questions. The standing committee, or whatever passes for it, needs to have a much larger staff. I think they should be working with the auditor general.

You know, the auditor general's reports have been tremendous wells of information about what's really going on in the military over the last five, six, seven years. And even the auditor general has a very small staff compared, for example, to the General Accounting Office in the United States, which oversees the work, the operations and the training of the armed forces very, very closely because the armed forces in the United States take up so much of the federal budget. If we had the auditor general working more effectively with a larger budget and a larger staff, working in co-operation with SCONDVA, you would get situations where they would know what questions to ask. They would know when the answers that they were getting were somewhat evasive and not necessarily revealing the truth. There's a lot of public relations and public opinion value there. There's a free press in this country. There's an opposition that can take information from SCONDVA hearings and use it. So there are ways of doing this without actually changing the Constitution.

Combat Capability
Combat capability is like beauty: it's in the eye of the beholder. What does combat capability mean? Does it mean that you've got soldiers that can fire bullets? Does it mean the navy has better equipment than it did 10 years ago? Does it mean the air force does this or does that? I don't know what combat capability means in anything other than in abstract terms. If we were to say, does the army have the formations that it had 10 years ago? Does it have a level of equipment that it had 10 years ago? Is it trained better or not so well as it was 10 years ago? Those are the kinds of questions that I think are answerable, but combat capability I think is just too fuzzy.

Today, in the fall of 2001, it's patently obvious that we cannot live up to the commitments that we made in the 1994 white paper. The reason is simply that we have allowed the military to run down, especially where numbers are concerned. The army does have some better kick than it had 10 years ago, but the army doesn't have the manpower, doesn't have the person power. We are in my opinion wasting a virtual brigade on the Bosnian mission, but we are trapped into the Bosnian mission because it's the only thing that we do of any consequence for NATO, and our NATO allies would be very upset if we decided that we were leaving Bosnia. But if we stay, there is no way that we can make a commitment of a brigade to send overseas anytime within virtually a year. We've just allowed the numbers to run down. We've allowed them to run down because we have taken money out of the budget, of course, but we have also seen the creeping in of questions like, what is our mission exactly? What are we here for? What sort of a career is there? Where is the future for anyone who wants to become a soldier in this country? That's also been a big part of it.

This government and a lot of governments that we've had back to the Trudeau era don't like to think of militaries as organizations that exist primarily to kill people and destroy things. But you can't get around that fact. The problem is, when you want to attract soldiers, you want to attract young men and, to a certain extent today, women who want to be warriors; who are not going into the military to become accountants. You've got to sell the military as an organization that is effective and trained and prepared to fight wars.

Look at this whole silly debate that we had for a few weeks after September 11 about whether or not we were engaged in a "war on terrorism." What does the word "war" mean? We can't use the word war — wars are nasty, wars are bad. Well, they are but occasionally they're necessary, as in September of 1939. Yet you've got this view, and it's primarily because the government orchestrates the view of the military, and the government doesn't want to emphasize war because if it does, it has to put more money into the military. So it de-emphasizes war, it talks about peacekeeping, peace support. The Canadian Armed Forces, as the prime minister said, are looked on as the international Boy Scouts. Then how do you sell the military to the folks out there who want a career that is physically challenging and, yes, maybe they'll see action? It's a mixed message and they know that.

The soldiers don't see themselves as civil servants in uniform. I think that's one of the great sources of disillusion in the military, especially in the ranks. I think that includes field level officers too. But then you get back into that mindset. When you're down in National Defence Headquarters, what are you there for? You're there for a lot of different reasons but one of the most important is to give your minister the information that he needs to fight with his Cabinet colleagues to get a larger share of the budget. You're there to make sure that the influence of the military is as expansive as possible in the making of political decisions. You're not there to fight anybody, that's the problem. There's a disconnect between what militaries do at the highest levels of civil societies in times of peace and what soldiers join the military for.

Understanding the Military
This phenomenon of what we use militaries for is particularly apparent in smaller countries like Canada. In this country — unlike the Europeans, who lived in the shadow of the Soviet Union for the entire period of the cold war — we've always been a little unsure of what our military was for, except during wartime. Canadians never really understood that the military in this country is our connection to the larger world in a very real and concrete sense. It's simply the price we pay for being a part of an international system that holds great value for us and pays great dividends for us. You can't expect to enjoy the benefits of that system without being prepared to put something on the table. That's what the military's always been for in this country.

Hitler was not coming over here with a rowboat in 1939 to conquer Canada. But there was no doubt in the minds of the people of this country when they were in the Second World War that there was an international system out there that was being challenged in a very real and terrible way, and that we were part of that system and had to respond along with our allies. We felt the same way in Korea. We're feeling the same way now, apparently, with this war on terrorism after 9/11. But then when the wars are over and all of that goes away, Canadians, like people in most democracies, think, OK, now we don't need to do that anymore. So we just let it fall apart. That is what we have done historically.

In a country like the United States they're very aware that they have global interests. They're very aware, through history but also through more current experience, that they sometimes need to resort to organized violence to either achieve their objectives or to defend their interests. There is more of a tendency to think of the military as what it really is, which is an organized force to pursue the state's violent interests, and less of a tendency to think of the military as a vehicle of experimentation or a way of keeping people at work.

In this country, because we don't think of ourselves as having global interests or we don't think of ourselves as needing to resort to violence in order to defend our interests or to project our interests, we tend to think of the military as a place where we're going to do social experimentation with a force that we're going to use to help people fight floods and ice storms. We think of defence contracting as a way to spread the wealth around. So we don't get the best helicopter but we get the best industrial offset package. That's more important than getting the best helicopter or the best fighter plane, or whatever the case may be. It's a lot easier to slip into that frame of mind in a country such as Canada where your enemies are not apparent and where you don't want to face the fact that, as Leon Trotsky said, "You may not be interested in war, but war is interested in you." Eventually it's going to grab you when you least expect it.

Canadian governments have known, pretty well since the end of World War II, that to a certain extent they do have to make military commitments. But I think they're torn in two ways. The first way is to always try to make the least military commitment that you can. Always budget for the cheapest threat. I think they've been doing that constantly for the last 50 years. Instead of preparing our soldiers for war, instead of withholding our soldiers from operations until there are actual combat operations that we can put them into, let's use them wherever we can. Let's put, say, 100 in the Golan Heights, or 30 in the Sinai Peninsula, package them out in small penny packets. This way we get broad representation, we can tell people that we've got peacekeepers in 26 countries all at once. That's been the way the governments have gone, more or less. They know you need to have some military commitment out there. You've got to show your allies to a certain degree that you're prepared to take up duties and responsibilities.

In any future commitment our military is going to be able to react well — and what I mean by "well" is by being there with the most and the best at the right time and the right place — only if the government

David Bercuson

continues year after year to act on the presumption that you need to
have a military force that is capable of reacting in a military situation for
an event that you cannot anticipate. That's a problem in a democracy
because you have to keep telling the voters that we've got to put money
into this new piece of kit, and that the Forces have got to reorganize, that
we've got to train and have more people ready. And they say, "For what?"
You say, "For the unexpected." And they say, " Sorry, we'd rather have
that money go to health care." So if you don't have the leadership and
you don't accept as a matter of principle that your country is going to
participate to the best of its ability whenever it is challenged internationally, or whenever its allies are challenged internationally, then you
cannot sustain that effort.

Unification

I think that the unification of the Armed Forces in the 1960s became the
great scapegoat for the high command of the Canadian military, so that
virtually anything that went wrong after that they could blame on unification, blame it on the Grits, blame it on the creation of National
Defence Headquarters, which was not Hellyer's doing. Blame it on
everybody but themselves. I don't think Hellyer was that far off base.
The problem with unification as we carried it out in this country was
that we did not give the Armed Forces any clear direction beyond the
rather silly and superficial directions that they should all wear the same
uniforms and have the same ranks and all lose their identification and
their identity in one big green mass. The problem with unification as we
carried it out is that it was a political act and it was not an act that was
designed to bring out the best and the most efficient in the military as a
fighting force.

But there was no attempt to integrate the Armed Forces beyond very
superficial measures, such as the uniforms. Did we attempt to create a
fighting force that would integrate and operate jointly — army, navy, air
force? No, we did not, and we do not have it today. I don't think there was
anything wrong with the concept of unification. I think there were a lot of
things wrong with the way it was introduced and I think today, in the fall
of 2001, we are seeing the unravelling of unification very, very rapidly.

Civilianization

The acts of mayhem that were carried out with the creation of NDHQ,
were acts of mayhem precisely because they were designed almost

313

exclusively as measures to make sure that the civil authority had total control over budgeting processes. Now, of course, everything contributes to budgeting processes, from how you let your defence contracts, to how you train people, to how you educate them and how you recruit. They let the budgetary process drive the creation of National Defence Headquarters. They did not create NDHQ as a joint operational command. It wasn't intended to achieve that. All it did was create a great sort of single administrative mass for taking care of budget issues and making sure that the civilians had their thumbs on the military in that regard. This is not a bad thing, but it didn't achieve anything other than just creating an administrative mess in Ottawa.

The question of who controls the military and the lack of political direction is an interesting one because sometimes it's the civil servants, and sometimes it's the high command who act like civil servants. In the last eight years or so I think we've gone through two different phases with regard to the civil service side.

We had a period in time in which the civil service was headed by a very powerful personality, the deputy minister of national defence, who really in a sense thought or acted as if his job was very much that of a senior commander, and not that of a senior bureaucrat and policy advisor to the minister. And the civil service side became very active in giving direction to the military side, and it got to the point where military decisions were being participated in, and military advice was being given, as much by the civil authority as it was by the military. It was very, very difficult for the government to separate out what the real soldiers, the professional soldiers, think of this as opposed to what the civil servants think about this. That's a very bad thing because the civil service side needs to be focused almost exclusively on the issue of budgetary control. That's what they're there for. The military's supposed to propose to the government and the government is supposed to then get the advice of the civil authority. What is this going to cost? Is it effective? Does it fit in line with the other policies of the government? Then the government decides to what extent it wants to meet the recommendations of the military side. Well, that was not happening.

That has changed to a certain extent over the last several years. We've had deputy ministers who have been much less intrusive in the policy-making process in the Department of National Defence, but we still have not had the direction that we need from the government, so we've had the soldiers acting as civil servants. And you've had a whole bunch of studies that have been published recently by NDHQ, by the CDS, for example, or for the signature of the CDS, which were internally generated documents that are as much documents of policy as they are documents of military advice.

I think there's a real dilemma for people who serve at the higher levels at NDHQ, and that is, if we don't begin to function as bureaucrats, how do we get the government to listen to us? The government seems to rely heavily on the advice of the bureaucracy. We're soldiers, we're strange people here. We're unlike any other people who are paid by the government, with the possible exception of the RCMP. But we're not here to give the government policy advice on spending issues, for example, or on how to institute this or that or the other thing, or to generate new policy ideas. We're here to fight the government's wars for it and give the government the best advice we can on how it ought to do that. That's something the government may not be interested in, so how do we get our influence? How do we maximize our influence? And sometimes the answer is, we need to act pretty much like bureaucrats.

There's another thing, too, that has invariably been the case in militaries, at war or at peace. The higher you go, the more politicized they become. It's especially true in democracies and it's not a bad thing because it means that at the very top of the ranks there's not a lot that separates the deputy minister from the chief of the defence staff in terms of their attitude toward civil authority. If you go to Latin America, for example, and they find out that you're the minister of national defence who used to be mayor of Canada's largest city, they ask, "How can you have an MND like that? He's got to be a general, surely." And one of the strengths of our system is that he's not a general. But it's also one of the weaknesses.

The Old Army and the New Army
I'm not enamoured of the old army. I think the old army was an army that was born of World War II and of the Korean War, and it did the job that it needed to do in World War II and in Korea. But there were certain attitudes that were at work in the old army. It was an army that just shuddered at the thought of independent thinking and strategic-level operations.

Somalia in a sense occurred during a time of transition between the old army and the new army. What I mean by the "new army" is what we are trying to develop today, in fits and starts because of budgetary problems, but we've got a better system of selection, better training, better education, the rules are much more clearly laid out for operations such as Somalia than they were before.

Somalia came in the middle of the transition. You had in Somalia a particular formation, although I think it was quite representative of the army as a whole, in which the old standards of discipline had broken down but new standards of discipline had not been put into place. In the old army you did something because you were told to do it. In the new army you are not only told to do something, but the high command or your commander also understands that the chances are that you're a young person who is pretty educated and pretty worldly and needs not only to be told something, but needs to be brought along. It's a different style of command, more suited to democracy. I don't think it's any less effective than the old style of command, but it is different. In the interim, however, you had no discipline. What you had in Somalia was a formation where the senior non-commissioned members were afraid of the junior non-commissioned members, and the junior officers were afraid of everybody. And I think it happened at a particular time and it was a time that I think is past, at least I hope so.

All armies in history have always had this phenomenon where the guys who are kicking up the dirt down at the bottom are to a certain extent disdainful of their commanders. It's especially true in peacetime because there is very little opportunity for commanders to form a true bond of brotherhood, as Shakespeare would have put it, between the guys who are fighting at the platoon level, or the company level, and the regimental commander.

Two trends developed in the 1990s that led to the undermining of the fighting frame of mind in the Canadian military. One of them was of course that the budgets got chopped. With the chopping of budgets the opportunities for good, solid, intensive military training deteriorated. To the best of my knowledge we haven't had a brigade-level exercise in this country in at least three years, and maybe longer. We basically train our people in small packets and they don't get a lot of training in certain kinds of warfare that they really need to know a lot about, like fighting in built-up areas for example.

But that's also gone parallel with the increase in the pace of peace support operations. The people have been rotated through Bosnia. If you go to Bosnia and sit in a room somewhere with 100 non-commissioned members and ask how many of them have been through Bosnia before on rotation, a whole bunch of them will stick their hands up. If you ask how many of them have been in there two or three times, another bunch of them will stick their hands up.

So when you are on that Bosnian mission you've been training for from six to nine months for that mission, but you are not training to fight a war. You're training for a certain kind of operation which is partly civil-military relations. Yes, you have to enforce the Dayton accords, but in Bosnia today there is no fighting. There is very little of what was going on that led to us getting in there. A lot of it is public relations; a lot of it is building schools; a lot of it is making sure you drive properly in the winter on the terrible roads over there. You are not training people to fight. And that's a big problem when you've got a very limited-size military. On the one hand we don't give our people enough real, or what approximates real, combat training. On the other hand we send people to peacekeeping operations more and more. So that's why our combat readiness is quite low right now.

The Gulf War
Canadian military participation in the Gulf War in my opinion was quite limited. We sent a handful of ground soldiers and medical personnel to guard bases, but we did not send combat troops. And we were asked to send them, but we refused to send them. A lot of different reasons have been advanced, but the real reasons are still hidden behind Cabinet secrecy, so I guess we won't learn for a while yet. But what it showed was that when we were asked to respond relatively quickly — let's remember that the buildup in the Gulf War took five to six months, not exactly a come-as-you-are war — we were not prepared.

Behind the scenes the allies always know what they are doing. There's no question that was true in the Gulf War. I'm sure that the Americans and the British knew the real reasons why we didn't send a brigade to war against Iraq. You know, it's their job to know what you're doing. And it's also their job to know what they can ask for. That's why I smile whenever I hear, "Well, we're doing what we're asked to do." They know that we're not capable of sending combat troops, so they don't ask us to send combat troops. They're not in the business of international embarrassment on the public stage. When they want to put pressure on the Canadian government, they put pressure on it from behind the scenes.

I think the reality of the Gulf War was that we had a military at that time that had 85,000 people. It was supposed to be at a level of preparedness that was at least as high as any other military right at the end of the cold war, but the Gulf War showed that we were a hollow force. Not only could we not send ground forces to the Gulf, but let's remember, our naval contribution came only after a lot of scrambling together of whatever we could to try to bolt on this and bolt on that so that these old steamships that we were sending out at the time might actually survive if they were attacked by anybody. Our air force was not prepared for ground operations in support of the troops, and we did not have a precision-guided munitions capability at the time. We were spending all this money for the military and we didn't have a capable military.

Leading a Mission

The Zaire mission in my opinion was one in which we were essentially being asked to provide administrative support and command for a large number of troops. It doesn't necessarily mean that you yourself are going to provide the bulk of the combat forces, but it could be that you are going to provide the headquarters, the signals, the communications and some of the ground troops. And it seems to me that's what we were being asked in Zaire. But I don't know that much about the Zaire situation. We took credit for solving it because of the threat that we were going to go in and blow everybody to bits.

My best take on Zaire is that in a way it was the prime minister compensating for Rwanda, and given how many Canadian troops were involved at that point in operations around the world, where were we going to find the extra troops? What were we thinking of, getting involved in the middle of a civil war, far from lines of supply and far from lines of communication? What particular contribution could we make? Do we have an interest in sending expeditionary forces into the heart of Africa? I think you can answer those questions in a variety of different ways, and I'm not opposed to Canadian intervention in Africa per se. But I think all of that was meant to compensate for the sense that possibly we had not done the best that we could, possibly at the command levels, to support General Dallaire in Rwanda.

I don't think there's anything wrong with the concept that Canadians from time to time will lead a mission. But where? It's entirely appropriate for Canadians to lead missions in the Caribbean, for example. It would be entirely appropriate if we were to say to the United States, "You know what? We will provide any rapid ready reaction force that is required anywhere around the Caribbean basin or in Central America, should some sort of military emergency arise, or some sort of internal dissension give rise to an overthrow of the democratic government, and we'll lead the way. You don't have to worry about that, we'll take care of that."

We have interests in the Caribbean. We have a lot of Canadians who come from that area. We have commercial and financial and industrial interests that we've had for the better part of a century. I'm not sure what our interests are in Africa. We have humanitarian interests everywhere and we should certainly participate to the extent that we can. We should have done everything we could to try to avoid Rwanda. But for us to be leading missions in areas of the world where we're not equipped, we're not trained and we don't have the capability, that's just foolishness.

Somalia

We have to look at Somalia in the context of the early 1990s. This was the new world order. Everyone was now co-operating — the Russians, the Americans, the Chinese. We were going to get things done. The UN was actually going to be an effective organization to save people from starvation and disease and what have you. That was the original impetus for going into Somalia. What people often forget about Somalia, looking back on it now, is that the nature of that mission changed very radically from the time that it was first proposed to the time that the troops actually got on the ground. It changed in two ways.

First of all, it was originally supposed to be what we call a Chapter VI, basically non-interventionist, sort of just-keep-the-dust-down kind of a mission. And then it changed into a Chapter VII mission, which is not peacekeeping but peace enforcement. You go in with loaded guns and you do not wear the blue beret, and no one mistakes you for being an international Boy Scout because if they do the wrong thing, you blow them away. The reason the mission changed was because there was a growing realization in the West that the situation on the ground in Somalia was not simply one of starvation by natural causes, but it was being caused by the total lack of any central political authority in that country.

So it was decided — it is not good enough just to distribute food. You need to guard the people who are distributing the food and you need to in a sense nation-build and create an environment in which that could happen. So knowing that, we selected a regiment that was supposed to be a combat-capable regiment and they thought they were going in to fight a war, but they weren't going in to fight a war. Most of the job that they were supposed to do in their area of responsibility was not very much different from traditional Chapter VI–style peacekeeping. So we take these guys with the tattoos and the rah-rah, gung-ho let's-shoot-'em-up sort of view toward life and we put them in a Chapter VII operation. Seemed appropriate for this kind of formation to do Chapter VII, but really we were asking them to do very much as was with Chapter VI. I don't think anybody knew what the hell the objective was in Somalia nine-tenths of the time.

Toward the spring of 1993 the situation throughout the country began to deteriorate. It's hard to know, particularly, as a response to what. Is it because the U.S.-led forces became more adamant about changing the political face of the nation, trying to in a sense establish and maintain peace and order in Somalia? Was that the beginning of it? Was it the warlords and the gangs whose chief intent was very much like the mafia itself — try to take as much of the food supply as you can for your own purposes, to buy weapons, to build your own political power bases? Clearly these were incompatible from the beginning, and toward March, April and so on, things began to escalate. You had a lot more incidents.

What we had in the Canadian area of responsibility was in part just a bunch of petty thievery. But what was going on in some of the other areas of responsibility were deliberate attacks: the placing of mines, ambushing of vehicles, killings of soldiers. As we now know, that eventually escalated to the point where the Americans decide they've got to get Mohammed Aideed and we had the disastrous incident of the Rangers and special forces in Mogadishu and what has become known since then as the Black Hawk Down episode. So we were on a slippery slope, by February, March, April of 1993, toward increasing chaos.

Now, you've got the Canadian Airborne Regiment. You have trained them for a certain kind of mission which you have asked them to do. They've been trained for combat; they were tough troops trained for combat. When they get in they're asked to do basically public relations work in the first couple of months that they're there. Then all of a sudden there's an increasing number of incidents. There were problems with the discipline within the regiment to begin with, and I think you had a very poisonous atmosphere where anything could happen and did.

I think two things happened. One was that the Somalis became more comfortable in engaging the UNITAF forces as they remained on the ground. But I also think that there was a growing realization of the extent to which they could use the public relations machinery, the mass media coverage. In a way, of course, Saddam Hussein pioneered that in the 1990s during the Gulf War, and CNN went along right with him. We showed pictures of civilian casualties and that undermines public opinion at home. What's the best way of getting the Americans out? Well, in the Vietnam War they were defeated not by the Vietcong or the North Vietnamese, but they were defeated by the American public. The biggest blow that Saddam Hussein could strike in the Gulf War was with TV pictures of innocent civilians being killed. They were very sophisticated in their use of the communications side of the confrontation. I think that was part of what was going on in Somalia.

We were messing around in their backyard. If you're going to save people, you've really got to get the co-operation of the local authorities to do it. I can't even go into this without trying to explain the more arcane points about logistics and communications and how you conduct military operations. But you've got to have the guys on the ground in back of you. You've got to have them supporting you or allowing you to operate because a very small number of them can do a lot of damage to a very large number of you, simply because that's their turf, they know it. What happened in Mogadishu to the Americans was a perfect example.

The Medak Pocket
Medak was important for two reasons. The first is that for the guys on the ground, and that goes right up to the battalion commander, Colonel Calvin, it was an object lesson of what they were really getting themselves into. This was no Cyprus — this was real war and they were in the middle of it. Not only was it real war in the sense that people were going

to try to kill them, but it was also real war in the sense that people all around them were being killed by bad guys, and nobody knew who the bad guys were because they were all bad guys and they were all killing everybody they could get their hands on. Our guys were basically forced to stand around and watch it happen. As Colonel Calvin said a number of times subsequent to that, "If we had done something to stop the ethnic cleansing in the Medak Pocket, it might have had an impact on the rest of the war in Bosnia."

I think that was a crucial turning point; I think that it caused the disconnect between the soldiers that went into Bosnia under the UNPROFOR banner from then on and the high command and the public who hadn't got a clue what was going on. And that's the second point. We didn't have a clue as to what was going on. For example, there was a time there when it came out by accident that we were sending snipers into Bosnia and people said, "What do we need snipers for? We are peacekeepers." Well, they knew they needed snipers in there, that's why they were bringing snipers in. But the public didn't know. And the government did its level best to suppress the truth about what kind of an operation Bosnia was. Why did they do that? I think because it ran against the image of blue helmet peacekeeping operations that are relatively cheap activities that you can participate in and there's no danger to anybody. I think part of it was simply that we don't do wars, that's not our sort of thing. There was suppression of the news of Medak Pocket, and even to this very day it's not something that is really talked about a great deal.

Keeping in Touch

Democracies at peace have always got this problem. The problem is that if the military loses touch with society, then society will not support the military, either in peace or at war, because they will see it as in a sense an alien creature. "What do we have to do with these people? Their values are not our values. They believe in things that we do not believe in." That's a problem.

But that's really not the issue. Canadians, as people in most democracies, I think, have always been perfectly willing to understand that there are times when they must resort to violence to defend their interests. We certainly understood that in 1914; we understood it in 1939; we understood it in 1950. Just as we understand that our cops out there have to have guns; just as we understand that we take bad people and we put them in jail; just as a large number of people in this country still support the death penalty, even though we don't have one. I don't think educated people in liberal democracies are naive. I think that they need to be reminded from time to time that there are certain realities that they need to face and pay for, and it's the leadership that reminds them or fails to remind them.

But once you do begin to build your military organization on the assumption that your people will, when the right time comes — or the wrong time, depending on how you look at it — countenance the use of force on their behalf, the military organization that you build needs to be one that reflects their values as educated, small "d" democrats, small "l" liberals, people who believe in the democratic process, free trade and so on. It's by no means an impossible task but it does take good, solid, imaginative leadership and leadership that cares about engendering an attitude that would be conducive to building an effective defence structure. And we don't really have that.

September 11, 2001
I think September 11 had a shocking effect on Canadians. First for the obvious reason of actually seeing this happen before your eyes. But more to the point, and the point that has been made over and over again by some of us during the last 10, 15 years, is that we cannot divorce ourselves from the larger world out there. It will impact us and it will affect us and we are part and parcel of that larger liberal, democratic, industrialized, trading, globalizing society.

It came home immediately when within hours of the collapse of the World Trade Center our trade was frozen, our airspace was frozen. Nothing crossed the border, nobody moved in this country and billions of dollars went down the tubes. In the subsequent weeks the economy has gone into the tank — it doesn't take a genius to figure out that an event that occurred outside of Canadian territory had a direct impact on the lives of millions of Canadians. It's tragic that we had to learn the lesson that way, but that's precisely what a lot of us have been saying to our fellow citizens for a long time: that you're not immune from this. And I think that's going to have a long-term change in the way the public reacts to security and defence issues.

The question is, what is the government going to do to translate that into action? And it's not simply the government. I think it's got to be translated into action at levels from Grade 6 and Grade 7 where we teach our kids — or we don't teach our kids — about security and defence issues and military heritage in this country. It's got to happen with the business community. Are they now going to start making demands on the government to make sure the Armed Forces don't deteriorate in the future because they too see a stake in this? It's not just the government that can do this. It's easy to blame the government, when it's the fault of 33 million Canadians.

Has there been a violent, dramatic, sudden demonstration of this lesson? Absolutely. Will we act on the change? That's the big issue.

Becoming Involved
It's been a matter almost of historical tradition in this country that the political leadership is forced into action with regard to military affairs in two ways. One is that our allies put pressure, unrelenting pressure, on us. The second is that the people get ahead of the government and put pressure on the government. Look, for example, at the first months of the Korean War, which I think is about as close a parallel as you're going to find to what is going on in the country right now. Public opinion in this country, as measured in public opinion polls, newspaper editorials and all those traditional sorts of things, was way ahead of the government in demanding Canadian participation in the Korean War, demanding that Canada send ground troops to Korea, while the government was shunting around and the prime minister was telling the press not to bother him while he was on his fishing vacation up in Quebec. At the same time, of course, the British and the Americans were putting tremendous pressure on the government behind the scenes because they were saying, "Even though this is Southeast Asia, this is a test of the new NATO and we have to show that we're up to the stuff."

That's exactly what's happening now, and I think that it's probably inevitable in this country that it will always happen that way because the government is going to continue to do what governments in this country have always done in military issues, and that is just go right down the centre of the board. It's only when the public gets upset or when our allies get upset that governments have been moved to action. Do I think Mackenzie King would have declared war in September 1939 under circumstances other than the ones that occurred? The public would never have stood for neutrality of this country in September 1939. This was a very pro-British public and the country saw its interests as being on the side of Britain and the Commonwealth and they wouldn't have stood it for five minutes. So he was really just bowing to public pressure and public opinion when he led Canada into war in September 1939, in the same way, I think, St. Laurent did in 1950 and Mr. Chrétien is doing now.

Lester Pearson cloaked the invention of peacekeeping as something that was done for humanitarian reasons, but it wasn't. The fact was that Canadian foreign policy in the 15 years or so after the end of World War II, and to a certain extent today, but certainly back in the 1950s, was based on maintaining harmony as much as possible between the United States and Britain. The worst nightmare for a Canadian government was to have the Americans going off in one direction and the British going off in another. This was because Britain was still an important country to Canada back in the 1950s. It still is today, but it was far more important to Canada in the 1950s than it is now.

What you had as a result of the invasion of the Suez Canal zone were the Americans on one side of the hill and the Brits and the French on another. That was a nightmare to a country that needed NATO as badly as we did. We needed NATO very badly because it was in effect the manifestation of our foreign and defence policy in 1956.

So how to bring them together? Pearson's answer was the United Nations Emergency Force. UNEF basically saved the British and French public image by replacing Britain and France in the Suez Canal zone. The whole use of UNEF between the Arabs and the Israelis, or the Egyptians and the Israelis was incidental to the main aim of UNEF, which was to go into the Suez Canal zone and give the Brits and the French an excuse for pulling out so that they could say, "We have achieved our objective of re-internationalizing the Suez Canal and the UN is there for us." There were good power-politics, national-self-interest reasons for us to invent peacekeeping in 1956. But of course you don't tell people that. You tell people that you're doing it for the good of the world. Not only did Lester Pearson do that, and very successfully and won a Nobel Peace Prize for it, but we've been doing it ever since.

Looking to the Future
If we continue to expand the mission with the force that we have or a shrinking force, we will effectively have disarmed ourselves. You cannot

continue to draw upon people to do more with less. It's a myth. We are overstretching our soldiers, our sailors, our airpersons to the point where a military career is no longer attractive except to a very small number of them. We have challenged them to choose between a real life and their lives as soldiers. Now, there was a time when the attitude of the military was that you've married the army and everybody else better get used to it, but you can't sell that in an all-volunteer force in a modern democracy. You can't sell that where the military members are 60 percent married. You can't sell that where you are forcing them to choose between having a wife and kids and a regular home life and a military career. If you want to force them to choose, they will choose to get out. The bumpkins and the bums to a large extent will dominate the Forces after that. The people who are there with a knife in their teeth, who want to go out and act like motorcycle gang members. You will not have a military that is highly professional and highly competent as is required today because it can't be done.

I don't want to make light of our military commitment to the war on terror. I think the government is doing the best that it can right now with what it's got. The problem is that it doesn't have what is required under these circumstances, which are ready-reaction, combat-capable, air-mobile forces. Ironically what we need today is a better Canadian Airborne Regiment and we don't have it. We don't have it because it was disbanded, largely for political reasons. So we send what we've got. I think most Canadians are glad we're sending as much as we're sending, but I don't think anyone should kid themselves as to what sort of a role we're going to be playing in this operation.

AFTERWORD

We are constantly reassured by the Department of National Defence that the problems of the Canadian military uncovered by the Somalia inquiry are behind us now. But the problems of the Canadian military, as this volume of interviews makes clear, are not problems that can be fixed by the Department of National Defence because they are problems that are not peculiar to the institution of the military in Canada. The problems of the military are in fact a byproduct of our way of governing ourselves.

The studies, commissions and treatises on how to fix the Canadian military that have been filling the bookshelves for decades seem to have missed this point. They have largely limited the scope of their inquiries to defence and defence policies. They have generated little resonance beyond those interested in the military, and the government has polls reporting that those who are genuinely interested and concerned about the military in Canada are few indeed.

One of the reasons the producers of *A Question of Honour* chose to look into the military was to reflect on our parliamentarians' abilities to keep the government in check. Another was to be a useful bellwether for public understanding of our Armed Forces. The military deals in blood and treasury, two matters one would think would interest constituents and therefore their representatives. But as the comments on Kosovo show, Parliament's interest in Canada's military commitments and its ability to oversee and hold the government accountable on them are minimal. Members of Parliament don't seem to be able to contribute much to holding government to account because our version of parliamentary government denies them the resources and the incentive to be little more than ciphers.

It is certainly not in anyone's interest to maintain the current arrangement.

Defence requires long-term commitments and planning over the life of several governments, and it requires consensus and commitment on the part of the public. This in turn requires a fully informed, ongoing debate and discussion of our options, which will naturally change as situations evolve. Such a process is necessarily time consuming, messy and expensive. But the alternative is to keep our heads buried in the sand.

Robert Roy
Producer, *A Question of Honour*
June 2002

GLOSSARY

CAST Brigade Group The Canadian Air-Sea Transportable Brigade Group was a commitment made to NATO at the time that Canada was planning to cut back on its European force, but according to many the commitment was always meant to be political tokenism. The Canadian troops that were to be withdrawn from Europe and returned to Canada were to be a main contribution to this brigade which, in the event of a Soviet invasion of Norway, would be sent to the northern part of the country to "beat off the Russian hordes." In 1968 the CAST Brigade Group committed troops from 2 Combat Group in Petawawa and later 5 Groupement de Combat in Valcartier. There was some question as to how the troops would get to Norway. It has been reported that at one time there was some suggestion to send them by Newfoundland ferries, but the idea was rejected.

What seems to have happened is that everyone forgot that this was supposed to be tokenism. In 1984 when the military put the plan under scrutiny on paper in Operation Bold Step, nothing was available; no ships, no ammunition and apparently not even a plan to get troops to the docks in Montreal. In 1986 a live-action exercise, Bold Lion, was carried out using Canadian soldiers stationed in Canada. The exercise met with some success, but it ultimately proved that the whole idea wasn't feasible. Some people have suggested that many senior military officers were hoping, in the lead-up to the 1987 white paper, that if the commitment to the CAST Brigade was shown to be unrealistic and was dropped, they could then reinforce and rebuild 4 Brigade.

CDS Chief of the defence staff.

CF-18 Canadian air force jet fighter. Also referred to as F-18.

Clausewitz, Karl von 1780–1831. Prussian general and writer on military strategy. He fought in the wars against Napoleon, including Waterloo, and was appointed director of the German War School in 1818. His masterpiece *On War* was published after his death. The doctrines expounded in it, including that of total war (that all citizens, territory and property of the enemy nation should be attacked in every way possible) had an enormous effect on military strategy and tactics around the world.

Franklin, Ursula Renowned physicist and professor emeritus at the University of Toronto. She was a vocal opponent to the NATO bombing of Yugoslavia in 1999 during the Kosovo crisis.

INF Treaty The Intermediate-Range Nuclear Forces Treaty went into effect on June 1, 1988. The fundamental purpose was to eliminate and ban U.S. and USSR ground-launched ballistic and cruise missiles.

JAG   Judge Advocate General. Canadian Military Prosecution Service.

KLA   Kosovo Liberation Army.

KVM   Kosovo Verification Mission.

Mujahideen   Muslim holy warriors.

NATO   North Atlantic Treaty Organization.

NGO   Non-government organization.

NORAD   North American Aerospace Defence Command. A binational United States and Canadian organization charged with the missions of aerospace warning and aerospace control for North America. Aerospace warning includes the monitoring of man-made objects in space, and the detection, validation and warning of attack against North America, whether by aircraft, missiles or space vehicles, utilizing mutual support arrangements with other commands. Aerospace control includes providing surveillance and control of Canadian and United States airspace. (Definition from the NORAD Web site: http://www.spacecom.af.mil/norad/.)

OSCE   Organization for Security and Co-operation in Europe.

Rugova, Ibrahim   Leader of the Albanian population in Kosovo.

UCK   Ushtria Clirimtare e Kosoves. The Albanian name for what became known as the KLA, the Kosovo Liberation Army. It first appeared in Macedonia in 1992.

UNIFIL — United Nations Interim Force in Lebanon.

UNPREDEP — United Nations Preventive Deployment Force in Macedonia. The mission was established in March 1995 and terminated in February 1999.

Ustashi — Fascist government of Croatia during World War II.

VJ — The new Serbian army which replaced the JNA, the Yugoslav National Army.

Weltanschauung — View or philosophy of life; ideology.

APPENDIX 1

Chapters VI and VII of the
Charter of the United Nations

CHAPTER VI
PACIFIC SETTLEMENT OF DISPUTES

Article 33

1. The parties to any dispute, the continuance of which is likely to endanger the maintenance of international peace and security, shall, first of all, seek a solution by negotiation, inquiry, mediation, conciliation, arbitration, judicial settlement, resort to regional agencies or arrangements or other peaceful means of their own choice.
2. The Security Council shall, when it deems necessary, call upon the parties to settle their dispute by such means.

Article 34

The Security Council may investigate any dispute, or any situation which might lead to international friction or give rise to a dispute, in order to determine whether the continuance of the dispute or situation is likely to endanger the maintenance of international peace and security.

Article 35

1. Any member of the United Nations may bring any dispute, or any situation of the nature referred to in Article 34, to the attention of the Security Council or of the General Assembly.
2. A state which is not a member of the United Nations may bring to the attention of the Security Council or of the General Assembly any dispute to which it is a party if it accepts in advance, for the purposes of the dispute, the obligations of pacific settlement provided in the present Charter.
3. The proceedings of the General Assembly in respect of matters brought to its attention under this Article will be subject to the provisions of Articles 11 and 12.

Article 36

1. The Security Council may, at any stage of a dispute of the nature referred to in Article 33 or of a situation of like nature, recommend appropriate procedures or methods of adjustment.
2. The Security Council should take into consideration any procedures for the settlement of the dispute which have already been adopted by the parties.
3. In making recommendations under this article the Security Council should also take into consideration that legal disputes should as a general rule be referred by the parties to the International Court of Justice in accordance with the provisions of the Statute of the Court.

Article 37

1. Should the parties to a dispute of the nature referred to in Article 33 fail to settle it by the means indicated in that Article, they shall refer it to the Security Council.
2. If the Security Council deems that the continuance of the dispute is in fact likely to endanger the maintenance of international peace and security, it shall decide whether to take action under Article 36 or to recommend such terms of settlement as it may consider appropriate.

Article 38

Without prejudice to the provisions of Articles 33 to 37, the Security Council may, if all the parties to any dispute so request, make recommendations to the parties with a view to a pacific settlement of the dispute.

CHAPTER VII
ACTION WITH RESPECT TO THREATS TO THE PEACE, BREACHES OF THE PEACE AND ACTS OF AGGRESSION

Article 39

The Security Council shall determine the existence of any threat to the peace, breach of the peace or act of aggression and shall make recommendations, or decide what measures shall be taken in accordance with Articles 41 and 42, to maintain or restore international peace and security.

Article 40

In order to prevent an aggravation of the situation, the Security Council may, before making the recommendations or deciding upon the measures provided for in Article 39, call upon the parties concerned to comply with such provisional measures as it deems necessary or desirable. Such provisional measures shall be without prejudice to the rights, claims or position of the parties concerned. The Security Council shall duly take account of failure to comply with such provisional measures.

Article 41

The Security Council may decide what measures not involving the use of armed force are to be employed to give effect to its decisions, and it may call upon the members of the United Nations to apply such measures. These may include complete or partial interruption of economic relations and of rail, sea, air, postal, telegraphic, radio and other means of communication, and the severance of diplomatic relations.

Article 42

Should the Security Council consider that measures provided for in Article 41 would be inadequate or have proved to be inadequate, it may take such action by air, sea or land forces as may be necessary to maintain or restore international peace and security. Such action may include demonstrations, blockade and other operations by air, sea or land forces of members of the United Nations.

Article 43

1. All members of the United Nations, in order to contribute to the maintenance of international peace and security, undertake to make

available to the Security Council, on its call and in accordance with a special agreement or agreements, armed forces, assistance and facilities, including rights of passage, necessary for the purpose of maintaining international peace and security.

2. Such agreement or agreements shall govern the numbers and types of forces, their degree of readiness and general location and the nature of the facilities and assistance to be provided.

3. The agreement or agreements shall be negotiated as soon as possible on the initiative of the Security Council. They shall be concluded between the Security Council and members or between the Security Council and groups of members and shall be subject to ratification by the signatory states in accordance with their respective constitutional processes.

Article 44

When the Security Council has decided to use force it shall, before calling upon a member not represented on it to provide armed forces in fulfillment of the obligations assumed under Article 43, invite that member, if the member so desires, to participate in the decisions of the Security Council concerning the employment of contingents of that member's armed forces.

Article 45

In order to enable the United Nations to take urgent military measures, members shall hold immediately available national air-force contingents for combined international enforcement action. The strength and degree of readiness of these contingents and plans for their combined action shall be determined within the limits laid down in the special agreement or agreements referred to in Article 43, by the Security Council with the assistance of the Military Staff Committee.

Article 46

Plans for the application of armed force shall be made by the Security Council with the assistance of the Military Staff Committee.

Article 47

1. There shall be established a Military Staff Committee to advise and assist the Security Council on all questions relating to the Security Council's military requirements for the maintenance of

international peace and security, the employment and command of forces placed at its disposal, the regulation of armaments and possible disarmament.

2. The Military Staff Committee shall consist of the chiefs of staff of the permanent members of the Security Council or their representatives. Any member of the United Nations not permanently represented on the committee shall be invited by the committee to be associated with it when the efficient discharge of the committee's responsibilities requires the participation of that member in its work.

3. The Military Staff Committee shall be responsible under the Security Council for the strategic direction of any armed forces placed at the disposal of the Security Council. Questions relating to the command of such forces shall be worked out subsequently.

4. The Military Staff Committee, with the authorization of the Security Council and after consultation with appropriate regional agencies, may establish regional subcommittees.

Article 48

1. The action required to carry out the decisions of the Security Council for the maintenance of international peace and security shall be taken by all the members of the United Nations or by some of them, as the Security Council may determine.

2. Such decisions shall be carried out by the members of the United Nations directly and through their action in the appropriate international agencies of which they remember.

Article 49

The members of the United Nations shall join in affording mutual assistance in carrying out the measures decided upon by the Security Council.

Article 50

If preventive or enforcement measures against any state are taken by the Security Council, any other state, whether a member of the United Nations or not, which finds itself confronted with special economic problems arising from the carrying out of those measures shall have the right to consult the Security Council with regard to a solution of those problems.

Article 51

Nothing in the present Charter shall impair the inherent right of individual or collective self-defence if an armed attack occurs against a member of the United Nations until the Security Council has taken measures necessary to maintain international peace and security. Measures taken by members in the exercise of this right of self-defence shall be immediately reported to the Security Council and shall not in any way affect the authority and responsibility of the Security Council under the present Charter to take at any time such action as it deems necessary in order to maintain or restore international peace and security.

APPENDIX 2
Suggested Further Reading

Prepared by Martin Shadwick, senior research fellow, Centre for International and Security Studies, York University, and Robert Roy, producer/researcher for *A Question of Honour*.

Journals (Canadian)

Behind the Headlines
Canada World View
Canadian Foreign Policy
Canadian Historical Review
Canadian Journal of Political Science
Canadian Military Journal
Canadian Public Administration
Canadian Public Policy
International Journal
Peacekeeping & International Relations
Policy Options

Journals (International)

American Review of Canadian Studies
Contemporary Security Policy
Current History
Foreign Affairs
Foreign Policy
International Security
Jane's Defence Weekly
Jane's International Defence Review
Journal of Ethics and International Affairs
Journal of International Affairs
Journal of Peace Research
Journal of Strategic Studies
NATO Review
ORBIS
Review of International Studies
The Washington Quarterly
World Policy Journal
World Politics

Also useful are the *SIPRI Year Book* and the International Institute for Strategic Studies publications, including *Strategic Survey* and *The Adelphi Papers*.

Web Sites

Government Departments and Agencies:
Canadian Security Intelligence Service (CSIS)
http://www.csis-scrs.gc.ca
Department of Foreign Affairs and International Trade (DFAIT)
http://www.dfait-maeci.gc.ca
Department of National Defence (DND)
http://www.dnd.ca
Office of the Auditor General of Canada (OAG)
http://www.oag-bvg.gc.ca
Office of Critical Infrastructure Protection and Emergency Preparedness (OCIPEP)
http://www.epc-pcc.gc.ca

Government Libraries/Research Centres/Publications:
Canadian Centre for Foreign Policy Development (CCFPD)
http://www.cfp-pec.gc.ca
Canadian Forces College (War, Peace and Security Server)
http://wps.cfc.dnd.ca
Canadian Military Journal (CMJ)
http://www/journal.dnd.ca

Parliamentary Committees:
Standing Committee on Foreign Affairs and International Trade
Standing Committee on National Defence and Veterans Affairs
Standing Senate Committee on Defence and Security
Standing Senate Committee on Foreign Affairs
http://www.parl.gc.ca

Non-Governmental Organizations:
Canadian Institute of International Affairs (CIIA)
http://www.ciia.org
Canadian Institute of Strategic Studies (CISS)
http://www.ciss.ca
Conference of Defence Associations Institute (CDAI)
http://www.cda-cdai.ca
Council for Canadian Security in the 21st Century (CCS 21)
http://www.stratnet.ucalgary.ca
Institute for Research on Public Policy (IRPP)
http://www.irpp.org
Lester B. Pearson Canadian International Peacekeeping Centre
http://www.Cdnpeacekeeping.ns.ca
Project Ploughshares
http://www.ploughshares.ca
Royal Canadian Military Institute (RCMI)
http://www.rcmi.org

International Organizations:
North American Aerospace Defence Command (NORAD)
http://www.spacecom.af.mil/norad
North Atlantic Treaty Organization (NATO)
http://www.nato.int
United Nations (UN)
http://www.un.org

Books of Note

Defence and Military Affairs:
Bland, Douglas L. *Canada's National Defence:* Vol. 1 *Defence Policy* and Vol. 2 *Defence Organization*. Kingston: School of Policy Studies, Queen's University, 1997 and 1998.

Bland, Douglas L. *Chiefs of Defence: Government and the Unified Command of the Armed Forces of Canada*. Toronto: Canadian Institute of Strategic Studies, 1995.

Davis, James R. *The Sharp End: A Canadian Soldier's Story*. Vancouver: Douglas & McIntyre, 1997.

DeWitt, David, and David Leyton-Brown, eds. *Canada's International Security Policy*. Scarborough: Prentice-Hall Canada, 1995.

English, John A. *Lament for an Army: The Decline of Canadian Military Professionalism*. Toronto: Canadian Institute of International Affairs, 1998.

Granatstein, Jack L. *Canada's Army: Waging War and Keeping the Peace*. Toronto: University of Toronto Press, 2002.

Gray, Colin S. *Canadians in a Dangerous World*. Toronto: Atlantic Council, 1994.

Horn, Bernt, ed. *Forging a Nation: Perspectives on the Canadian Military Experience*. St. Catharines: Vanwell, 2002.

Hunt, B. D., and R. G. Haycock, eds. *Canada's Defence: Perspectives on Policy in the Twentieth Century*. Toronto: Copp Clark Pitman, 1993.

Jockel, Joseph T. *The Canadian Forces: Hard Choices, Soft Power*. Toronto: Canadian Institute of Strategic Studies, 1999.

MacKenzie, Lewis. *Peacekeeper: The Road to Sarajevo*. Vancouver: Douglas & McIntyre, 1993.

Maloney, Sean M. *Canada and UN Peacekeeping: Cold War by Other Means, 1945–1970*. St. Catharines: Vanwell, 2002.

Maloney, Sean M. *War Without Battles: Canada's NATO Brigade in Germany 1951–1993*. Toronto: McGraw-Hill Ryerson, 1997.

Middlemass, Danford, and Joel Sokolsky. *Canadian Defence: Decisions and Determinants*. Toronto: Harcourt Brace Jovanovich, 1989.

Milner, Marc, ed. *Canadian Military History: Selected Readings*. Toronto: Copp Clark Pitman, 1993.

Morton, Desmond. *A Military History of Canada: From Champlain to Kosovo*. Fourth edition. Toronto: McClelland & Stewart, 1999.

Pugliese, David. *Canada's Secret Commandos: The Unauthorized Story of JOINT TASK FORCE TWO*. Ottawa: Esprit de Corps, 2001.

Rempel, Roy. *The Chatterbox: An Insider's Account of the Irrelevance of Parliament in the Making of Canadian Foreign and Defence Policy*. Toronto: Dundurn, 2002.

Taylor, Scott, and Brian Nolan, *Tarnished Brass: Crime and Corruption in the Canadian Military*. Toronto: Lester, 1996.

Taylor, Scott, and Brian Nolan. *Tested Metal: Canada's Peacekeepers at War*. Ottawa: Esprit de Corps, 1998.

Foreign and Defence Policy:
Cooper, Andrew. *Canadian Foreign Policy: Old Habits and New Directions*. Scarborough: Prentice-Hall Canada, 1997.

Hampson, Fen Osler, Norman Hillmer and Maureen Appel Molot, eds. *Canada Among Nations 2001: The Axworthy Legacy*. Don Mills: Oxford University Press, 2001.

Hillmer, Norman, and J. L. Granatstein. *Empire to Umpire: Canada and the World to the 1990's*. Toronto: Copp Clark Longman, 1994.

Keating, Tom. *Canada and World Order: The Multilateralist Tradition in Canadian Foreign Policy*. Second edition. Toronto: Oxford University Press, 2001.

Nossal, Kim Richard. *The Politics of Canadian Foreign Policy*. Third edition. Scarborough: Prentice-Hall Canada, 1997.

Rempel, Roy. *Counterweights: Canada's German Policy*. Kingston: McGill-Queen's University Press, 1996.

International Security Policy:
Gray, Colin S. *Modern Strategy*. London: Oxford University Press, 1999.

Hampson, Fen Osler, et al. *Madness in the Multitude: Human Security and World Disorder*. Toronto: Oxford University Press, 2002.

Irwin, Rosalind, ed. *Ethics and Security in Canadian Foreign Policy*. Vancouver: University of British Columbia Press, 2001.

Tucker, Michael J., Raymond Blake and P. E. Bryden, eds. *Canada and the New World Order: Facing the New Millennium*. Toronto: Irwin, 2000.

The Gulf:
Deere, David, ed. *Desert Cats: The Canadian Fighter Squadron in the Gulf War*. Stoney Creek: Fortress, 1991.

Somalia:
Bercuson, David. *Significant Incident: Canada's Army, the Airborne and the Murder in Somalia*. Toronto: McClelland & Stewart, 1997.

Desbarats, Peter. *Somalia Cover-up: A Commissioner's Journal*. Toronto: McClelland & Stewart, 1997.

Loomis, Dan G. *The Somalia Affair: Reflections on Peacemaking and Peacekeeping*. Ottawa: DGL Publications, 1996.

Rwanda:
Off, Carol. *The Lion, the Fox and the Eagle: A Story of Generals and Justice in Rwanda and Yugoslavia*. Toronto: Random House, 2000.

The Balkans — Bosnia/Croatia and Kosovo
Cohen, Lenard. *Serpent in the Bosom: The Rise and Fall of Slobodan Milosevic*. Vancouver: University of British Columbia Press, 2000.

Appendix 2

Maloney, Sean M. *Chances for Peace: Canadian Soldiers in the Balkans 1992–1995*. St. Catharines: Vanwell, 2002.

Maloney, Sean M. *Operation KINETIC: The Canadians and Kosovo 1999–2000* (forthcoming).

Taylor, Scott. *INAT: Images of Serbia and the Kosovo Conflict*. Ottawa: Esprit de Corps, 2000.

INDEX